Bob Roshier and Harvey Teff

LAW AND SOCIETY IN ENGLAND

Tavistock Publications

First published in 1980 by
Tavistock Publications Ltd
11 New Fetter Lane, London EC4P 4EE
Published in the USA by
Tavistock Publications
in association with Methuen, Inc.
733 Third Avenue, New York, NY 10017

Typeset by Red Lion Setters, Holborn, London
Printed in Great Britain at
the University Press, Cambridge

British Library Cataloguing in Publication Data

Roshier, Robert
  Law and society in England.
  1. Law – England.
  2.   Sociological jurisprudence
  I. Title   II. Teff, Harvey
  340.1'15'0942   KD660   80-40090

  ISBN 0-422-76720-4
  ISBN 0-422-76730-1 Pbk

To Shlomit
H.T.

To David, Helen, and Iona
B.R.

Contents

Acknowledgements		*viii*
Table of Cases		*ix*
Table of Statutes		*xii*
1	Law and Society	1
2	The Emergence of Legal Rules	19
3	Legal Rules in Operation: (1) The Criminal Process	78
4	Legal Rules in Operation: (2) The Settlement of Disputes in Civil Law	145
5	The Provision of Legal Services	178
6	Some Limits and Social Consequences of Law	201
7	Conclusion	222
Bibliography		226
Name Index		243
Subject Index		249

Acknowledgements

We would particularly like to thank Bob Sullivan for reading substantial parts of the text and making many valuable suggestions. We are also indebted to Colin Munro for his comments on Chapter 4. Our very warm thanks are due to Susan Hancock for her skilled typing of the bulk of the manuscript and tireless help in the final stages of preparation. We would also like to thank Susan Spence and Ann Mitchell for additional secretarial assistance. We are most grateful to the publishers for all their help.

Table of Cases

Anisminic Ltd. *v.* Foreign Compensation Commission
  [1969] 2 A.C.147   67
Att.-Gen. *v.* Leveller Magazine Ltd. [1978] 3 All E.R. 731   125
Baker *v.* Carr (1962) 369 U.S. 186   71
Black-Clawson International Ltd. *v.* Papierwerke
  Waldhof-Aschaffenburg A.G. [1975] 1 All E.R.810   59
Bonsor *v.* Musicians' Union [1956] A.C.104   68
Brown *v.* Board of Education (1954) 347 U.S.483   71, 209
Brutus *v.* Cozens [1973] A.C.854   129
Cassell & Co. *v.* Broome [1972] A.C.1027   62
Charter *v.* Race Relations Board [1973] A.C.868   60, 67
Congreve *v.* Home Office [1976] Q.B.629.   67
Constantine *v.* Imperial Hotels Ltd. [1944] 2 All E.R.000   170
Davis *v.* Johnson [1978] 1 All E.R. 1132   58
Duport Steels Ltd. *v.* Sirs [1980] 1 All E.R. 529   69
Elias *v.* Pasmore [1934] 2 K.B. 164   100
Entick *v.* Carrington (1765) 19 St.Tr.1030   99
Firman *v.* Ellis [1978] Q.B. 886   57
Fitzpatrick *v.* Kelly (1873) L.R.8 Q.B.337   33
Ghani *v.* Jones [1970] 1 Q.B.693   100
Gouriet *v.* Union of Post Office Workers [1978] A.C.435   69, 175
Grainger & Son *v.* Gough (1894) 3 T.C.311   63
Home Office *v.* Dorset Yacht Co. [1970] A.C.1004   62
Jeffrey *v.* Black [1978] Q.B. 490   100
Jones *v.* National Coal Board [1957] 2 Q.B.55   162

Laker Airways Ltd. *v.* Department of Trade [1977] Q.B.643   67
Magor and St. Mellons Rural District Council *v.* Newport
    Borough Council [1952] A.C.189   64
Marbury *v.* Madison (1803), 1 Cranch. 137   71
Miranda *v.* Arizona (1966) 384 U.S.436   71
Padfield *v.* Minister of Agriculture, Fisheries and Food
    [1968] A.C. 997   67
Portec (U.K.) Ltd. *v.* Mogensen [1976] I.C.R.396   61
R. *v.* Allen [1977] Crim.L.R. 163   103
R. *v.* Atkinson [1978] 2 All E.R.460   116
R. *v.* Bass [1953] 1 Q.B.680   101
R. *v.* Bird [1978] Crim.L.R.237   116
R. *v.* Brown [1977] R.T.R.160   102
R. *v.* Coe [1969] 1 All E.R.65   115
R. *v.* Feely [1973] 1 Q.B.530   129
R. *v.* Howell [1978] Crim.L.R.239   116
R. *v.* Lemsatef [1977] 2 All E.R.835   102, 103
R. *v.* Llewellyn (1978) *The Times*, 3 March   116
R. *v.* Prager [1972] 1 All E.R.1114   104
R. *v.* Ryan [1978] Crim.L.R.306   116
R. *v.* Sang [1979] 2 All E.R. 46   100
R. *v.* Sheffield Crown Court, ex. p. Brownlow (1980)
    The Times, 4 March   125
R. *v.* Sutton [1977] 3 All E.R.476   48
R. *v.* Turnbull [1976] 3 All E.R.549   105
Race Relations Board *v.* Dockers' Labour Club and Institute
    [1974] 3 All E.R. 592   59, 60, 67
Regents of the University of California *v.* Bakke (1978)
    S.Ct.2733, U.S.   210
Rice *v.* Connolly [1966] 2 Q.B.414   102
Roe *v.* Wade (1973) 410 U.S.113   71
Rookes *v.* Barnard [1964] A.C.1129   68
Santobello *v.* New York (1971) 404 U.S.257   114
Secretary of State for Education and Science *v.* Tameside
    Metropolitan Borough Council [1976] 3 All E.R.665   67
Science Research Council *v.* Nassé [1978] 3 All E.R.1196   174
Shaw *v.* Director of Public Prosecutions [1962] A.C.220   64
Spartan Steel & Alloys *v.* Martin & Co. (Contractors)
    [1973] Q.B.27   57

Thomas *v.* Sawkins [1935] 2 K.B.249   100
Todd *v.* British Midland Airways Ltd. (1978)
   The Times, 22 July   61
Wall's Meat Co. Ltd. *v.* Khan [1979] I.C.R.52   168
Wilson *v.* Maynard Shipbuilding Consultants A.B.
   [1978] Q.B.665   61

Table of Statutes

Vagrancy Act 1824	30, 92, 102
s.4	102
Factories Act 1833	30
Metropolitan Police Act 1839	99
s.66	99
County Courts Act 1846	154
Food & Drink Act 1860	33
Sale of Food and Drugs Act 1875	33, 34
Conciliation Act 1896	170
Poor Prisoners Defence Act 1903	189
Official Secrets Act 1911	39
s.2	39, 40
Harrison Act, United States 1914	26
Sex Disqualification (Removal) Act 1919	173
Marijuana Tax Act, United States 1937	24, 25, 26
Legal Aid and Advice Act 1949	188
Magistrates' Courts Act 1952	103, 104, 106
s.38(1)	106
s.38(4)	103
s.40	104
Clean Air Act 1956	35, 36, 37
Sexual Offences Act 1956	48
s.14, 15	48
First Offenders Act 1958	52
Tribunals and Inquiries Act 1958	167

Indecency with Children Act 1960	48
Law Commission Acts 1965	7
Race Relations Act 1965	170, 208
Voting Rights Act, United States 1965	209
Road Safety Act 1967	212, 213
Criminal Law Act 1967	100, 101
s.2	101
s.2(6)	100
Sexual Offences Act 1967	82
Criminal Justice Act 1967	52, 104
s.33	104
Race Relations Act 1968	171, 208
Children and Young Persons Act 1969	135, 137
Divorce Reform Act 1969	156, 157, 158, 159
Equal Pay Act 1970	173, 208
Misuse of Drugs Act 1971	99, 215
s.23	99
Industrial Relations Act 1971	211, 218, 220
Local Government Act 1972	175
s.222	175
Legal Advice and Assistance Act 1972	189
Administration of Justice Act 1973	164
s.7	164
Matrimonial Causes Act 1973	157
s.25	157
Fair Trading Act 1973	175
s.35	175
Legal Aid Act 1974	189
Prevention of Terrorism (Temporary Provisions) Act 1974	102
Sex Discrimination Act 1975	171, 172, 173, 208
Domestic Violence and Matrimonial Homes Act 1976	48
Bail Act 1976	52, 112
Race Relations Act 1976	60, 171, 172, 208
s.25	60
Criminal Law Act 1977	104, 125
Housing (Homeless Persons) Act 1977	48
s.1(2)(b)	48
Domestic Proceedings and Magistrates' Courts Act 1978	159

Employment Protection (Consolidation) Act 1978   61
    s.141(2)   61
Legal Aid Act 1979   190

1
Law and Society

The Paradox

The legal practitioner has to cope with the law as he finds it and is naturally inclined to take many aspects of the legal system for granted. Faced with a mass of rules, at times obscure and intractable, he operates on the assumption that they can in principle be elucidated in accordance with the law's own internal logic. The law presents itself to him as an essentially self-contained body of knowledge waiting to be ascertained and applied. The academic study of law, though less constrained, has also in the main focussed on law divorced from its social context. The academic lawyer has traditionally seen as his main task the exposition and analysis of the law as it appears in statutes and cases. Until very recently, little attention has been paid by lawyers to the underlying processes which help determine the content and form of law, how it functions as a mechanism of social control, and the unintended consequences which it may have.

The relative lack of inquiry along such lines is at first sight surprising. Reflection on law in its social context is as old as the Greeks. In more modern times one can find a wealth of sociological material on the nature of law, admittedly somewhat fragmented and scattered, in the works of the founding fathers of sociology. Durkheim's theory of social solidarity and his analysis of sanctions were concerned with the ways legal institutions are created and function. The bureaucratic nature of modern societies poses problems about the processing of cases and the proper role of discretion in decision making which can be better appreciated in the light of Weber's work on bureaucracy and his distinction between formal and substantive rationality. The Marxist stress on the primacy of economic relations and on law as an instrument of oppression challenges more conventional views of the nature of the legal order.

From the field of social anthropology, studies of social organization in primitive societies have highlighted the elusive nature of the distinctively legal. At the same time, the social dimension of law has been a dominant theme in several strands of juristic thought. These include the work of the historical school, with its emphasis on cultural relativism; the call from within sociological jurisprudence to study the 'living law' and the 'law in action'; and the influential American realist movement, which challenged orthodox notions about the legal process in general and legal reasoning in particular. Why has this formidable array of learning never been welded together to create a more clearly defined whole?

The Basic Divide: Solving Problems or Constructing Theories

In working towards an answer to this question, one must first appreciate that the nature of the relationship between law and sociology has been the source of much definitional controversy. The subject matter of what is commonly called the 'sociology of law' is simple enough to describe in very general terms. It is concerned with the functioning of law in society and the way in which people behave in relation to the law. More specifically, it investigates the social processes of law creation and the social consequences of law in operation. It is, in short, the study of the interaction between the legal and the social. But within this broad framework, two major and distinct approaches are discernible. On the one hand there are those, not surprisingly lawyers for the most part, who stress the value of socio-legal research as an aid to decision making or problem solving. They will want to know, for example, what outcome may be predicted from legislating in a particular way on race relations, or on the rights and duties of landlord and tenant, or the likely consequences of employing various methods of punishment. They will want to see the results of empirical research on such matters reflected in legislation and in the organization of the legal system and the provision of legal services. Others would deny that such practical concerns are properly termed sociology of law. Law, they would argue, is merely one, admittedly important, form of social control. It may be a valuable source for understanding the nature of social systems generally, but ought not to be singled out as if it were an appropriate subject of sociological study in isolation. The real task of the sociologist of law in this view is the study of the social order in its widest sense. In the same way, though the study of lawyers as a profession may produce useful insights, it is the place of such study within the wider concerns of the sociology of occupations which is seen as the proper interest of the sociologist of law.

The two phrases 'socio-legal studies' and 'sociology of law' have then, in the words of Campbell and Wiles (1976), 'been flown as standards in the battle for whatever resources and intellectual or practical prestige might be at stake' (p.548). They reflect a difference of attitude which is at root ideological. Implicit in the problem-solving approach is an acceptance, to a greater or lesser extent, of the values of the existing social system and a belief in the value of empirical studies in helping to improve it. Its proponents have, for the most part, been concerned with ways of redressing inequalities evident in the system, notably in the administration of criminal justice and welfare law and in the provision of legal services. Their inspiration derives from the liberal ideals of due process and equality of treatment before the law.

The main difficulty inherent in this approach is that where there is structural *inequality*, the extension of procedural *equality* is prone to mask and perpetuate substantive injustice. Thus among liberal reformers there has been a tendency to assume that the problem of inadequate provision of legal services can be overcome merely by providing more of them and by making them more easily accessible to those most in need. At the individual level, and in the short term, measures of this kind are undoubtedly beneficial. But to the extent that the problems, legal or otherwise, of the socially disadvantaged result from their relative lack of resources, remedial measures could be seen as merely cosmetic, even counter-productive, if they leave the basic social and economic framework squarely entrenched.

The pragmatic, reformist stance has therefore increasingly come under attack from theorists who aspire to an enhanced understanding of the legal and social order. For those who see the law and its socio-economic setting as problematic, the law ceases to be the main focus of inquiry. Instead, the emphasis is on the structures and processes which dictate or permit its emergence in a particular form. Such a view need not entail an explicit ideology. But it does presuppose that the attempt to improve the system simply by altering its formal rules is doomed to failure, precisely because it ignores the social and economic structure within which the rules operate.

But if the 'problem solvers' are open to the charge of sacrificing theory to expediency, their opponents are not without their shortcomings. Not least among these, as we suggest later, has been their failure to provide any theoretical framework capable of transcending their ideological sectarianism, or even of achieving an agreed position from which the theoretical inadequacy of the 'problem solvers' can be specified.

Other Barriers to Collaboration

The sharp differences of purpose embodied in these competing views of the field go some way towards explaining the lack of coherent development. But there are several additional considerations. Progress has been impeded by the relative insularity of academic lawyers and sociologists when confronted with the prospect of inter-disciplinary study. As Schur has put it, 'Lawyers and sociologists "don't talk the same language"' (1968: 8; see also Willock 1974). Anxious to preserve control in their respective domains, they are mistrustful of each other's discipline, not just through fear of encroachment as such, but also because of what they perceive to be academic dilution. Where the sociologist might feel that the purity of his theoretical concerns is undermined by the mundane priorities of the lawyer, the latter is disposed to resent constant questioning and cavalier treatment of what he takes to be the hard data of the law. In the case of the legal practitioner the gulf is readily understandable. For him the court is a place where legal disputes are settled, not a structured social situation characterized by role playing. He is impatient of theorizing, interpreting it as a self-indulgent exercise engaged in by someone unaffected by the need to reach a decision between two litigants in the here and now. Faced with the perennial conflict created by the need both for certainty and flexibility in law, judges often feel compelled to rely on an established precedent, even though doubtful of its merits, or of the justice of applying it in the particular case before them. In this respect 'it is in the nature of law that its devotees are for ever condemned to live in a pre-Baconian world' (Kahn-Freund 1966: 124).

The sociologist then is disturbed by the lawyer's readiness to assume that the facts speak for themselves and that the law may be legitimately viewed in relative isolation from the social structure within which it functions. The legal practitioner has traditionally been suspicious of empirical evidence in general, in part perhaps through the fear that techniques which reduce the human element in legal proceedings represent a threat to the autonomy of the legal system. A minor example might be the English judiciary's aversion to actuarial tables as a guide to the assessment of damages in personal injury cases. The law, fundamentally normative and instrumental, almost of necessity elevates finality in litigation and continuity of legal principle above considerations of strict logic. Unlike sociology, it does not purport to be a descriptive pursuit of the truth.

There have also been many practical obstacles to academic collaboration, not least a sheer lack of mutual understanding. The sociologist cannot be unaffected by the general image of the law as a somewhat arcane pursuit, clothed in impenetrable language. He may feel inhibited by the mass of legal detail of which he is ignorant and by the need to acquire the special techniques involved in legal method. Conversely, many lawyers subscribe to the conventional wisdom that sociological writing consists of high-sounding jargon covering up trite knowledge. Thus Lord Hailsham (1971), while expressing himself in favour of 'cross-fertilisation at every point between the serious student of civics and the academic and professional lawyer', has described law as 'the bony structure of sociology . . . without which social studies will become the flabby and irresponsible thing that, in the universities, sociology too often is' (p.624). Nor does it help matters that there is more than a grain of truth in each side's accusations of mystification.

Law, innately conservative, remains wary of sociology. Sociology, conscious of its relative newness as a form of academic study, has been equally wary of making incursions into a realm which has such a long history and established reputation. Isolationism has been reinforced by the constraints of departmental politics and practical considerations within institutions of higher education. There are powerful forces inhibiting precisely the kind of interdisciplinary approach necessary to stimulate the research and written texts indispensable for academic development and consolidation (Wilson 1973). The scholar who devotes the time needed to acquire expertise in two traditionally separate fields of study risks losing touch with the mainstream of his 'primary' field. The difficulties are accentuated when law is involved. This is because of the degree of tacit control exercised by the legal profession over the nature of syllabuses, in return for granting exemption from equivalent professional examinations in the more vocational subjects. Partly as a result of this vocational link, law schools have generally lacked a strong tradition of graduate teaching and research. The Bar Council and the Law Society, representing the two branches of the legal profession, not unnaturally think of law schools as training grounds for legal practice, rather than as sources of research. In consequence, most law students have been loath to pursue courses of no immediate relevance to legal practice.

The Development of the Sociology of Law in the United Kingdom

Yet despite all these barriers to fruitful collaboration, the last decade has seen a sudden growth of interest in Britain in the sociology of law and socio-legal studies, in striking contrast to their earlier neglect (Cain 1974; Campbell and Wiles 1976). In the 1960s one would have searched in vain for courses in the field, and research was minimal; by 1976 twelve university law departments and three social science departments were teaching sociology of law at undergraduate level.

A meeting of academic lawyers in Cambridge in 1967 paved the way for recognition of socio-legal studies on an institutional footing. In the following year, Birmingham established its Institute of Judicial Administration, as an interdisciplinary undertaking. In 1971 the Nuffield Foundation set up a research unit and the Centre for Socio-Legal Studies was launched at Oxford under the aegis of the Social Science Research Council (1972). At around the same time, the Society for Public Teachers of Law formed a separate socio-legal group, which was soon to absorb a study group from the British Sociological Association.

Further testimony of growth has been provided by several publishing ventures. Various new series of books have emerged under rubrics such as *Law and Society, Law in Context*, and *Law in Society*, and in 1974 there appeared the first issue of the *British Journal of Law and Society*. In its report on Legal Education, the Ormrod Committee (1971) stressed the need to broaden legal education so that law students should be able to relate law to the wider context of the social sciences generally, and there have been developments in this direction, sometimes on an interdisciplinary basis. Courses in areas such as welfare law, housing law, consumer protection, planning and the environment, and human rights are now common. A broader social perspective than would be required for purely vocational purposes is now frequently adopted, together with some reshaping of more traditional subjects, to take account of the 'law in action' as well as the 'law in the books'. The challenge has been most directly met in the new style of degrees introduced at the universities of Kent, Sussex, and Warwick, with their major emphasis on the social function and context of law, and by some small-scale attempts to develop clinical legal education, so that students are exposed to actual cases and can, for example, advise clients or represent them at tribunals.

Another contemporaneous development was the increasing interest shown by both professional and academic lawyers in law reform itself. The 1960s marked a turning point in willingness to examine how efficiently laws and the machinery of justice were operating. Considerable impetus came from the publication in 1963 of *Law Reform Now* (Gardiner and Martin 1963), a major influence on the decision to establish the Law Commissions (1965), with their remit to 'keep under review all the law ... with a view to its systematic development and reform' (Law Commissions Act 1965). The English Law Commission has expressed the hope that it might 'harness the social sciences to law reform' and its establishment put paid to the belief that law reform was 'something that could be entrusted to a group of legal practitioners, academics and judges in their spare-time moments on Friday afternoons' (Wedderburn 1965). The main focus of recent socio-legal research in England has been on the provision of legal services, clearly stimulated by the experience of the American neighbourhood law firms from the mid-sixties onwards. The Civil Rights Movement was then at its height. From 1965 the 'war on poverty' included Federal funding of legal services programmes through which a growing number of young radical lawyers represented the underprivileged. By 1973 over two thousand lawyers were working in neighbourhood law firms and there has been a steady stream of research into the nature of their work and the discrepancies which it has brought to light between the law in theory and in action.

This was the background to the demand for improved services in England, outlined in two pamphlets in 1968, *Justice for All*, a Fabian tract, and *Rough Justice*, produced by the Society of Conservative Lawyers. Mounting concern about shortcomings in the administration of justice and organization of the legal profession was articulated in works by Zander (1968) and Abel-Smith and Stevens (1967), which condemned the profession for providing an inadequate and outdated service for the general public. In 1971 the Legal Action Group (LAG) was formed. As a pressure group concerned to improve legal services to the community especially in deprived areas, LAG has done much to sustain the momentum for reform, which had not been assisted by the lack of systematic information about the operation of the legal system. The vast mass of evidence accumulated by the Royal Commission on Legal Services (1979) has provided a basis for more informed debate, though the findings of the Report itself scarcely reflect the degree of disquiet expressed (see pp.199–200).

The Sociology of Deviance and the Sociology of Law

Another major source of the revived interest in the sociology of law came from developments within the academic discipline of criminology, or rather 'the sociology of deviance', as it came to be known. In the late 1960s and early 1970s, first in the United States and then in this country, the emergence and temporary dominance of the 'interactionist' and 'labelling' perspectives had a profound influence on academic criminology and at the same time laid some of the necessary foundations for the subsequent revival of interest in the sociology of law. In the United States this process was manifested in the work of writers such as Chambliss and Quinney, which cut across both fields (Quinney's *The Social Reality of Crime* (1970) being particularly influential in this respect). In this country it was evidenced by developments within the National Deviancy Conference, which emerged initially as a forum for bringing the new perspectives of the sociology of deviance to this country and subsequently went on to nurture and encourage a reviving interest in the sociology of law.

Before considering these academic currents in more detail, however, it is perhaps worth looking at the way in which they, in turn, were predicated on and reflected the practical confrontations with 'the law' which were characteristic of that same period in both the United States and Britain (see Pearson 1975). This was a time when civil rights and liberation movements, based on such issues as black power, the Vietnam war, the drug laws and, more recently, gay liberation, were bringing new and articulate groups into direct confrontation with the law and its agents. Such confrontations highlighted an obvious and fundamental, yet much neglected, feature of laws – they are man-made. That is, they are not divinely ordained, nor are they the natural outcome of some form of societal consensus on right and wrong. In these confrontations laws stood out as being selective, both in their definitions of what constituted crimes and in the way such definitions were applied and enforced. Above all, such selectivity clearly reflected socially structured power differences in society. Thus, the anti-Vietnam war movements were able to make much of the way their protest activities could be criminalised, while the pursuance of the war itself could not. Similarly, the hippie drug culture was able to draw attention to the selective and discriminatory manner in which some drugs, such as marijuana and LSD, were made illegal, while others, such as tobacco and alcohol, were not.

These direct insights into the nature of legal definitions, combined with some experience of the manner of their enforcement, helped to produce among the radicals, students, and young academics involved, an intellectual climate very much out of line with the central concerns of traditional academic criminology as it was operating at that time. In the first place, academic criminology had taken its subject matter very much for granted. It was not so much that, as some writers tried to suggest, it took existing legal definitions as being in some sense objectively, or divinely, 'correct'; it was rather that it simply was not concerned to discuss them at all. In its quest for a scientific explanation of criminal behaviour, it took existing criminal law definitions as its unquestioned starting point.

This implicit acceptance of existing definitions was allied to an apparent acceptance of crime as being obviously 'wrong'. And this gave rise to a second significant feature of traditional criminology – what Matza (1969) has termed its 'corrective stance'. That is, because crime was obviously wrong, the role of criminology was to ascertain the causes of crime, in order that it might be corrected. Consequently, both crime and the criminal were seen as being pathological, either in the sense that they were caused through something going wrong in the offenders themselves, or through something going wrong in their social environment.

Finally, underlying this enterprise of traditional academic criminology was a determinist conception of man. Man's actions (in this case his criminal actions) were 'caused' and were hence mere outcomes of underlying social, psychological, and genetic forces.

Whatever might be said for or against these implicit assumptions of traditional criminology – and it could be argued that its critics both caricatured it and dismissed it too glibly (Roshier 1976; Cohen 1979) – they were clearly antipathetic to the spirit of the 1960s. The lack of concern with the way in which laws came about and were applied and the interests they reflected, and the denial of the possibility of seeing the so-called criminal as a free agent fighting a corrupt and immoral society, made academic criminology appear stifling and reactionary.

It was against this background that the new 'sociology of deviance' arose. As with most 'new' movements, it was based not so much on new ideas as on the rediscovery of old ones – in this case the interactionist theory of G.H. Mead. In the United States the key figures were Becker (1964) and Lemert (1967). In this country it is best represented by the two collections of essays emanating from the National Deviancy Conference (Cohen 1971 and Taylor and Taylor 1973). Obviously, the various writers offered differing interpretations, but there was a general underlying acceptance of interactionist theory, particularly in the way in which it opposed virtually all the fundamental assumptions of traditional criminology. The crucial significance of this movement for the emergence of the new sociological interest in law derives from the actual substance of interactionist theory. Thus, at the risk of seeming a little discursive at this point, it is worth spelling it out in a little more detail.

The basic assumption of interactionist theory is a simple one: men construct their actions in a process of social interaction with others. Consequently, the responses of others to our initial actions are crucial in shaping our subsequent actions. One important way in which people respond to the actions of others is to 'label' them (i.e. classify them in some stereotypical way): hence the tie-up between interactionism and 'labelling' theory. One very significant label that is sometimes attached to actions is that of being 'criminal' or 'deviant' (the new writers preferred the broader category of deviance since, they insisted, there were important continuities in terms of societal response between crime and other forms of deviant behaviour). Such labels have important implications both for the way in which others subsequently react to the person so labelled and, ultimately, to the way the person labelled sees himself.

Clearly, from this perspective, crimes do not exist as objectively 'given' actions which we can take for granted. Rather, they consist of labels *applied* to actions. And anything could be (and perhaps at some time or other has been) so defined. Particular actions are designated as crimes through a process of interaction (a 'transaction') between the actor concerned and those responding to and labelling his actions. Thus, to really understand crime and deviance we must examine *both sides* of this process – the labellers as well as the labelled. Traditional criminology, it was pointed out, had focussed almost exclusively on the latter.

The interactionist and labelling theorists thus directed attention to the nature and implications of the societal response to crime and deviance. Within the sociology of deviance, one of its main contributions in this respect was the suggestion that this response, by altering the way society treated the labelled deviant and ultimately by altering the deviant's conception of himself, actually created *more* deviance rather than correcting it (which was the formal aim). Unfortunately, this particular contribution tended to violate one of the initial aims of the new perspective: the reassertion (contrary to the determinism of traditional criminology) of man's 'freedom' to direct his own actions. In the event, it tended to take on a more and more deterministic appearance, merely providing a new causal explanation of crime and deviance in terms of the consequences of societal labelling (a point later admitted by Lemert (1974)).

The new deviance was also something of a disappointment in another respect. Although it allowed for a concern with the wider, political questions of how laws come to be formulated and operated,

it in fact focussed its attention almost exclusively on the more immediate implications of the interaction between offenders and lower-
level functionaries in the process of societal response (a criticism
made by Gouldner (1975)).

However, while it is true that the interactionist and labelling
perspectives on the whole failed to live up to expectations and have
now largely been abandoned in the sociology of crime and deviance,
they have certainly had a lasting impact as far as the sociology of law
is concerned. Indeed, from the sociological side, they were probably
the most important influence on the resurgence of interest. It is not
difficult to see why. Their emphasis on the 'other side' of crime
directed attention to precisely those areas which constitute the core
of the sociology of law – the social processes involved in the formulation, application, and change of legal norms (the main limitation
being the exclusive focus on *criminal* law). In this respect, the sociology of law became the natural counterpart of the new sociology of
crime and deviance. As Chambliss (1974) has recently put it:

> 'It is now recognised . . . that the starting point for the systematic
> study of crime is *not* to ask why some people become criminal
> while others do not, but to ask first why is it that some acts get
> defined as criminal while others do not. Criminology begins,
> then, with the sociology of law: the study of the institutions which
> create, interpret and enforce the rules that tolerate one set of
> behaviour while prohibiting and discouraging another' (p.7).

Much of the sociological work we will be concerned with in later
sections of this book dealing with both the emergence of legal rules
(e.g. Carson 1974a; Gunningham 1974; Chambliss 1970) and legal
rules in operation (e.g. Piliavin and Briar 1964; J. Young 1971) owe
at least some of their impetus to the impact of the interactionist and
labelling perspectives on traditional criminology.

As we have seen, these developments in sociology and criminology
had their counterpart in the law. A new breed of 'radical' lawyers
was to emerge in the newly established law centres, with a commitment to changing society, instead of pursuing the traditional
lawyer's role. As Pearson has pointed out, in the 1970s the radical
lawyer has joined forces with, among others, the radical social
worker, psychologist, therapist, and architect, in building up an
ethos of community action, to tackle issues as diverse as tenants'
rights, entitlement to welfare benefits, the rights of mental patients,
and opposition to motorways.

In so far as the confrontations of the 1960s provided a common source for a revived interest in the sociology of law on the part of both lawyers and sociologists, it might have been expected that a new level of cooperation and integration would have been achieved. The fact that this has not happened, and that we are left with the sociology of law/socio-legal problems dichotomy, reflects an ambiguity in the attitude towards law that was implicit in the various movements of the Sixties. On the one hand, law was seen as an instrument of oppression or discrimination (for example in the Black Power movement, the more politically-conscious manifestations of the anti-Vietnam war movement, and the anti-drug law and gay liberation movements). On the other hand, law was also seen as a means of redressing wrongs, of achieving desirable social changes (for example in the various civil rights movements seeking legislative changes to combat racial and later sexual discrimination).

The 'oppressive' view of law led naturally to a wider questioning of the role of law in society, in particular its relationship to the state and capitalism. As such it was the natural precursor of an important, Marxist-oriented concern in the current theoretical branch of the sociology of law (as in the work ·of Bankowski and Mungham (1976a) and the more recent writings of Chambliss (1975) and Quinney (1975)). The 'problem-solving' approach has, on the other hand, led to reformist-oriented research into the operation of the law (see e.g. Zander 1978).

This division within the sociology of law to some extent corresponds to the different interests of sociologists and lawyers noted earlier. But its significance must not be exaggerated, since it also relates to a wider, longer-standing division between the 'theoretical' and the 'practical' within the social sciences generally – for example, the unresolved division between the wider theoretical and philosophical issues which have always preoccupied sociology and the policy-orientated concerns of social administration.

To this account of the growth in sociology of law studies might be added the more cynical view of Bankowski and Mungham, that the traditional areas of legal scholarship have been over-researched to the point of market saturation and that careerism has dictated a 'need' for 'socio-legal studies', 'law for the poor', and 'welfare law'. On this analysis, academics involved in sociological approaches to law have defined their own scholarship as centrally legal, in order to legitimate their own activity. But while as White (1973) also notes, cynics are talking of a 'legal services industry', nurtured by the Social Science Research Council, and akin to the 'race relations industry', and while no doubt all new ventures of this kind produce a bandwagon (not excluding, one might add, the 'Marxist critique industry'), the argument is vastly overstated. Not only is the premise that traditional legal areas have been over-researched highly debatable, but there are no signs of sociology of law or socio-legal studies challenging the supremacy of the long-established legal subjects; nor are there any grounds for anticipating such a development, as long as the study of law is geared to a significant extent – as will surely continue to be the case – to legal practice.

Sociological Theory and the Sociology of Law

Perhaps as a result of the failure of the interactionist perspective to provide a generally acceptable theoretical framework for the resurgent sociology of law, there is now a confusion of perspectives and practical demands. Carson (1974a) warns: 'There is a danger that in the current climate the sociology of law will become prematurely harnessed to the demand of immediate legal applicability and will not be guided by significant theoretical concerns' (p.68). The problem is, of course, what constitutes a 'guiding' and 'significant' theoretical concern? Or, more realistically, what sociological theories seem to be offering such guidance, in terms of inspiring empirical research and theoretical development? The founding fathers of sociology – even when specifically concerned with law, as were Weber and Durkheim – do not currently appear to be inspiring very much. This is perhaps because their sociology of law is inextricably bound up with their wider substantive theoretical concern – to analyse the emergence of modern industrial society. And their theories for understanding this process have been far less influential than other aspects of their sociology, such as their ideas on modes of sociological analysis.

Thus, for Weber, law is one of the many areas of social life subject to the 'rationalization' which he saw as characterizing the emergence of modern industrial society. His sociology of law consists primarily of chronicling this process (see Bendix 1960). But the extent and nature of rationalization is not now an issue which stimulates much sociological interest. It certainly shows no sign of doing so in the sociology of law today.

Durkheim's sociology of law is similarly tied up with his wider concern with the transition from simple to modern industrial forms of society. He was primarily interested in the differing forms of solidarity which bind these two kinds of society together: 'mechanical' solidarity in simple societies and 'organic' solidarity in modern industrial ones. A major index of the degree of transformation from mechanical to organic solidarity, according to Durkheim, was the extent to which law had changed from a predominantly 'repressive' form (relying on punitive sanctions) to a predominantly 'restitutive' one (concerned more with reparation). His sociology of law was, consequently, central to his general sociology. The theme of transition from repressive to restitutive forms of law as society has become more complex has inspired a limited amount of subsequent research (in particular Schwartz and Miller (1964); see also, for useful summaries, Clarke (1976) and Cotterrell (1977)). On the whole, Durkheim's main argument has not found very much support. Indeed, Chambliss and Seidman (1971), starting from similar assumptions about simple and industrial societies, come to exactly the opposite conclusion: that the intimate relationships of simple societies require restitutive forms of law, while the impersonal relationships of modern industrial society are more associated with repressive forms. But once again, apart from this limited and not very complimentary follow-up, there is absolutely no sign that Durkheim's work on the sociology of law is likely to provide a significant and guiding theoretical theme.

Despite the fact that law was not a central concern of Marx and Engels (so that, some Marxist writers claim, a Marxist sociology of law is not possible: e.g. Hirst (1972)), Marxist themes do seem to be providing some inspiration for the new interest in sociology of law (see Cain and Hunt (1979) for a compilation and analysis of the scattered references to law in Marx and Engels' writings). Various recent studies have taken as their theme the way in which law supports the capitalist ruling class both directly, as norms legislated and enforced in their interests, and indirectly, as ideology legitimizing their position. Consequently, these arguments will play an important part in the next chapter when we look at the way legal norms emerge and change.

Apart from the various forms of Marxist sociology, the currently most influential trend has been the development of equally varied forms of phenomenologically inspired 'interpretive' sociology. They have in common the rejection of deterministic conceptions of man and of positivist methods for studying him, and insist that human action can only be understood in terms of the meanings that men attach to actions and situations. As such, they primarily represent a stance on what constitutes proper sociological knowledge. Thus, Grace and Wilkinson's contribution to the sociology of law (1978a) consists of a critique of previous sociological theory and research on law from an interpretive standpoint, and a set of criteria for doing acceptably 'sociological' work on law. The more phenomenologically committed strands of interpretive sociology, on the other hand, seem to rule out any specific interest in particular substantive areas of human action at all. Their concern is with their own microscopic analyses of action and meaning construction. Consequently, even when such work is carried out in legal contexts (see, for example, Atkinson 1979) the contribution is to a particular branch of phenomenological sociology rather than to anything that might be termed the sociology of law.

With the exception of some forms of Marxist sociology, then, there does not seem to be much available in the way of 'guiding' theoretical concerns for the emerging sociology of law. The trend is likely to be a continuing divergence between its theoretical and practical branches: the theoretical consisting mainly of re-analyses of old sociological approaches to law, and the practical continuing with its problem-solving approach without confronting the theoretical problems implicit in what it accepts as problems and solutions. Indeed, the currently emerging literature already divides fairly uniformly into one of other of these categories (e.g. Grace and Wilkinson (1978a) and Hunt (1978) on the one hand and the various publications of Zander, Baldwin, Bottoms, and McConville on the other).

Conclusion: an Approach to the Study of Law and Society

It will be apparent from the following chapters that we do not adhere to either a fully indeterminate conception of man or any particular Marxist or anti-Marxist conception of legal and social change. There is nevertheless a unifying theme underpinning the subject matter of this book.

We can describe this theme in terms of two questions. First, how is law, in reality, formulated and applied? Second, whose interests does it express in these processes? The first question involved empirical, descriptive work, but also frequently entails making the kind of distinction insisted upon by the legal realists – between 'law in the books' and 'law in action'. That is to say, the reality of law is measured against some 'ideal', usually taken to be implicit in the formal 'book' content of the law, or in the constitutional procedures available for formulating and changing laws. Often this kind of analysis takes the form of measuring the reality in terms of ideals of justice, equality or democracy. Since such conceptions cannot necessarily be derived from the formal content of law and constitutional procedures, the researcher is usually, implicitly at least, introducing his own version of these ideals as a measuring rod (this was self-consciously the case with the legal realists). It is at this point too – the introduction of ideological considerations into the analysis – that we can discern an underlying theoretical dispute. Arguments about the existence of disjunctures between the reality of law and its ideal forms reflect varying conceptions of the nature of power in society – from Marxist at one extreme, through pluralist to consensual at the other, and it is in these terms that the second question (whose interests does the law reflect?) is answered.

However, the 'disjunctures' approach is not without its critics (quite apart, that is, from those pointing to its failure to be guided by a significant theoretical concern). Grace and Wilkinson (1978b), for example, argue against concentrating on 'law in the books as against law in action; legal as against social rules: formal as against informal rules', claiming that ' . . . utilising the disjunctures renders organisational activity unproblematic, a mere comparison of 'what should be the case', and leads to a position of organisational activity never being analysed in its own terms but only by reference to the disjuncture' (p.38).

This is certainly true, but it is difficult to see why it is the problem they claim it to be. Certainly the disjunctures approach is a *different kind of interest* in the law from that which they propose, but there is no reason at all, and they give none, to regard it as more problematic, any worse or any better. Interestingly, Abel (1973), arguing from a similar rejection of the disjunctures or 'gap' approach, comes to a very different conclusion as to the appropriate alternative: namely a policy-orientated, problem-solving approach.

McBarnet (1978), in the context of the criminal law, makes a rather more fundamental criticism – denying, in effect, that there are disjunctures at all, and claiming that analysis which proceeds on the basis that they do exist rests on a curiously liberal view of formal law: 'That formal legal rules are organised around civil rights is taken for granted by both the champions and the critics of the status quo' (p.30).

In other words, 'the critics' see any disjunctures as being between formal law, which embodies the principles of due process, and the law in action, which involves the subversion of these principles by those who apply the law in favour of an almost exclusive concern with crime control.

McBarnet claims, giving various examples, that:

' . . . A good many of the practices in criminal justice described as informal perversions of the formal rules are in fact allowed, facilitated or upheld in the formal rules of statute and precedent. . . . The operation of the law is not a subversion of the substance of the law but exactly what one would expect it to produce; the law in action is only too close a parallel to the law in the books; due process is for crime control' (pp.30–1).

It is difficult to see how one can derive the conclusion that 'due process is *for* crime control' (emphasis added) from the premise that the formal rules 'allow' or 'facilitate' it! Nevertheless, there is much that we would agree with in McBarnet's thesis. Certainly, as we have already suggested, it is implausible in practice to identify formal law with a simple due process model. Nor does it make sense to chronicle the law in action without careful reference back to its relationship with the formal provisions. But we would argue that, in the end McBarnet's view is based on a version of the relationship between formal law and law in action which is equally simplistic (though opposite to) the one she criticizes. We would suggest both that it is *sometimes* possible, and useful, to analyse the law in action in terms of its deviation from the intent of the formal law, but that more usually the formal law is insufficiently specific to be seen as necessarily implying any particular form of 'law in action' at all. That is to say, the relationship is usually a problematic one, where it would be just as unrealistic to assume equivalence (as does McBarnet) as it would be to assume disjuncture.

It is clear, then, that any analysis of law and society must concern itself with the description of the law in action. This will be the subject matter of most of this book. However, regardless of whether it can be specifically related to a disjuncture between intent and reality, we would insist on the necessity for discussing the reality of law in action in the context of the competing demands of due process, bureaucratic imperatives, and social control. This is simply because they represent demands made of it in the real world and neglect of them would consequently make the analysis sterile or, worse still, resemble an attempt at a spurious scientific objectivity. This means, of course, that we are nearer to the 'socio-legal problems' end of the spectrum we described earlier in the chapter.

Suggested Reading

Bendix, R. (1960) *Max Weber: an Intellectual Portrait*. London: Heinemann.

Cain, M. (1974) 'The Problem of Teaching the Sociology of Law in the U.K.' International Sociological Association VIII World Congress of Sociology and Law, Toronto.

Cain, M. and Hunt, A. (1979) *Marx and Engels on Law*. London: Academic Press.

Campbell, C. and Wiles, P. (1976) The Study of Law in Society in Britain. *Law and Society Review* **10**: 547.

Clarke, M. (1976) Durkheim's Sociology of Law. *British Journal of Law and Society* **3**: 246.

Cotterrell, R. (1977) Durkheim on Legal Development and Social Solidarity. *British Journal of Law and Society* **4**: 241.

Durkheim, E. (1964) *The Division of Labour in Society*. New York: Free Press.

_____ (1973) Two Laws of Penal Evolution. *Economy and Society* **2**: 285.

Grace, C. and Wilkinson, P. (1978) *Sociological Inquiry and Legal Phenomena*. New York: St. Martin's Press.

Hunt, A. (1978) *The Sociological Movement in Law*. London: Macmillan.

Lloyd, Lord (1979) *Introduction to Jurisprudence* (4th. ed.). London: Stevens.

McBarnet, D. (1978) False Dichotomies in Criminal Justice Research. In J. Baldwin and A. Bottomley (eds.) *Criminal Justice: Selected Readings*. London: Martin Robertson.

Open University (1972) *Social Interaction* (The Sociological Perspective Units 5–8). Milton Keynes: Open University Press.

Roberts, S. (1979) *Order and Dispute: an Introduction to Legal Anthropology*. Harmondsworth: Penguin.

Twining, W. (1974) Law and Social Science: the Method of Detail. *New Society* **758**: 27 June 1974.

Willock, I. (1974) Getting on with Sociologists. *British Journal of Law and Society* **1**: 3.

2

The Emergence of Legal Rules

How Legal Rules Emerge

INTRODUCTION

In this chapter we will be looking at the dynamic aspect of the relationship between the legal and the social – the process whereby new legal norms emerge, or old ones change. Under this heading we will be concentrating on both legislation and judicial interpretation as sources of creation, leaving the rest of the legal process to be dealt with under the heading of the 'application' of legal rules. However, it should be emphasized that this distinction is a matter of degree rather than a hard and fast one, since one of our basic assumptions is that some element of creativity occurs at virtually all levels of the legal process.

As we have just seen, much contemporary sociology of law involves the identification of discrepancies between some formally accepted or ideal state of affairs and the reality, together with some underlying ideological position on how and why these discrepancies have come about. We can roughly locate the different positions on a continuum ranging from a consensualist position at one extreme, through to a more or less pluralist position in the middle, to a more or less Marxist one of ruling class dominance at the other extreme. Essentially, the difference between them lies in their answer to the question of whose interests are represented in the emergence or change of legal rules.

The consensual view coincides, in this case, with what may be regarded as the formal, or ideal state of affairs. That is, a position which sees all such change as reflecting 'public opinion' in some way.

In the contemporary English context it implies that the political processes of the liberal democratic state express this consensus (see, for example, Friedmann (1972) Ch. 1). Such a position can be allied to an equally formal or ideal view of judicial interpretation of law: that it is simply a matter of an objective clarification of its literal meaning. Alternatively, if some creativity is allowed for in this process, again it is carried out in a way which purports to express an underlying social consensus, as when a statutory provision is interpreted in accordance with the 'intention of Parliament'. (We will be looking in more detail at such arguments about judicial interpretation later in this chapter.)

The middle or pluralist position sees conflict, to some extent at least, as a central feature of the emergence or change of law. One problem posed by, the consensualist view is what proportion of supportive public opinion is presumed to be reflected in such change? Does it mean everyone, or a simple majority? If the latter, then it would allow for a considerable amount of opposition – sufficient to make the consensual concept rather misleading. More importantly, perhaps, the consensualist position overestimates the degree to which 'public opinion' is ever mobilized in relation to particular issues. The pluralist view, consequently, sees change as being the outcome of competing groups, with differing power bases, mobilizing themselves to achieve changes in line with their interests. It covers a wide range of possibilities, from one in which the 'winner' varies widely from case to case, to one where a particular power group usually predominates. Nor does it rule out 'public opinion', in so far as it does organize and express itself, being a competitor and power base. The 'pure' form of pluralism (which is often implied when the term is used) is the middle position, where power is more or less equally divided among a number of (minority) groups. But in terms of the continuum it obviously covers a wide range, shading into consensualism at one extreme, as majority popular opinion asserts itself and into the Marxist model of ruling class dominance at the other extreme.

It follows that, on the pluralist model, judicial interpretation, in so far as it occurs, would be expected to reflect the particular interests of the judiciary which certainly could not be assumed to itself reflect some generalized 'public opinion'. Thus Weber, for example, who held to a version of the pluralist conception of social change, believed that the self-defined intellectual needs of the legal profession were an important influence in the development of law in Western Europe. Since the pluralist position does not claim at the outset to know who the winners are in the conflict over legal change, nor what effective power is based on, or how it can be effectively used, these questions become its focus of attention. Much more than the two other positions, it necessarily requires detailed analysis of the actual processes whereby law emerges and changes.

Finally, at the other end of the spectrum from consensualism is the Marxist position; this typically sees all manifestations of legal change as an expression of the interests of an identifiable ruling class, which are themselves dependent on the requirements of the underlying mode of production. Alternatively, law is employed to sort out disputes *within* the ruling class, in their interests as a whole. The judiciary, as members or servants of that class, similarly interpret the law in its interests.

Carson (1974a), although not ultimately favouring an uncompromising Marxist interpretation, provides some useful support for it by noting various ways in which apparently contradictory evidence (for example legislation which places constraints upon the behaviour of the ruling class – such as the Factories Acts, the Companies Acts, etc.) is in fact often nothing of the sort. Thus he notes that such legislation may in practice be rarely enforced, or that barriers to efficient implementation are subtly built into the legislation itself. Alternatively, the legislation simply may not be as inimical to ruling class interests as it appears on paper (by providing, for example, some rational rules which, though individually restrictive, are in the interests of overall efficient operation). Once again, Carson points to the need to look at what actually happens, rather than what appears to be the case on paper.

However, other techniques for salvaging a Marxist interpretation in the face of apparently contradictory evidence are rather more problematic. Two in particular require some attention. First, there is the 'tokenism' argument. That is, when evidence of legislation which *does* operate against ruling class interests is brought forward, it is written off as a 'token' concession designed to ward off any real opposition, and hence reinforcing the ruling class power position. The problem with this contention is that it could be argued, and indeed we would argue, that such concessions when made through fear of more fundamental opposition are precisely examples of opposition forces exercising power. Consequently, we would count all such examples as being incompatible with a strict Marxist interpretation.

Closely allied to tokenism is the 'irrelevance' argument: all changes which do not operate to challenge or alter the economic basis of capitalism are written off as irrelevant – in a sense as not being changes at all. The most obvious examples are provided by 'social' legislation such as homosexual or abortion law reform. But the argument is also applied to quite substantial economic changes, affecting the quality of life of the working class, but not substantially altering the private property, profit orientation of capitalism. A further complication is the fact that the *desire* to leave the fundamental basis of capitalism unchanged is apparently shared by all classes – that is, it *appears* to be consensual. Contemporary Marxists tend to argue that this is because ruling class hegemony is not simply over power and coercion, but also over all sources of legitimizing ideology, for example the mass media, and consequently is able to manipulate consensus over what constitute legitimate areas of change.

The problem, once again, is that the parameters of change allowed for even under these circumstances would, in our view, still make possible significant changes affecting the quality of peoples' lives, which are intrinsically important and worthy of consideration. But, more importantly, are there not changes which admittedly still leave the *formal* structure of private property capitalism intact, yet make sufficient inroads into the actual *meaning* of private property to count as 'real' changes? We will revert to this issue later when we consider the views of Renner.

Although much of the work which has been done on the emergence and change of legal norms relates to this consensualist – pluralist – ruling class continuum it is very much an oversimplification in the form in which we have considered it so far. Other important themes have also been suggested: it remains to look at some of these, and explore their relation to the continuum.

SYMBOLISM

In his book *Symbolic Crusade* (1963) Gusfield attempts to explain what would otherwise be rather paradoxical features of some examples of legal change: as when new law does not seem to serve any particular material interests of the dominant class and is a remarkable failure as far as enforcement is concerned. Gusfield's archetypal example is Prohibition in the United States. His point is that it did not particularly matter whether it succeeded or not as far as enforcement was concerned; more important was what the successful passage of the Act *symbolized*. As Gusfield (1967) puts it: 'Legal affirmation or rejection is . . . important in what it symbolises as well as or instead of what it controls. Even if the law was broken, it was clear whose law it was' (p.178).

Prohibition symbolized the continuing dominant status of an

abstinent, Protestant middle class, by showing that it was still able legally to define morality. Such moral assertiveness, Gusfield suggests, is particularly likely when such groups feel themselves under threat.

He argues that this is an additional kind of interest that is sometimes expressed in legislation – an interest in status assertion, of showing who is boss. Additional, that is, to an economic class interest, although presumably part of the interest in status assertion is that it facilitates the expression of more material interests. Gusfield, however, is clearly arguing that an interest in status assertion, particularly when it takes the form of defining public morality, can act as a driving force behind legislation in its own right.

Hay (1975) on the other hand, in his study of English Criminal Law in the eighteenth century, points to the way in which such symbolic qualities of law illustrate its significance as *ideology*, legitimizing and reinforcing the position of the ruling class.

Hay starts with a rather similar paradox to that of Gusfield. The eighteenth century in England was a period of massive increase in capital offences (to protect the property of the emerging propertied middle class). Yet in practice, the incidence of enforcement was extraordinarily low – hangings being fewer in number than in Tudor times. Indeed, it was argued at the time that the very severity of the punishments was responsible for the high level of impunity. Hay concedes that the contemporary reformist argument that less severe punishment would have led to more certainty of conviction, and hence more coercive efficiency on the part of the law, was probably correct. But, he claims, this argument overlooked the important symbolic functions that this apparently irrational system had for the bourgeoisie. The extremely harsh formal punishments provided an important backdrop of terror which helped to endow the law with its quality of majesty, while at the same time providing the judiciary with the opportunity to temper justice with mercy. It was the manipulation of these qualities of the law, Hay suggests, which enabled the ruling class to legitimize their position in the eyes of the ruled; to command the deference and establish the authority which constituted the basis of their successful hegemony throughout the eighteenth century.

Burman (1976) makes an essentially similar point with reference to the enforcement of colonial law in South Africa in the nineteenth century. While officially there was no recognition at all of tribal law, in practice its use was widely countenanced. Burman suggests that this apparently ineffective policy enabled the colonial ruling class to establish their authority symbolically, while at the same time averting excessive conflict and a consequent loss of deference.

Both Hay and Burman thus claim to show how the coexistence of official harshness and inflexibility with discretionary enforcement could be manipulated to legitimize the position of the ruling class. The apparent (and actual) inefficiency of the law as a *coercive* instrument was not as important as the symbolic and ideological functions that it performed. In this sense, their views are similar to those of Gusfield, who argues that the coercive failure of the law on prohibition was also less important than the symbolic function it performed for the group whose law it was. Gusfield, on the other hand, clearly does not imply that such a situation is necessarily peculiar to a Marxist conception of a ruling class.

Between them Gusfield, Hay, and Burman point to the fact that if we are to discern the interests that are being served by particular legal changes, we must often look beyond both the formal content of the law and whether it is successful or not in achieving its aims. However, according to Hay and Burman it is clear that the benefit to be derived is in the reinforcement of the power position of the ruling class, so that, presumably, its opportunities to pursue its material interests are enhanced. Gusfield's view is rather different. For him, status-assertion through legislation is an autonomous interest. If he is right, then the concept of an 'interest' must be extended beyond that of a straightforward material benefit. We will now look at an argument which suggests precisely that.

MORAL ENTREPRENEURSHIP

In his analysis of the emergence of the Marijuana Tax Act (1937) in the United States, through which the legal control of marijuana was introduced, Becker concentrates on the role of the Treasury Department's Bureau of Narcotics, whom he describes as 'moral entrepreneurs'. That is, 'they perceived an area of wrongdoing that properly belonged in their jurisdiction and moved to put it there.' He describes the techniques they used to achieve this: providing information and propaganda on 'the problem' via Departmental reports which were given directly to newspapers who then featured them as 'horror' stories and demanded action; cooperating with state authorities, and ensuring minimal effects on powerful 'legitimate' business interests (such as bird seed suppliers). Marijuana users, on the other hand, being unorganized and powerless, were unable to provide any opposition, and the Bill passed both the House and The

Senate unopposed. Becker (1963: 219) draws some general conclusions from this example:

> 'I have given an extended illustration from the field of federal legislation. But the basic parameters of this case should be equally applicable not only to legislation in general, but to the development of rules of a more informal kind. Wherever rules are created and applied, we should be alive to the possible presence of an enterprizing individual or group. Their activities can properly be called *moral enterprise*, for what they are enterprizing about is the creation of a new fragment of the moral constitution of society, its code of right and wrong.'

It is clear, however, that moral entrepreneurship is only successful when it comes from an economically and politically powerful source. Further, the moral opposition to drug use, as Becker himself suggests, itself derives from the protestant ethic, with its disapproval of behaviour indulged in purely for pleasure, especially if not 'earned'. Consequently, in Marxist terms, moral entrepreneurship would be seen simply as the ideological manifestation of economic power, but Becker does not seem to see it as being reducible in this way. Rather he portrays moral enterprise as an interest in its own right – arguing that people have an autonomous interest in the 'moral constitution of society', which is not simply an expression of their economic interest, despite the fact that it is the economically powerful who usually dominate it. This view is perhaps better supported by examples of what might be called 'liberal' moral enterprise – such as homosexual and abortion law reform – which are not so easily portrayed as manifestations of economic power. Becker's concept of moral entrepreneurship seems to us to be a useful way of conceptualizing the sources of such legal changes (which, as we argued earlier, cannot be written off as irrelevant). It does not, however, in itself explain what determines whose moral entrepreneurship should succeed. Becker does explore this important question to some extent, in his description of the power of the Bureau in terms of the contacts and propaganda opportunities which its status afforded.

BUREAUCRATIC IMPERATIVES

The conclusions drawn by Becker from the case of the Marijuana Tax Act provide a partial explanation, then, of its passage. A further

₺ element is suggested by Dickson (1968) who points to an additional dimension of the interests expressed in legislative change.

The Narcotics Bureau emerged as a separate unit in 1930. Its powers and jurisdiction were relatively limited, however, and at the same time public concern about drugs was low. Dickson, arguing from an assumption that all bureaucracies have some kind of intrinsic need for expansion, described the Bureau's strategy for expanding its jurisdiction. First, it mounted a campaign against narcotics: a barrage of reports and newspaper articles generated a public outcry, and a series of test cases (sponsored by the Bureau) resulted in a reinterpretation of the 1914 Harrison Act, broadening the Bureau's powers. Narcotics clinics were closed, and doctors brought under more effective control. The Bureau's success, Dickson suggests, resulted from the strong powers of legitimation which attach to a public body.

The later Act was not, says Dickson, the outcome of a prior moral crusade. Indeed, marijuana was already under the legal control of state authorities (due to earlier pressure from the Bureau) and without the generation of much public concern. The Act was inspired by more simple considerations: economic pressures had led to a low budgetary appropriation to the Bureau. The Act was pushed through by the Bureau and *followed* by a propaganda campaign because it needed to make itself appear more necessary and attract funds for survival and expansion.

Dickson is careful not to deny the force of moral factors as well. He sees the Marijuana Tax Act, as well as the earlier jurisdictional expansion of the Narcotics Bureau, as the outcome of a combination of moral and bureaucratic factors. His analysis, however, suggests a significant additional interest lying behind some forms of legal change: the need for self-aggrandizement and expansion which is intrinsic to bureaucracies. It is an extension of Parkinson's Law – whereas Parkinson was primarily concerned with the self-generated needs for expansion of personnel in bureaucracies, Dickson is interested in demonstrating the (obviously related) need for jurisdictional expansion. He also demonstrates that it is particularly *state* bureaucracies, with their power to generate publicity and easy access to legislators, who are especially likely to be successful in translating this need into reality. This is an important point since it suggests a need, and a source of power to realize that need, which are characteristic of *all* state bureaucracies. It would consequently be as applicable to state bureaucracies in socialist societies as to those in capitalist societies, if not more so. However, there does appear to be an important proviso: the need for expansion of control seems more compelling where those who are being controlled are 'outsiders' (as in the case of marijuana users) or at least of relatively low status. As we will see later, where state bureaucracies are set up to control the powerful (as in the case of the Factory Inspectorate and Alkali Inspectorate) they have a tendency to identify with those they are supposed to control, thereby reducing the desire for jurisdictional expansion.

LEGAL CHANGE AND LEGAL FUNCTIONS: RENNER

Carson's warnings about the interpretation of legal change were essentially that we should be wary of formal change since it need not necessarily represent *real* change. Karl Renner's argument (1976) is the obverse: that formal legal norms which have remained unchanged may in fact alter dramatically in their social and economic implications. Indeed, Renner argued more generally that as new ruling class interests emerge, they characteristically express themselves through existing legal norms. Formal legal change, recognizing the real change that has taken place, usually lags well behind. On this view, if we are to understand the way in which power and interests are reflected in legal norms, we must look at the way they function, rather than at their form.

Renner begins by looking at how the interests of the rising capitalist class expressed themselves through legal norms. Thus, although institutions such as 'property' and 'contract' retained essentially the same legal definition from the eighteenth century to the twentieth century, yet, he argues, during that period their social and economic implications became almost entirely different. The original formulation of property laws was related to controlling 'matter' or 'things' only. But as property came to include capital under the emergence of capitalism, it also came to include the control of wage labourers – that is, the control of human beings. Similarly, the 'freely entered into' private contract became, in fact, 'an indirect power relationship, a *public* obligation to service, like the serfdom of feudal times.'

Renner's subsequent analysis is also of interest. He argues that things have changed again since Marx wrote. There have been further transformations in the social functions of these legal institutions – private property in *fact* becoming transformed into 'public utility'. To illustrate this he contrasts the feudal manor and the peasant's farm, with their clearcut, fenced-off, unequivocally 'private' property, with a privately owned railway of the period in which he was writing (the beginning of this century). The latter, in the way it presented itself to the user, had none of the characteristics of being privately owned: the user was not aware of the fact that he was on private property, that he had entered a contract with the owner (who was nowhere apparent); the railway had all the characteristics of a public utility (Renner's point being reinforced by the fact that none of these characteristics changed when railways later *were* nationalized and became an *actual* public utility). Renner saw such changes as part of a determined trend towards full public ownership. But it was only *after* the event that they began to be recognised by legal changes.

Renner saw a similar process taking place in relation to labour. In Marx's time, the labour relation was based entirely on individual regulation. But in Renner's time, 'thanks to a century of struggle', workers had achieved a collective status which gave them a certain amount of power. Again, the translation of this power into legal rights followed some time after the event.

Quite apart from its intrinsic interest as an important statement about the relationship between legal change and social change, Renner's analysis is of equal interest for its Marxism. It is clearly an unusually optimistic, evolutionary version of Marxism (he was explicitly critical of Bolshevism). It is also an effective response to the 'tokenism' and 'irrelevance' arguments with which hard-line Marxists respond to social and legal changes which do not appear to favour ruling class interests. We asked earlier – at what point does giving in a little to reinforce your general power position become loss of power to your opponents? And at what point do changes which leave the formal institutions of capitalism intact nevertheless become significant changes?

Renner answers both of these questions by insisting that we look *behind* the formal legal provisions and ask how they operate. Just as formal legal definitions in relation to property and contract concealed the emerging power interests of the capitalist class in the last century, so too, he argues, they conceal the emerging assertion of working class interests in the present century. Thus, for Renner, the 'century of struggle' *has* altered the position of the working class, despite the fact that the formal institutions of capitalism are still intact. Renner implies in his analysis that to consider the existing form of such legal institutions as private property and contract to be evidence of the continuing existence of unfettered capitalist exploitation is as naive as to see them as guarantors of individual freedom, in the way that the nineteenth-century laissez-faire capitalists did. In both cases, to understand them properly, it is necessary to see how they *operate*. Renner was in no doubt that changes in the operation of such legal institutions (together with piecemeal, belated changes in the legal forms themselves) produced inroads into the dominant power position of the capitalist ruling class, even though they did not remove it.

We have now encountered some important qualifications to the rather simplistic consensus-pluralist-Marxist framework with which we started this chapter. Gusfield, Becker, and Dickson suggest that we must take a wider view of the interests expressed in legal change than is implied simply by economic interests, despite the fact that they may often stem from the same power source. Carson and Renner remind us of the discrepancy between legal form and legal reality – Carson warning that changes in legal forms do not necessarily lead to real changes in terms of the expression of interests; Renner the obverse, that unchanging legal forms may come to express very different interests. Bearing these points in mind, we will now turn to some case studies of the emergence and change of legal norms.

SOME CASE STUDIES

Theft, Vagrancy, and the Emergence of Commercial Capitalism: Hall and Chambliss

Hall's study of theft (1952) and Chambliss's of vagrancy (1970) can be taken together since they make essentially the same points. Both chronicle the historical reinterpretation of particular legal norms to accommodate the emerging interests of the rising capitalist class. And both, consequently, fit in with a fairly straightforward Marxist interpretation.

In fifteenth-century England there was no conception of theft as we know it today. Hall's analysis shows how a new definition emerged in response to the needs of the rising merchant middle classes (championed by Edward IV – himself a merchant). The problem crystallized around the carrier's case of 1473: a merchant hired a man to carry bales (presumed to be of wool) to Southampton. Instead of doing so, the carrier ran off with them. At that time no crime was involved under common law. The carrier was in legal possession of the bales – the assumption being that it was up to merchants to ensure they hired trustworthy carriers. But this was particularly problematic at the time. It was a period of rapidly increasing trade which required the continual movement of merchandise in safety and security. The interests of the developing merchant class were at stake. Consequently, Hall shows, the judges in the case effectively created new law. They decided that because the carrier 'broke bulk' by opening the bales he was carrying, they reverted to the possession of the merchant. There was no precedent whatsoever for such an interpretation; new law was clearly being created by expanding the law of larceny to include a wide range of acts formerly excluded.

Chambliss's analysis of the English vagrancy laws shows how, for similar reasons, old legal rules which have fallen into disuse may be resurrected to serve new interests. The vagrancy laws arose in the fourteenth century to control the mobility of labour which resulted from the labour shortage caused by the black death. That is, they arose to protect the interests of a feudal, landed ruling class threatened by a natural disaster. In the following century a decline in the demand for such control led to the vagrancy laws falling into disuse.

By the sixteenth century, however, a new need arose for which, with a little adaptation, the vagrancy laws were ideally suited. Once again, it was the interests of the emergent commercial class that were at stake. It was a period when the great increase in the transporting of goods meant constant danger from footpads and robbers. Consequently, the vagrancy laws were resurrected to serve as a preventive measure – to allow for the picking up of suspicious and dangerous-looking people before they could commit their crimes. The current use of the Vagrancy Act 1824 to arrest on suspicion might be seen as a modern counterpart (see p.92).

Dealing with this period of English history, Hall and Chambliss have little difficulty in demonstrating the significance of dominant class interests as determinants of legal change, though they illustrate different ways in which change may be achieved. Hall shows how, despite a common law formally based on precedent, the judiciary were able to find room for reinterpretation which effectively created new law. Chambliss, on the other hand, illustrates the point we have already encountered in Renner's work: how the same legal forms may be utilized to serve quite different dominant class interests.

Symbolic and Instrumental Dimensions of Early Factory Legislation: Carson

In his analysis of the 1833 Factories Act, Carson (1974b) reveals a complex interplay of moral, instrumental, and symbolic forces to account for its passage. He is particularly concerned to clarify the nature of the symbolic aspects of this process, since he is unhappy with Gusfield's formulation of the 'symbolic crusade'. He points out that although Gusfield accepted that most movements involved both instrumental and symbolic elements, he failed to explore the dynamics of this relationship. In particular, since symbolic status goals are rarely, if ever, articulated as being the initial motivating force behind legislative change, it is necessary, as he puts it 'to portray symbolic meaning as an *emergent property* of the interactional sequences occurring in connection with particular pieces or types of legislation' (p.113).

First, Carson allows for moral entrepreneurship having played its part in the passage of the Act. He sees the moral and humane concern expressed by the powerful figures who pressed for reform as both a genuine and important force behind its success. At the same time, however, there were undoubtedly instrumental reasons for the powerful manufacturers allowing its passage. Carson shows that even before the Act they had recognized that it was in their own interests to have a 'moral, sober, well-informed, healthy and comfortable body of workmen' and that many of the larger manufacturers had already made various reforms. But, as a consequence, they regarded the competition of smaller producers, who were the more exploitative, as unfair and in need of regulation. The Act thus came to be seen as being in their interests – as a means of eliminating unfair competition and of producing stability by ensuring equality in the conditions of production.

However, Carson is more concerned with the symbolic connotations which the debate acquired as it progressed. The protagonists of reform were, on the whole, 'traditionalists' – ideologically opposed to the new economic order represented by the manufacturers. Consequently, it is tempting to see them as 'moral crusaders' in Gusfield's sense – a group concerned with asserting their status via moral legislation. But, Carson argues, such a view would be mistaken – or, at least, premature, for this was not the motivating force. As he had already stressed, the reformers were genuinely motivated by humane considerations. In any event, at the outset there was no such clearcut division between traditionalists and pro-manufacturers. Symbolic overtones of this kind emerged only *in the course of* the debate which, ironically, when it did come to symbolize traditionalism versus manufacturing, deprived the proposals for reform of the initial, instrumentally based support which they had had among some manufacturers. They then saw the aim as being to 'criminalize' some of their activities and symbolically indict all that they stood for. It was only when a Royal Commission was set up whose report totally exonerated the moral status of the manufacturers and explicitly rejected the 'penal' aspects of the bill that the way was made clear for it to be passed.

Carson's analysis thus shows the complexity of the forces underlying this piece of legislation. Moral, instrumental, and symbolic forces (sometimes the last two operating in opposition to each other) all played their part. The final outcome, however, distinctly favoured the big manufacturers. Not only did it serve their economic needs, but it also symbolically reinforced their dominance by showing that the new system was humane and caring, and therefore not in any real need of control by the 'criminal law' (reflected in the setting up of the Factory Inspectorate, whose extreme reluctance to use criminal procedures and sanctions to enforce factory legislation has been a significant feature to the present day, see Carson, 1970). Nevertheless, the Act did also serve the interests of the working class and did, as Carson insists, reflect genuine moral and humane concerns. Indeed, the argument that it served the instrumental needs of the manufacturing class by clarifying, stabilizing, and equalizing the conditions of competition, does not otherwise explain why this had to be achieved by moving in the direction of more humane hours and conditions. The alternative argument – that it benefited the manufacturers by creating a more contented and stable workforce – is merely an acceptance of the ability of the workforce to influence change by threatening (passively or actively) some material loss by expressing their discontent (see our earlier remarks on the 'tokenism' argument).

The Search For Pure Food: Paulus

Rather than concentrating on a particular Act, Paulus (1974) examines the whole range of legislation enacted between 1850 and 1900, to prevent the adulteration of food and drink. She examines in some detail both the forces behind the legislation and the factors determining its relative success or failure. One similarity with Carson's work is that Paulus clearly demonstrates the 'emergent' character of legal control – as Rock puts it in his introduction to the book:

> 'Laws do not arise full grown . . . They do not enjoy an uncomplicated and unproblematic relationship with the settings and intentions of their original drafting . . . Indeed, the "final" form of the law could never have been foreseen because it accommodates conflicts and understandings that had not been imaginable at first' (p.10).

In 1850 there was no general legislation aimed at protecting the consumer, despite the fact that adulteration was known to be rife. Various attempts at legislation between 1820 and 1850 had foundered against the opposition of the growing representation of business interests in parliament, with their resistance to state intervention and the fact that, in the highly competitive food and drink trade, adulteration was perceived as 'fair' business practice. The consumers who were being cheated and poisoned presented no opposition, not only because of their lack of direct power but also through ignorance and prejudice about diet.

The first development followed the publication in the prestigious medical journal *The Lancet* of a series of articles publicizing adulteration, between 1851 and 1854. A parliamentary inquiry in 1855 resulted in the first Food and Drink Act of 1860. However, the high status and power of the potential law breakers meant that enforcement was fraught with difficulty. The 1860 Act was denied effective enforcement machinery: control was vested in local authorities, with power to appoint inspectors and analysts, who proved reluctant to take action against their status equals.

An amendment in 1872 strengthened the provisions for the appointment of inspectors, but the crucial issue in effective enforcement was the need to prove 'intent' on the part of the offender (that he *knew* his goods to be adulterated). It became clear that as long as this remained necessary effective enforcement would be impossible. An important victory for the controllers was thus achieved when it was decided (*Fitzpatrick* v. *Kelly*, 1873) that in one part of the Act at least, businessmen were to be strictly liable for the goods they sold (i.e. proof of intent was not necessary). This ensured the possibility of conviction and was bitterly opposed by the business community, whose agitation for repeal led to the 1875 Act.

By that time however, according to Paulus, 'public opinion' had persuaded the House of Lords that strict liability was necessary, and the 1875 Act embodied this principle. Large numbers of inspectors and public analysts were subsequently appointed. Interestingly, Paulus points out that this gave rise to powerful Government bureaucracies whose status was tied up with control, and that they formed effective opposition to subsequent attempts by the business community to nullify the Act.

But the battle was not won. However effective the efforts of the inspectorate, control was doomed to failure without full cooperation from the 'secondary law enforcers' – the magistrates. Their status identification with offenders meant that the low level of enforcement and avoidance of criminal stigmatization continued. In time, however, enforcement became more frequent. Strict liability came to be 'redefined' as prevention of adulteration, rather than as punishment (the very fact that it excluded 'intent' facilitated relatively stigma-free conviction, thus allowing the magistrates to exercise control without coming too directly into conflict with their status equals). This process was assisted by the fact that, as in the earlier example of factory legislation, influential businessmen came to realize the advantages of control (regulating competition) and so themselves came to redefine adulteration as 'unfair trade practice'. Finally a clarifying amendment followed in 1879, making the 1875 Act effectively enforceable.

The final outcome was effective control of food and drink adulteration, without harm being done to the status of the business community. As this brief summary illustrates, it involved complex interweavings of business interests, public interest, moral entrepreneurship, bureaucratic need, and status symbolism. Paulus ends with a fifteen-point 'model' of this legislative and enforcement process (p.133). As Rock says of her study:

> ' ...It makes the stock devices of the sociology of law appear somewhat skeletal, incomplete or misleading. They typically rest on a master terminology which attempts to embrace great tracts of legislative work with simple ideas. ... In the instance of anti-adulteration law, at least, little clarity flows from a blanket application of the vocabulary of "interest", "conflict", "crusade" and the like ... The usual invocation of these concepts comes to be seen as only obliquely illuminating.'   (Paulus 1974: 9)

However, this is perhaps going a little too far. Like Carson, Paulus illustrates the fact that we need a wide interpretation of 'interest' and, above all, that we must be conscious of the fact that legislation is a *process* during which new, unforeseen interests sometimes emerge, and old ones sometimes disappear. Bearing these important points in mind however, concepts such as 'interest', 'moral crusade', and the like still seem to be rather more than 'obliquely illuminating'.

Anti-Pollution Legislation: Gunningham

Gunningham's study (1974) is of particular interest since it concentrates on much more recent legislation than we have looked at so far, and also because he is explicitly concerned with determining the interests that are involved, and with the applicability of the consensualist and pluralist models. Although he is interested in the prob lems associated with anti-pollution legislation generally, his analysis deals mostly with the Clean Air Act of 1956.

Gunningham sees the emergence of 'environmental consciousness' as an important influence on anti-pollution legislation and its enforcement, in both the United States and Britain. Such figures as Rachel Carson and Paul Ehrlich in the United States, the National Smoke Abatement Society (and more recently the Friends of the Earth) in this country, have acted as moral entrepreneurs, providing the mass media with expert, technical information on environmental damage. This, however, could only produce a background pressure for reform, and has probably been more influential in the United States than here. The more important precipitating factors have been the massive growth in production and technology which have provided both a more dramatic environmental threat and, at the same time, more sophisticated means of measuring and monitoring it. Particularly important in this respect have been specific 'disasters'. Thus an important influence on the 1956 Clean Air Act was the 1952 London 'killer smog' (estimated to have been responsible for 4,000 deaths) and, equally important, the publicity given to information about its effects provided by the National Smoke Abatement Society.

In the struggle for legislation, Gunningham suggests, the pressure groups that have emerged in support of control defy specific social class location. They consist of various groups of moral entrepreneurs drawn from the academic, scientific, and technological 'middle levels' of society. The opposition, on the other hand, is easily class located: big business interests. Pollution control is both expensive and unproductive, and hence unprofitable and intrinsically unattractive. Government interests have been similarly averse to it, due to their preoccupation with economic growth and budget-balancing as a means of winning votes. Using Dickson's argument, Gunningham also shows that Government bureaucracies have often been powerful opponents (for example in the United States the Department of Agriculture has seen control as both a criticism of its past behaviour and a threat of future shrinkage in its responsibility). He also points out, however, that once the barrier has been broken and control gets underway, bureaucracies then emerge which have a similar interest in *expanding* control (signs of which are already emerging in the United States).

The initial response of industry (for example prior to the 1956 Act) was implacable hostility. Yet subsequently, Gunningham argues, there has been considerable cooperation, particularly from larger firms, and important advances have been made, often on a purely voluntary basis. He explains this in terms of Burnham's theory of the 'managerial revolution'. That is, industry in most Western societies has come increasingly under the control of non-owners (i.e. 'expert' managerial staff) who do not have the same simple profit-orientation of traditional owner/controllers. Gunningham acknowledges the counter-arguments (that top managers *are*, in fact, often shareholders, and that in any case their interests are their career prospects which are tied up with their contribution to profitability and are hence identical to those of traditional capitalists). Nevertheless, although it is not clear how he arrives at this conclusion, he argues that manager /controllers *are* more free from 'immediate pressures and interests in high profitability' and are 'able to think in the long-term', and this has led them to a more positive response to the long-term threat of environmental pollution. Thus, he argues, where profit margins are sufficient to cover the costs, and where anti-pollution pressure is strong, big business does tend to give way.

Gunningham sees no evidence in relation to pollution control to support Carson's theory that big business tends to come round to seeing legislative control as a useful means of eliminating competition from smaller firms. Big business support, such as it is, seems to have come from a genuinely more responsible attitude than seems to exist in the United States for example. He suggests this is partly because the influence of middle managers is stronger here (they are less likely to be large stock-holders) and partly because the physical constraints of living on an island (*sic*) tend to generate a greater awareness of long-term interests.

Despite all this, however, Gunningham shows how the 1956 Clean Air Act was effectively sabotaged by big business interests at the legislative stage. The Act provided so many let-outs for them that it was only the private householder who came under effective control. In addition, the Alkali Inspectorate have tended to regard themselves as 'partners in industry', have rarely used the penal process and have shown little enthusiasm for expansion of the kind envisaged by Dickson. They have argued that informal methods are necessary if the law is to be enforced sensitively enough to avoid damaging industry and creating unemployment. Gunningham gives several examples, however, which suggest that they have been over-lenient in applying this principle (pp.67–9).

This style of enforcement (or rather non-enforcement) is particularly characteristic of 'white collar crime' (see Carson on the Factory Inspectorate). However, the mere fact of widespread violation does not suffice to establish its ineffectiveness. 'Conventional' laws which are enforced by the penal process are also widely violated and many offenders evade sanctions altogether. Consequently it is difficult to tell from Gunningham's evidence whether a rigorous penal process would be more effective (see Chapter 6). More important, perhaps, in relation to the power of big business interests, is how they contrived to have a wide range of polluting activities excluded from legislation altogether.

In conclusion, Gunningham looks at the evidence in relation to consensualist and pluralist models of the legislative process. Rather surprisingly he rejects even the pluralist model in favour of a ruling class explanation. However, this is because of his definition of pluralism as a situation in which 'power is scattered among the diversity of interests, none of which is dominant.' The fact that big business interests clearly exerted the most powerful influence on the course of events obviously does not fit this definition of pluralism. In terms of our continuum his findings would fit within the pluralist range, but biased towards the ruling class end. Gunningham confirms this by his admission that he is not entirely happy with a ruling class explanation, since he allows for a significant and separate influence being exerted by the managerial middle-range group (he also allows for at least some influence from outside moral entrepreneurial groups and even public opinion).

An important theme common to Carson's work on the Factory Acts, Paulus' on pure food legislation and Gunningham's analysis of the 1956 Clean Air Act, is the need to understand the dynamics of the legislative process itself, for it is here that interests emerge, assert themselves, and disappear. The actual form any piece of legislation takes is the outcome of contests between interests, fought within the context of the formal institutional arrangements that prevail (though once again we might expect some discrepancy between the formal arrangements and what actually happens). Consequently, we will now turn our attention to the legislative process in contemporary England, and try to assess how interests are represented there, and what seems to determine their relative success or failure.

Decision-Making and the Legislative Process

The American legal realists directed attention to the courts, both higher and lower, as sources of law creation, while the sociological interactionists found similar processes operating even further down the scale, in police work. But there has been little inclination, at least on the part of lawyers, to conduct inquiries of a similar kind into the legislative process.

✗ There are several reasons. In the first place, the legislative process was not so plainly in need of demystification. Whereas the realists were consciously striving to refute the widely held view that judges merely declared pre-existing law, the political processes involved in legislation could hardly be so plausibly characterized as a largely mechanical exercise. Constitutional lawyers have always acknowledged the various influences at work in the enactment of bills, though it is fair to say that they have in the main concentrated on the mechanics of legislative procedure, leaving analysis of outside influences to political scientists. Though this academic division of labour is understandable, it has meant that the politics of legislation has been examined from the perspective of its significance for the political process as a whole, rather than for any light it may shed on the nature and operation of law. The analysis usually takes the passing of a bill as the note on which to end rather than as a further point of departure.

The relative lack of interest shown by lawyers also reflects the low status historically accorded to statute law by judges and academics alike. In both formal and functional terms, Acts of Parliament are superior to the common law (that is, judicial precedent created by custom and the decisions of the judges). They are a higher source of authority than the decisions of any court and far more pervasive in their effects. But there remains a very real sense in which the common law, with its ancient tradition, has been perceived as the core of our legal system, however misconceived such an attitude is in modern times.

In the case of the judiciary, this perspective derives partly from its historical conflicts with Parliament and, more recently, from an aversion for the encroachment of the welfare state. As recently as 1974, Lord Justice Scarman felt able to write: 'The modern English judge still sees enacted law as an exception to, a graft upon, or a correction of, the customary law in his hands...' (p.3). In legal education too, statutes used to be treated as some kind of aberration, an appendix to the common law, while delegated legislation, in reality the typical product of legislative power, received no more than passing mention. Even today, private law subjects such as contract and tort are frequently taught with a strong emphasis on their common law origins and minimal reference to their social and economic setting and the ways in which the importance of common law rules has been eroded by statutory developments.

Naturally, the absence of hard data on how legislation emerges primarily stems from the intangible character of the process itself. Judicial decisions at the appellate level are readily accessible in the form of reasoned judgements, which can be evaluated by reference to past cases and authoritative statements of the law. The issues between the parties will usually be clearly delimited and specific. Judicial influence on the moulding of law is therefore of high visibility. The numerous influences on legislation, on the other hand, are often hard to assess, or even trace at all, especially since much of it is drawn up within government departments with little or selective regard to the views of interested parties, and subject to only nominal parliamentary scrutiny. The greatest obstacle to unravelling the process is the degree of official secrecy which, despite mounting criticism, still surrounds it.

The whole ethos of the administrative process in Britain is conspicuously – many would say excessively – hostile to the disclosure of official documents. It is epitomized by the resilience of our restrictive Official Secrets Act, with the far-reaching presumption contained in section 2 that no information may be disclosed without authorization. Even if it is rarely invoked to launch a prosecution, the very existence of such a sweeping provision has encouraged the marked tendency within the civil service to regard secrecy and confidentiality as the norm. Some prospect of change was held out in 1974, when the Labour Party Manifesto promised 'to replace the Official Secrets Act by a measure to put the burden on public authorities to justify withholding information'. In line with this pledge on more open government, in 1977 all government departments were instructed to prepare background material on policy studies, with a view to publication unless ministers objected (Allen 1977). But there has been little discernible change in practice, and, at the time of writing, no reform of section 2. In fact, the following year, a White Paper on reform of the Official Secrets Act (1978) was published without any accompanying policy papers. This irony was compounded by the extreme secrecy which surrounds the Cabinet committee system from which the White Paper emerged. Decisions on a wide range of policy issues are taken by Cabinet committees, reported to the full Cabinet and rarely altered. As de Smith (1977) observes:

' . . . the secrecy enveloping this system is even harder to penetrate than the working of the Cabinet itself. In no official publication is there so much as a full list of these committees, let alone the names of their chairmen and members, a statement of their functions, or their relationships with the Cabinet as a whole' (p.160).

An article which revealed the composition of the Cabinet committee concerned with Official Secrets reform – a matter within the Prime Minister's discretion – claimed that its somewhat pallid proposals were partially explained by 'creative manipulation' of the system of appointing members (Page 1978).

Moreover, though the Government is committed to reform of section 2, no further legislation is envisaged on open government generally, despite growing pressure for a Freedom of Information Act comparable to that passed in the United States in 1966 and strengthened in 1974 (see for example, Outer Circle Policy Unit 1977; Justice 1978). The distinctive features of the Federal statute are its general presumption in favour of disclosure of information held by the executive branch of government (subject only to exceptions relating to aspects of national security and other confidential material), and the provision for judicial review of administrative refusal to disclose (the Act does not apply to legislative or judicial information). In 1979, a private member's Official Information Bill which sought to establish a general right of access to official documents, along broadly similar lines, lapsed with the fall of the Labour Government, whose last proposals on the subject fell far short of the United States model (Open Government 1979, and Disclosure of Official Information 1979). It is difficult to see how legislative processes could, even in principle, be satisfactorily analysed without some such measure. Yet, perhaps even more than the trial process, they merit investigation along 'realist' lines, because of the impact of legislation on people's lives. Furthermore, undue secrecy in decision-making precludes informed debate on the policies themselves and thus makes for ineffective government.

INVESTIGATING THE LEGISLATIVE PROCESS

The procedural framework for the passage of Bills can be summarized as follows. The bulk of proposed legislation is drawn up in government departments, at the instigation of the Cabinet. The ministers and civil servants concerned consult with the Treasury and appropriate government departments. Discussions take place with a variety of interested and influential outside bodies, and eventually Parliamentary Draftsmen will produce a Bill. It will then go through the required parliamentary procedure – three Readings in each House; Committee and Report Stages – before receiving the Royal Assent. A number of Private Members' Bills will also be introduced, but under much less favourable conditions. Their sponsors do not normally have the advantages of departmental consultations and drafting facilities. Little parliamentary time is set aside for them and government authorization is needed if they would require public expenditure. In the circumstances, few are ultimately enacted (for a recent account of some factors affecting their prospects of success see Gray (1978)).

How can one evaluate the forces at work in all of this? Just as consensual, pluralist, and ruling class models are invoked to explain the emergence of legal norms in general, similar characterisations are possible of the more specific processes involved in the passage of legislation. The formal constitutional structure envisages a consensual ideal – the democratic aspiration towards representative government, to be achieved by means of parliamentary scrutiny. The operative reality is of course highly complex and often belies the ideal. Among the most distinctive features of the dynamics of modern legislation are, typically, the domination, if not by-passing, of parliament by the government of the day and the government's own need to accommodate the demands of powerful interest groups. Pluralist and ruling class explanations of the legislative process naturally derive their strength from the extent to which the power of unrepresentative, sectional interests is reflected in particular pieces of legislation.

The democratic ideal asserts that legislative policy derives from the government's electoral mandate and that parliamentary scrutiny acts as an additional safeguard. But as Walkland (1968) has pointed out, legislation will only partially reflect government mandates, which are in any event expressed in broad terms, while parliamentary scrutiny is often far from effective. Nor can it be convincingly argued that the major political parties as a whole are particularly influential in the formulation of policy, still less the bulk of individual Members of Parliament (Mackintosh 1978).

Legislative policy then is largely explicable in terms of the relationships between the Cabinet, Government Departments, and powerful pressure groups (Walkland), and subordinate legislation by government departments has become the typical regulatory instrument of our society. The picture is further complicated by certain other key pressures on government. Domestic economic policy is increasingly dictated from abroad and heavily constrained by the requirements of institutions such as the International Monetary Fund and the European Community. While at home there is the impenetrable relationship between the Bank of England and the Treasury, as well as the elusive influence of powerful City institutions. All this clearly has serious implications for public accountability. As Street (1975) has said: 'The Government and the senior members of the Opposition are agreed on one thing: that the less the public knows about the process of decision making the better' (p.226).

If this is the operative reality, scepticism about the representative nature of democracy is readily understood. Even the most influential pressure groups such as the CBI and the TUC will be expressing a sectional view, and not necessarily one which is truly representative of their own members. On many issues, the air of secrecy which we have described is incompatible with meaningful consultation; the less influential pressure groups and the public at large will not normally be in a position to make their voices heard until crucial decisions have been taken, such that alternative proposals to those outlined by government are unrealistic. The dynamics of the legislative process are well summed up by the Outer Circle Policy Unit (1977):

'The government announces its intention to look at an issue – say housing. Specialists are employed and some outsiders consulted. Evidence may be submitted, some may be published. But the discussion, digestion and conclusions on the issues are private internal matters. A year or two may pass. The government issues a paper – White or Green. Public discussion is invited. But by that time the civil service and the government will have made up their minds: the civil servants will be tired of the subject and in no mood to look at new or old views that emerge in the public debate, or to upset the compromises and bargains laboriously struck between departments by reopening questions settled between them. And many inquiries do not result in any statement of policy and never come to public knowledge at all' (p.5).

Once one understands the process in these terms, the relative impotence of Parliament is readily appreciated. 'Information is power' and in disclosing it a government loses its initiative. In theory the government is accountable to Parliament by means of procedures such as Question Time in the House and the work of Parliamentary Select Committees. But their effectiveness too is undermined by lack of detailed information. In practice Question Time is widely acknowledged to be something of a charade and an exercise in stonewalling. Select Committees, too, have been the subject of much criticism for their failure, as constituted, to provide effective scrutiny (see for example Griffith 1974a), especially in matters of public expenditure. Very recently, the House of Commons, implementing proposals of a Select Committee on Procedure (1978) approved the establishment of 14 Departmental Select Committees to 'shadow' the main Departments of State, employing independent consultants and with considerable power to scrutinize matters of expenditure in detail. The whole problem is now seen as one of urgency, the more so given the increasing mass of regulations and directives emanating from the European Community, many of which are implemented as English Law virtually unchecked.

As yet we have made only passing reference to pressure groups. It should be clear from what has been said about the decision-making process so far that the influence of pressure groups cannot be assessed with much precision. But some account should be given of the forms they take and the circumstances in which they are likely to be most effective.

If Parliament often finds it difficult to influence the legislative process, it would not be surprising if other bodies seeking change through governmental processes favoured a direct approach to administrators and government departments. This is in fact the preferred strategy of the more powerful and established pressure groups. Proposals for legislation on matters of great import for the economy are subjected to the continual scrutiny of the TUC and CBI, who will also frequently influence subsequent modifications. Departmental consultation with certain interest groups is common practice in the preparation of delegated legislation, in many instances being a statutory obligation of the Minister. But there are also isolated Acts of Parliament which reflect the persistent campaigning of one or several minority groups, who tend to concentrate their efforts on winning over MPs and the public, as, for example, with the abolition of capital punishment and abortion law reform. It is also important not to overlook the notable success of certain determined bodies, such as the Lord's Day Observance Society and the hunting lobby, in *preventing* changes in the law. It is easier to persuade governments to do nothing than to convince them of the need to introduce new laws.

As state involvement in citizens' affairs grows and social and economic planning becomes more complex, government policy is increasingly modified by the claims of interest groups. Several political systems are showing more flexibility in accommodating them. In West Germany, the Netherlands, and Scandinavia, extensive consultation is encouraged, as well as direct pressure group administration of some public programmes. In this country, the possibilities are perhaps most apparent in what is sometimes described as a trend towards 'corporatism', in supplementing, if not by-passing, representative government in certain spheres. 'Corporatism' denotes something more than the conventional role of pressure groups in seeking influence through consultation with policy makers. It implies active cooperation between bodies to help shape, even determine, policy. In England it is most evident in the increasingly accepted notion that key decisions on economic policy should be agreed upon by the Government, the CBI, and the TUC (the doctrine of 'Tripartism'). In this capacity the CBI and the TUC function rather as negotiators than as pressure groups in the normal understanding of the term, as when using the formalized machinery of the National Economic Development Council. But as Grant has pointed out (1977: 173), the most concrete acknowledgement of a corporatist approach is to be found in the recent establishment of relatively powerful tripartite institutions – the Manpower Services Commission (1974), the Health and Safety Commission (1975) and the Conciliation and Arbitration Council (1976). These bodies contain a balance of CBI and TUC nominees and exercise effective executive functions of a kind formerly undertaken by government departments and Ministers. The current proliferation of Quangos (quasi-autonomous non-Governmental organizations, appointed by Ministers) carries with it similar implications. This is, of course, far from saying that Britain is on the way to becoming a corporate state. In particular, the relationship between CBI and TUC seems too fragile, the areas of potential accord too limited, for that.

Pressure groups have conventionally been divided into two major categories: sectional or interest groups, representing particular sections of the community – for example the TUC, CBI, or BMA – and promotional or 'cause' groups, which focus on particular issues or areas of concern – such as the Abortion Law Reform Society, the Howard League for Penal Reform, the Association for Vaccine Damaged Children, the Legal Action Group, and the Friends of the Earth.

Clearly, such is the variety of groups trying to exert pressure that it is fruitless to generalize about the methods they adopt, all the more so because the same group may operate simultaneously on several different levels. The TUC and the CBI represent interests powerful enough to exploit the government's dependence on their cooperation. In addition, they exercise influence directly either through membership of Parliament, or by enlisting sympathetic MPs, through representation on advisory bodies, access to Ministers, senior civil servants, and the media. This combination of power and contacts normally enables them to have a substantial effect *before* a government Bill is drawn up. At the other end of the spectrum there are 'ginger' groups with no access to the corridors of power, insufficient funds or inclination to employ MPs as consultants to promote their interests, and little expectation of being consulted at the formative stages of legislation, if at all. Their very existence however serves as a continuing reminder of minority grievances.

At a time when lip-service, at least, is paid to 'participatory democracy' it is easy to overestimate the significance of most pressure groups. Their pervasiveness and increased access to the media can be misleading. Quite apart from the predominance of government-inspired legislation, the ideology of a political system places unspoken limits on the extent of feasible reform. But it is still of interest to ask why some groups succeed and others fail. For example in explaining the success of the Consumers' Association as a pressure group, Gray (1978) stresses its strong research and publicity base, professionalism, independence, and good national image. In particular, the admittedly rare instances of legislated norms which do not reflect government policy, powerful vested interests, or widespread popular demand, are precisely those which should excite the interest of the sociologist of law. The abolition of capital punishment, and abortion law reform, were changes which seemed to challenge the conventional wisdom that law follows public opinion. It is a reasonable hypothesis that pressure groups played an important role, as seems to be suggested by case studies of these reforms (see Christoph 1962; Hindell and Simms 1971).

One of the complicating features in analysis of pressure group influence is that several organizations may be pursuing similar but not identical aims in different and even contradictory ways. The pattern is noticeable in the context of prison reform (Wright 1975) where there is an uneasy coexistence of gradualists and radicals. The National Association for the Care and Rehabilitation of Offenders (NACRO), funded mainly through the Home Office is able, as a voluntary organization, to conduct experimental projects with official backing. Its closeness to the authorities gives it access to information, 'the most valuable commodity in the reform business'. The Howard League for Penal Reform acts as an independent body, with influential parliamentary links, which carries out research and produces educational material on prison reform. Preservation of the Rights of Prisoners (PROP) is run by and for ex-offenders, focussing on prisoners' rights and at times resorting to direct action. Finally, Radical Alternatives to Prison (RAP), fuelled by allegations in the late 1960s of harsh prison conditions, brutality in detention centres, and force feeding, concentrated its attention on the more fundamental question of whether it is right to incarcerate people at all.

Ryan (1978) in a comparison of the performance of the Howard League and RAP, illustrates the limits of pluralism. He shows that Governments and top bureaucrats grant differential access to pressure groups, according to their willingness to abide by unwritten rules about what can be questioned and the limits of permissible change. RAP, because they have not kept to such rules, but demanded total abolition of the prison system, have been defined out of the reform process. The Howard League on the other hand, has obeyed the rules, maintained access to the powerful (and, as a former Secretary Hugh Klare, 1979, concedes, has steered clear of what it has always regarded as hostile public opinion) and has consequently achieved some, though limited, success. In doing so, however, Ryan concludes, the Howard League has been contaminated by the Establishment and has buttressed a system which tolerates only gradualist reforms.

It is hardly surprising that such limits exist. Pluralism, after all, does not imply that all pressure groups are equally powerful. The fact that pressure groups with no power base (whether in terms of supportive public opinion or access to legislators and administrators) fail to exert an influence is only to be expected. Fringe, radical groups will fail as much under pluralism as under any other system of power distribution. Indeed, what is perhaps more instructive from Ryan's account is the degree of success achieved by the Howard League despite negligible support from either public opinion or the mass media.

The Pressure Group as Moral Entrepreneur

With the passage of time, the genesis of numerous Acts of Parliament fades into obscurity. Occasionally one bears the stamp of an individual's single-minded devotion. Even if the effects are often slight, close examination can provide a rewarding insight into certain aspects of the decision-making process, while also serving as a corrective to the tendency of later generations to think of such changes as having in some way been dictated by public opinion.

An instructive example is the Protection of Children Act 1978 (see Lennon 1978). In the summer of 1977 the English press published a number of scare stories about the exploitation of children for pornographic purposes in America. There was however no hard evidence of a sizeable increase in such exploitation in

England. Mrs Mary Whitehouse, under the aegis of the National Viewers and Listeners Association (NVLA), approached the deputy leader of the Conservative Party, Mr William Whitelaw, to see if he could suggest a Conservative back-bencher interested in putting through a Private Member's Bill to deal with the problem in England.

In the meantime, she employed a well-worn technique. She sent letters to 270 provincial daily and religious newspapers, exhorting readers to stamp out 'kiddie porn' and claimed that over 200,000 children were being used by pornographers (a much-publicized report of an eight-year-old Manchester girl on a list of children available for unlawful sexual activities was later shown to be wholly misleading). Child porn, she has said, is 'like an outbreak of rabies', a menace against which the Government must be forced to act. A Conservative backbencher, Cyril Townsend, who came fourth in the draw for Private Members' Bills, agreed to put forward Mrs Whitehouse's Protection of Children Bill, to make it an offence to take an indecent photograph of a child under sixteen.

Mrs Whitehouse's next move is revealing for one's appreciation of the frailty of the concept of public opinion. She cited the many newspaper cuttings of her own letters and the responses to them as evidence of 'widespread alarm', and wrote back to the papers asking readers to write to MPs and lobby them to be in the House of Commons for the Bill's Second Reading. She also cited a list of over 200 MPs who had answered readers' letters as further evidence of support. The Bill obtained an unopposed Second Reading. When its progress was subsequently impeded by a procedural wrangle, she sent a telegram to the Prime Minister stating: 'The country will never forgive any failure on the part of the Government now to ensure that this Bill safely reaches the Statute book.' There were similar appeals from the Archbishop of Westminster and other church leaders. The Bill duly became law.

The importance of this relatively minor episode in the wider debate over the legislation of morality must not be exaggerated. Few people would be disposed to denounce the substance of the statute, which had all-party support and whose protagonists' sincerity is not in doubt. But it does teach us something about the emergence of legislated norms. Mrs Whitehouse's claims of 'public anxiety' largely reflected the alarm which she had herself activated. Her contention that this was 'an immense social problem' was not borne out by extensive inquiries carried out by the Home Office to determine the incidence of child pornography, which concluded that 'no evidence has been produced that such practices are wide-spread, or that they are growing.'

Even the assumption of prolonged traumatic effects on children who had been the subjects of indecent photography is itself more problematic medically and psychologically than would appear to the layman. The market for the magazines will presumably not disappear with the advent of the Act, but merely provide a fresh instance of the 'crime tariff' (see p.215), in which illicit supply merely increases the profits of the illicit entrepreneur.

Nor were the deficiencies in the previous law commensurate with the degree of passion aroused by this issue. Indecent assault against children under sixteen was already an offence under the Sexual Offences Act 1956 (Ss.14, 15), as was indecency falling short of assault against children under fourteen (Indecency with Children Act 1960). The only real gap was that children between fourteen and sixteen could be photographed or filmed naked provided they were not touched in an indecent manner against their will (*R. v. Sutton*, 1977). Even then, it would probably have been illegal to sell the photographs. The Act is thus a prime example of law as symbolic affirmation.

The 'new' phenomenon of 'battered women' is another instance of an issue being embraced by the media and precipitating legal change. Here too, one may observe how the efforts of a determined campaigner, Erin Pizzey, have helped to shape legislation. The Domestic Violence and Matrimonial Homes Act 1976 elevated the personal rights of a battered wife or mistress above the proprietary interests of the owner of the home. In the Select Committee Report which preceded it (Violence in Marriage 1975: paras. 22, 25), Mrs Pizzey's Chiswick Women's Aid refuge was singled out for its 'pioneering role'. The Housing (Homeless Persons) Act 1977 contains a special definition of 'homelessness' (s.1(2)(b)) to include as a 'priority need' a 'battered wife' who has left home (the Code of Guidance on the Act's implementation specifically cites battered women without children as a priority).

Our concern is not to assert a simplistic direct causal link between Mrs Pizzey's activities and legislative change, but to note that the role of tenacious reformers is apt to be overlooked once the concepts built into a statute become common currency. No doubt Mrs Pizzey has both used and been used by the media. To some extent the recognition of the 'battered woman' is traceable to strands within the women's liberation movement, which itself reflects changing patterns in the socio-economic structure. The new provisions for the homeless stem partly from dramatization of their plight, notably in the documentary-drama *Cathy Come Home*, the work of Shelter and the squatters' movement, and revelations of the inadequacy of housing policy as evidenced by the hotel and hostel placements necessitated by the lack of housing stock.

A NOTE ON ADVICE TO GOVERNMENT

The Role of Official Reports

In a society which claims to encourage the representation of interests, and in which governments feel bound to justify their actions by appeal to rational argument, one might have assumed that expert advice and official reports of various kinds would be important sources of legislative change. Inevitably, in practice, it is their immediate political appeal, their compatibility with the usually short-term aims of government, which is normally the measure of their influence. Partly for this reason, official inquiries are often cynically dismissed as the stock device for conveying an impression of concern while ensuring inactivity. But even reports which are not implemented may indirectly influence subsequent policy, while those of the Law Commission, which is admittedly something of a special case, are often followed by legislation which closely corresponds to its recommendations.

An examination of the emergence of legislated norms would therefore be incomplete without some reference to the findings of Committees and Commissions. In particular, are there any general factors which help determine the conclusions they reach and whether or not these are acted upon, and how do they fit into consensual, pluralist, and ruling class models of decision making?

We suggested earlier that the broad ideology of the political system places unspoken limits on the possibilities of reform. This is often reflected in the terms of reference of official inquiries. As Hood notes (1974), in the context of penal reform, a committee formed to consider ways of *improving* the *administration* of custodial institutions is virtually precluded from pursuing in any depth questions related to the ideology of custodial treatment and its acceptability. The parameters of permissible change then are often predetermined.

More generally, the conclusions reached in such inquiries will be shaped by the very nature of the investigating body. 'The English', in the words of Bagehot, 'are born with a belief in a greencloth, clean pens, and twelve men with grey hair.' In her study of the Royal Commission on the Police, Jenifer Hart (1963) identified certain limitations of Royal Commissions as *investigative* bodies, in contrast to their undoubted value in making recommendations of broad policy. They tend to have vague terms of reference, too many part-time members and minimal staff resources. Protracted oral hearings are common, producing evidence preponderantly from interested official bodies to Commissions themselves over-represented by interest groups. These are not ideal ingredients for the thorough investigation of sensitive issues, which really requires effective power to compel the production of evidence.

Thus, for example, the Royal Commission on Standards of Conduct in Public Life (the Salmon Report 1976), largely inspired by the Poulson affair, decided 'to survey the field broadly', doubtless reflecting its unsuitability for the task of establishing the extent of corruption in public life. The officially perceived need to sustain morale in the public service, reinforced by the mass of evidence from central and local government authorities and national industries must presumably have influenced the Commission not to recommend the establishment of an independent inspectorate, but rather to continue to place trust in internal policing procedures. Whether morale is in fact better sustained in the absence of an independent body with powers of scrutiny is itself open to question. But the key criticism of the Salmon Report is simply that a Royal Commission is unfitted to examine a problem which demands investigative powers (Pinto-Duschinsky 1977). There is an instructive contrast between the methods of American state crime commissions, such as the Knapp Commission on police corruption in New York (1972), which made use of informers, and the handling of similar malpractices in the Metropolitan police force here, with its heavy reliance on timely resignations.

Another obvious constraint on committees is the lack of financial resources at their disposal, which often greatly limits the use they can make of social research. Consider for example the contrast between the scale of the English Wootton Report (1968) on the use of cannabis and the comparable report of the Canadian Le Dain commission (1972). The full Wootton Report is a very brief document, the fruits of the labours of a small group of people, meeting sporadically and, despite the technical nature of the subject, reaching their conclusions with relatively little research back-up. As one member put it: 'at [the] first meeting I asked if we could initiate some original research to supply information in some of the areas where this was not available. Another member of the committee felt that this was not necessary and all we had to do was work out ways to stop 'the spread of this filthy habit' (Scofield 1971: 92–3), and 'I was surprised by the ease with which most of [the witnesses] made assertions unembarrassed by the small amount of evidence to support their claims' (p.93). The Canadian Commission, on the other hand, produced an exhaustive report on cannabis and commissioned research on a vast scale. It made numerous tours of the country, holding public meetings, meetings on university campuses and in coffee houses frequented by drug users.

In his book, Scofield brings out another feature of the committee system which has been insufficiently explored, namely the way in which issues are actually thrashed out, the psychology of meetings, the shifts of opinion, the element of give and take, and how the quest for unanimity, to avoid the report becoming a dead letter, usually tones down its final version:

'One of the so-called softies agreed with me and still felt the penalties were too high, but he also felt that unanimity was even more important. He talked to me privately and produced strong historical evidence to show that minority reports rarely had any influence and the impact of reports which were not unanimous were often seriously weakened' (p.96).

Quite apart from a committee's own perception of its remit – or rather the assortment of perceptions of its individual members – there is the more basic complication that the social background of its members is bound to affect their selection and interpretation of material. The actual process of choosing members of committees remains somewhat obscure. Whitehall is known to have its list of 'the great and the good'. This is composed largely of people who have achieved eminence in the relevant fields, with evident bias towards age and respectability. The choice of chairman can be very significant, especially as he or she is normally consulted about who the other members should be and kept in close touch with the Government as to its aims. While the system avoids the evils of direct political patronage, its very secrecy leaves it open to criticism.

Whether or not a particular report is implemented depends, as we noted earlier, on a whole host of political considerations. To take just one example, the Finer Report (1974) on One Parent Families, though widely praised as humane, well-researched, and constructive, gathers dust for lack of political support. In a climate of general public indifference, it was condemned to obscurity by the economic recession which was at its height shortly after its publication. On the other hand, governments may be prompted by extrinsic considerations to invoke research findings in order to give their own policies a veneer of respectability. Hood contends that: '... the belief that expert advice based on criminological and penological research is the foundation for penal change, is only a screen behind which ideological and political factors, perhaps inevitably, shape those attitudes which imbue legislation'. (Hood 1974: 417). Thus a whole series of measures, such as the First Offenders Act 1958, the introduction of suspended sentences in the Criminal Justice Act 1967 and the Bail Act 1976 are most plausibly explained as attempts to cut down the rate of growth in the prison population for both economic and ideological reasons.

The Role of the Law Commission

The Law Commission merits separate treatment both because of its direct involvement with legal change and because in practice its reports do have a unique potential for generating legislation. Indeed the reports often contain a model bill drawn up by parliamentary draftsmen seconded to the Commission and the authors of reports are available for consultation while a Bill passes through Parliament. It is true that in much of the Commission's work elements of public policy are less evident than legal technicalities. However, that has not been the case, for example, with the radical reform of matrimonial law in the early 1970s, in which the Commission was largely instrumental, or with its contribution to increased consumer protection (see for example Law Commission 1966; 1969a; 1969b; 1975).

The Law Commission has a mandate: 'to take and keep under review all the law . . . with a view to its systematic development and reform . . .'. If the Commission has a 'quasi-legislative' role, albeit of a limited kind, a number of questions seem pertinent. How is it constituted and how are its members selected? The English Law Commissioners are persons 'appearing to the Lord Chancellor to be suitably qualified by the holding of judicial office or by experience as a barrister or solicitor or as a teacher of law in a university' (Law Commissions Act 1965: s.1(2)). Disparaged in advance in the House of Lords as consisting of 'a High Court judge, a practising barrister and three leftish dons' (Lord Tangley 1965), the Commission is in fact entirely staffed by lawyers, though making use of non-lawyers in sub-committees and for consultation. The suggestion of Lord Wedderburn that one Law Commissioner should be a sociologist has not so far been adopted.

How does the Commission decide which areas of the law are in need of reform and in what order of priority? To what extent can it decide such matters free from express or implicit governmental pressures? The official view is that matters which are politically controversial or concerned with broad social trends are more suitably dealt with by Royal Commissions or committees of inquiry. Thus permission was not granted to investigate the principles governing accident compensation because of the policy issues involved. But any attempt to draw hard and fast lines between law involving a 'broad social trend' and what has been mysteriously termed 'lawyers' law' is unlikely to be convincing, has been condemned by leading Law Commissioners (for example, Lord Scarman, 1968: 26–37, and Professor Diamond 1977: 400–02) and, as indicated above, is belied by the record of the Commission itself.

To what philosophy of law reform, if any, does the Law Commission subscribe and how does it go about its work? In has been suggested that the plea in its First Programme for simpler, more accessible and certain law, and the general emphasis on the value of codification, argues 'a strong Benthamite influence' (Farrar 1974). In contrast to the traditional procedure of *ad hoc* committees of inquiry, the Law Commission initiates its own research. It issues a working paper, which is circulated for comment to 'appropriate' organizations and individuals, the press and broadcasting media, and then published. Only later does it produce its Report. It its 7th Annual Report (1972) it expressed a 'hope to evolve a standard procedure for harnessing the social sciences to law reform which will become as much a part of our method as the working paper procedure itself.' But though it has subsequently acknowledged (11th Annual Report 1976) the immediate practical value of social research for particular reform projects, it seems to be more impressed by its wider, indirect role in influencing the climate of opinion.

Any analysis of the Commission's work from a social scientific standpoint would want to know how research on which it relied was conducted, on what basis groups and individuals are selected to give evidence, and how representative they are in fact of the particular causes they espouse. Certainly as a mode of operating its general method marks some advance. The laissez-faire stance adopted by so many Royal Commissions and departmental committees in the past works to the advantage of those with most access to the committee in question. Many groups or individuals likely to be affected by changes in the law will not read the 'quality' press where evidence is solicited, may not be tightly organized into effective pressure groups or be able to communicate their feelings adequately through the medium of a written memorandum.

Judicial Legislation

THE DECLARATORY THEORY

We have been considering the emergence of legislated norms in the strict sense of enactment via Parliament. We now turn to the role of the judges as creators of law.

A mere thirty years ago the very phrase 'judicial legislation' would have been anathema to the English judiciary. The reigning orthodoxy, never more sedulously cultivated than in the first half of the twentieth century, was the declaratory theory, according to which judges 'discover', but do not 'create', law. On this view, the law consists of a *pre-existing* body of rules and principles, to be found in the common law and statutes (and the vast amount of delegated legislation authorized by Act of Parliament). The judge merely applies the rule or principle appropriate to the facts before him. In England the theory drew some intellectual support from a now discarded feature of positivist jurisprudence: the more extreme assertions of a rule-based conception of law, divorced from social policy or morality, helped to sustain the notion that adjudication was a largely mechanistic process. Though now largely discredited, the doctrine has had a deep impact on judicial attitudes and is not without its adherents even today.

To explain the persistence of a view which seems so plainly inconsistent with the continued adaptation of law to meet changing social needs, we must first indicate briefly the formal framework within which judges operate. Obviously a judge has to conform to the rules of the decision-making process recognized in the legal system. In England this means that he must decide cases in accordance with the doctrine of precedent and the rules of statutory interpretation. Precedent requires him to follow previous decisions which are similar in material respects to his own; that is, where the point of law established in the earlier case covers the facts of his case. All courts are bound to follow decisions of courts above them in the judicial hierarchy, the appellate courts (though not, since 1966, the House of Lords) are bound by their own previous decisions.

The rules of statutory interpretation require the judge to implement the intention of Parliament as expressed in the wording of the Act. In the event of conflict, legislation prevails over the common law.

We will shortly look at a few examples of the process at work. This cursory outline may make it seem somewhat mechanical, but it should soon become clear this is not the case. When are similarities to be deemed material? What exactly is meant by the intention of

Figure 1 Outline Structure of the Courts

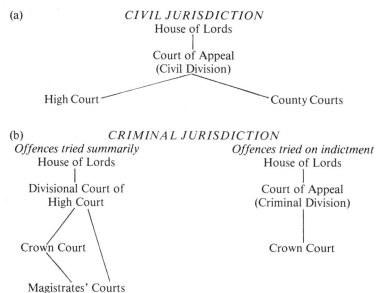

(a)   *CIVIL JURISDICTION*

House of Lords

Court of Appeal
(Civil Division)

High Court   County Courts

(b)   *CRIMINAL JURISDICTION*

Offences tried summarily   *Offences tried on indictment*

House of Lords   House of Lords

Divisional Court of   Court of Appeal
High Court   (Criminal Division)

Crown Court   Crown Court

Magistrates' Courts

Parliament and how is it to be discovered when the language of the statute is ambiguous? The making of value judgments is in practice unavoidable.

The process of adjudication then allows considerable scope for flexibility and judicial manoeuvre. The weight to be attached to seemingly binding precedents, for example, will vary according to how developed the relevant principles of law are. The wording of a statute may legitimately be given a restrictive or liberal meaning, depending on the particular rules of interpretation which the judge relies on. Certain general standards, for example broad principles of justice, will at times be invoked.

Nonetheless, at the lower court level, and the overwhelming majority of cases go no higher than the magistrates' or county court, the declaratory theory retains a certain plausibility. The bulk of the work does consist of ascertaining whether or not the facts in dispute fall within some well-established legal rule. At the appellate level however and especially in the House of Lords, where the court is normally exclusively concerned with legal, not factual, issues, it is much more difficult to deny that judges can have a creative role.

The declaratory theory accorded with public expectation. The essential role of a judge is to resolve disputes between individual litigants in civil matters and between the State and the accused in criminal matters, *in accordance with the law*. It is the reasonable expectation of the citizen that he will not be punished unless he *has* broken the law; that he will not lose his civil action unless he *was* wrong in law. He therefore naturally sees the judge's function as determining whether this *has* happened or not. He does not expect to be confronted with some new principle of law, mysteriously conjured up from nowhere, or perhaps reflecting some particular concept of justice to which the judge is wedded. No system of law can be said to operate satisfactorily unless the citizen is able to conduct himself and arrange his affairs without risk of being in breach of a relatively stable and fixed set of rules. He therefore expects from the judge 'the disinterested application of known rules' (Jaffe 1969). Nor should it be overlooked that the judge, too, benefits from being able to distance himself from his decision, the appeal to authority acting as a useful, arguably necessary, psychological mechanism.

The political advantages which accrue from being able to portray the judiciary as impartial arbiters of justice are self-evident. They are reflected in the constitutional struggles over centuries to establish a 'government of laws, not men.' Our doctrines of parliamentary sovereignty, the rule of law, the separation of powers – however much open to qualification in practice – have helped sustain the moral authority of the law, by projecting the image of an independent judiciary eschewing a legislative role.

From the 1930s through to the immediate postwar years, the judicial self-restraint implicit in the declaratory theory was especially marked. It manifested itself in different ways. At times it seemed to involve a self-conscious 'political neutrality' as a reaction to the dramatic increase in legislative social engineering. Yet it also reflected a subservience to executive discretion at a time of national emergency and waning Parliamentary control. In earlier times judges had been less reticent about invoking policy considerations, albeit couched in the language of 'natural law', or 'reason' or general principles.

It is in part this very image of impartiality which has encouraged successive Conservative and Labour governments to call upon high-ranking judges to preside over Royal Commissions, Committees, and Inquiries, often of a highly political nature. Precisely because he is not a politician committed to some creed or manifesto, the judge is trusted to use his acknowledged skill as a craftsman in sifting arguments to achieve an authoritative and acceptable result. But though this image of a totally value-free judiciary is doubtless a comforting one, it does not unfortunately correspond to reality.

THE CREATIVE ROLE

Today it is commonly accepted that judges do quite legitimately exercise discretion. The most influential modern exposition of this view is that of Professor Hart (1961). In hard cases, Hart argues, the open texture of rules and of language, and the human inability to anticipate future situations, sometimes require judges to exercise a creative function, though not in an arbitrary way. 'Displaying characteristic judicial virtues', they invoke and evaluate in an impartial, neutral, and reasoned manner acknowledged standards of, for example, fairness and reasonableness in endeavouring to identify the aims of the rules under consideration.

As a description of judicial practice this seems eminently reasonable, though one must never underestimate the difficulties of actually achieving impartiality. But it is an indication of the resilience of the declaratory theory that Dworkin, Hart's successor as Professor of Jurisprudence at Oxford, has developed an implicit defence of it in his elaborate depiction of the judicial process as a vehicle for establishing *existing* legal rights and obligations (1977). It is the judge's duty, he asserts, even in hard cases, to discover what the rights of the parties are, not to invent new ones retrospectively. However, we are here concerned with what judges do, and for practical purposes, even assuming that one theoretically correct conclusion did exist in hard cases, judges, being human, would not always reach it. In fact, in some, admittedly rare, cases they will explicitly state that their decision has been made on policy grounds (Lord Denning being the most forthright exponent of this approach. See in particular his judgement in *Spartan Steel & Alloys Ltd* v. *Martin & Co.*, 1973); in others, the arguments in terms of precedents and principles seem so evenly balanced that it is difficult to see how any objectively 'correct' determination is possible (see Cross 1977: 220).

It seems more realistic to conclude that judges do have a creative role which involves the exercise of discretion; that they are to a degree law-makers. Indeed legislation will often itself confer such discretion in terms, though of course in such circumstances no question arises as to the legitimacy in principle of exercising it. In the recent case of *Firman* v. *Ellis* (1978), the Court of Appeal held that Parliament had conferred on the court a virtually unfettered discretion to allow any action for damages for personal injuries to proceed after the normal three-year limitation had expired, if it appeared to the court 'equitable' to do so. Lord Denning observed:

> 'In former times it was thought that judges should not be given discretionary powers. It would lead to too much uncertainty. The law should define with precision the circumstances in which judges should do this or that. Those days are past. In statute after statute, Parliament has given powers to the judges and entrusted them with a discretion as to the manner in which those powers should be exercised' (p.905).

But even when Parliament purports to circumscribe the judges through precisely worded and detailed legislation, it cannot anticipate the infinite variety of factual situations which may arise. It cannot, in a complex and fast-changing society, guarantee that what would have been a straightforward interpretation of a phrase when the Act was passed remains so. Such is the ambiguity of language – compounded by frequently convoluted and occasionally careless drafting – that the ideal of a crystal-clear and all-embracing set of statutory rules is of necessity a chimera. The point is reinforced by the elusiveness of 'the intention of Parliament', an abstraction which cannot meaningfully be identified with any specific group of people in respect of a particular Act or section of it, and which, by definition, would be non-existent in regard to circumstances not envisaged at the time the Act was passed.

In the face of such difficulties, the stock judicial approach is to confine analysis of intention to the wording of the Act. The suggestion, made from time to time, that the court should be permitted to consult Hansard or the report of a Parliamentary Select Committee as direct evidence of Parliament's intention was firmly denied in the House of Lords decision of *Davis* v. *Johnson* (1978), one reason being the imprecision and lack of uniformity of expression which characterizes parliamentary debate.

An interesting sidelight on the quest for objective interpretation is to be found in two letters to *The Times* (1977, 1978) from the draftsman of the Sex Discrimination Act 1975, claiming that in two cases courts had 'defied the clear words of the Act'. As a later correspondent observed: 'Everybody knows that Members of Parliament, for the most part, haven't the faintest idea what their enactments mean; they just hope that the parliamentary draftsman has got it right (whatever 'it' might be).'

Confronted with unclear statutory provisions and virtually precluded from reliance on extrinsic sources, what is a judge to do? Traditionally he is armed with three main rules of statutory interpretation – the literal rule, giving words their plain meaning; the golden rule, giving them a feasible alternative meaning, where the literal approach reveals internal inconsistency in the Act, or entails an absurd result; and the mischief rule, which interprets the intention of the Act by reference to the 'mischief' it seeks to correct. Various official reports may be consulted to identify the mischief, but not for any solutions which they recommend (*Black-Clawson International Ltd.* v. *Papierwerke Waldhof-Aschaffenburg A.G.* (1975)). As we shall see, further guidance may be obtained from certain presumptions about statutes in general – for example, that they should not be retrospective – and about the meaning of words in their particular context (see Cross 1976).

However, there is no single authoritative statement either of the three rules themselves, or of the appropriate circumstances or order of priority of their use. The same holds true for the presumptions. It follows that the legal system itself envisages both narrow literalist interpretation of statues and functional creativity. Since, within reason, both styles of judging are legitimate, the temperament of the individual judge to some extent dictates his approach.

SOME INSTANCES OF JUDICIAL CREATIVITY

A few examples from recent cases illustrate some of the difficulties. A dockers' club was linked with 4,000 other working men's clubs in a union. Any member of one club was entitled to become an associate of the union, which meant he could enjoy the facilities of any of the other clubs, unless lawfully excluded by its committee. Mr Sherrington, a coloured member of one of the clubs and an associate was excluded from the dockers' club because it operated a colour bar. Had the club contravened the Race Relations Act 1968? Under the Act it was unlawful for anyone concerned with the provision of goods, facilities, or services 'to the public or a section of the public' to discriminate in providing them. The sole point at issue then was whether or not associates constituted 'a section of the public'.

In *Race Relations Board* v. *Dockers' Labour Club* (1974), the Court of Appeal, affirming the decision of the county court, *unanimously* held that associates, as they were not personally selected by the dockers' club and as they comprised a very large body of people (approximately 1 million), did constitute 'a section of the public' within the meaning of the Act. The House of Lords *unanimously* reversed this decision, holding that as the Act covered discrimination in the public as opposed to the private sphere, associates came within the private sphere because they had been personally selected by *a* club in the union, and the proportion of associates *in fact* making use of the dockers' club facilities was not large enough to alter its private character. A similar problem had arisen over a colour bar in a Conservative social club (*Charter* v. *Race Relations Board*, 1973). There too a unanimous Court of Appeal had been reversed by the House of Lords. In the Court of Appeal Lord Denning had stressed the essentially impersonal nature of Conservatism as indicating that members were 'a section of the public'. But the House of Lords held that a private club where rules provided for genuine personal selection did not contravene the Act by operating a colour bar.

Both cases illustrate several of the points we have made about judicial interpretation. The Act sought to reduce racial discrimination, while acknowledging that legal controls would be unworkable in certain domestic and private spheres, which were specified. But it contained no express reference to clubs, so the judges had to decide whether members (in *Charter*) or associates (in the *Dockers Labour Club* case) constituted 'a section of the public'. The literal rule could not provide an adequate·answer, since it would cover *any* two or more associated persons. The judges therefore took into account the policy behind the Act. Lord Reid characterized it as being 'to separate the private from the public sphere' and by emphasizing the formalities of club procedures, rather than the substance of club activities, excluded the operation of the Act. Lord Diplock said (*Dockers Labour Club and Institute Ltd*. v. *Race Relations Board*): 'This is a statute which, however admirable its motives, restricts the liberty which the citizen has previously enjoyed at common law to differentiate between one person and another in entering or declining to enter into transactions with them', and: ' . . . in discouraging the intrusion of coercion by legal process in the fields of domestic or social intercourse, the principle of effectiveness joins force with the broader principle of freedom to order one's private life as one chooses' (p.598).

These passages are significant not merely in invoking general principles of effectiveness and a right to privacy, but for the underlying inference that an Act which, in Lord Diplock's judgement, potentially threatened those principles, must be interpreted in a restrictive manner. One might equally, at a higher level of abstraction, have stressed the fundamental aim behind the Act (its 'admirable motives') of minimizing racial discrimination, and the general principle of social justice, so as to achieve results more in accord with the spirit of the legislation (the decisions were later reversed by the Race Relations Act 1976, s.25.). Certainly one can speculate about inarticulate premises within the individual judgements. But what remains crucial is that in neither of these cases was the decision of either court manifestly wrong in law.

We will turn briefly to another area of law – labour relations – for an example of literal interpretation so draconian that it made subsequent judicial creativity almost inevitable (see Forde 1978). Statutory protection against unfair dismissal does not apply ' . . . to any employment where under his contract of employment the employee ordinarily works outside Great Britain.' (See now Employment Protection (Consolidation) Act 1978, s.141(2)). In *Portec (U.K.) Ltd* v. *Mogensen* (1976) the plaintiff was summarily dismissed. He did almost half of his work in great Britain and the rest in France. The court held that though he 'ordinarily worked' in Great Britain *when there*, nonetheless, when in France he 'ordinarily worked' outside Great Britain and therefore was caught by the literal meaning of the wording! Bristow J. commented: 'If it had been the intention of Parliament to exclude those who ordinarily worked *only* outside Great Britain it would have been easy to say so' (italics supplied).

In support of this interpretation, Bristow J. pointed to the subsequent clause which expressly provided that merchant seamen employed on United Kingdom registered ships are to be treated as 'ordinarily work[ing]' in Britain where they do not work 'wholly' abroad. He inferred that a similar provision could have been, but was not, inserted to protect other employees. But in a subsequent case (*Wilson* v. *Maynard Shipbuilding*, 1978) the Court of Appeal overruled *Portec*, on the ground that Parliament could not have intended 'ordinarily works' to have a different meaning in the two clauses. Thus by using a different canon of construction, the Court of Appeal reached a diametrically opposed conclusion, but one which seems both fairer and more in accord with the general aims of the Act. As Lord Denning was to comment in a later case (*Todd* v. *British Midland Airways Ltd.*, 1978): 'The construction put on [the statute] in the *Wilson* case was plain commonsense. It might be giving a liberal construction to the Act, getting away from the literal meaning of the words; but that was all to the good.'

Much of what we have said about the open texture of legislation applies with even more force to the common law. The very wealth of cases, the difficulty at times of extracting, let alone interpreting, the relevant principle, the selective nature of reasoning by analogy, the need to reinterpret antiquated precedents, all make for open-endedness. It is reflected in the frequency of dissenting judgements in cases which go to appeal, most pointedly when they are decided by 3 to 2 in the House of Lords.

Also important is the belief, often voiced by judges, that they are more entitled to develop the common law. ' ... in the common law there is a general warrant for judicial law-making; in statute law there is not' (Lord Devlin 1976a: 9). The main argument here is that controversial issues, in a democratic society, should be settled by the legislature; 'lawyers' law' may be developed by the judges. In addition, Lord Diplock (1965) has suggested that the common law is more amenable to judicial innovation than legislation because it lacks the constraints of the rules of statutory interpretation and precise statutory wording.

On this last point, though precedent is less limiting in a formal sense – especially now for the House of Lords – one may legitimately doubt if the difference is very marked, given the flexibility of the rules of interpretation and the ambiguity of much statutory language. In the words of the American writer Jaffe: ' ... the law is all of a piece whether enforcing constitutions, written or unwritten, interpreting statutes or applying the common law, the job is much the same ... '. Each allows the 'opportunity for creative manipulation or resigned impotence' (1969). Also, as Wade (1977) notes in the context of administrative law: 'It is a paradox that the nearer judges come to [the law's] fundamentals, the more prone they are to speak with discordant voices.'

JUDICIAL OBSERVATIONS ON INTERPRETATION

One of the most striking and, we would argue, healthy developments of recent years has been the increased willingness of senior members of the judiciary to admit to an innovative role. It facilitates discussion of the criteria and values underpinning their creativity, not least because they have to produce reasoned decisions. If judges are law-makers we are entitled to know whether or not we can trust their judgment.

There is still, however, a wide spectrum of opinion as to the scope of legitimate judicial choice. At one extreme there are still a few appellate judges who espouse the declaratory myth (see, for example, Lord Dilhorne in *Cassell & Co.* v. *Broome* (1972) and in *Home Office* v. *Dorset Yacht Co.* (1970)) and at the other we have Lord Denning's blunt admission that in some cases he employs an almost wholly policy-based approach. The majority however do not adhere to either of these extremes.

Lord Diplock (1965) has drawn a distinction between different kinds of legislation. He suggests that tax statutes, for example, lend themselves to a narrow semantic approach. A morass of detailed technical provisions, they spawn litigation on points which Parliament has often not foreseen and judicial rulings which 'legislate' for all other taxpayers in the same position. Statutes which contain clear indications of general principle or policy, on the other hand, merit a more flexible approach. In practice, the House of Lords hears an average of fifty or sixty cases a year, mostly revenue, town and country planning, housing, and charterparty appeals. Lord Diplock notes with some regret that in modern times the restrictive approach which he sees as justified in these areas tends to carry over into the others.

One may question the extent to which judicial practice really does reflect this distinction. If one considers judicial attitudes to tax legislation from a historical perspective, for example, there is evidence of significant shifts of emphasis, partly on policy grounds. In 1809, admittedly despite several dicta to the contrary, the editor of Blackstone felt able to say : 'It is considered a rule of construction of revenue acts, in ambiguous cases, to lean in favour of the revenue'. In the Victorian period, on the other hand, there was a pronounced movement towards literal interpretation, favouring the taxpayer, and in one case the Master of the Rolls described the revenue officials as 'unpleasant tyrannical monsters'. (*Grainger and Son* v. *Gough* (1894)). In the last few years there have been signs of a return to purposive pro-revenue interpretation. It has been argued (Williams 1978) that part of the explanation lies in changing perceptions of the nature and purpose of taxation. In Victorian times, 'Tax avoidance was not a problem. The economic effects of taxes were rarely of concern' (p.411).

The type of statute under consideration will not then always be a sure guide. Indeed the value of adopting a historical perspective when trying to assess judicial attitudes is precisely that they cannot be fully understood in isolation from the prevailing economic and social climate; nor, in some matters at least, without examining the contemporary relationship of the judiciary to the legislature and the executive. In the important field of administrative law, for example, the courts were conspicuously more reluctant during the Second World War and the period of immediate post-War reconstruction to challenge the exercise of administrative discretion than they had been in much earlier times, or have been since (Wade 1977; cf. Allott 1977).

A further judicial contribution to the general debate on interpretation is the defence of judicial restraint advanced by Lord Devlin (1976a). Creativity, he maintains, demands enthusiasm, a quality inconsistent with impartiality and the appearance of it. The judge, he says, must not abandon 'his role of arbiter between the government and the governed'. He contrasts *activist* judicial law-making – 'keeping pace with change in the consensus' – which is acceptable, with *dynamic* or creative, law-making – judges generating change in the consensus – of which he disapproves. In a democratic society, he says, judges are not entitled to be dynamic leaders, nor are they usually temperamentally equipped to be. In any event, even in areas of 'lawyers' law', they lack the appropriate resources and do not operate in a suitable forum. The first priority of the litigation process, in other words, is the proper resolution of particularized disputes between individuals, not the advancement of social change.

But the undoubted force of these arguments is undermined both by the assumption that the consensus of the community is a readily identifiable and unproblematic notion and the broad definition of it as consisting of 'those ideas which its members as a whole like, or if they dislike, will *submit* to' (p.2, italics supplied). 'Consensus' normally connotes a more positive response to issues than mere submission. Defined so widely, it allows for much law-making that many people would deem creative. Indeed, it is difficult to see, in the light of *his* definition, what Lord Devlin means by saying that 'there was no consensus, probably not even a bare majority, for the abolition of capital punishment or the reformation of the laws against homosexuality'. First, there surely was submission to these reforms. Second, he implies here that consensus involves *more* than a bare majority positively in favour of them.

Numerous instances of a conscious and articulated policy role are to be found in the judgments of Lord Denning (see *The Discipline of Law*, 1979) who, as presiding judge of the Court of Appeal, is a living negation of the declaratory theory. In a famous judicial clash nearly thirty years ago, his assertion of a right to 'fill in the gaps' was described by Lord Simonds (on appeal in *Magor and St. Mellons R.D.C.* v. *Newport Corp.* (1952)) as a 'naked usurpation of the legislative function under the thin disguise of interpretation'. Yet in *Shaw* v. *D.P.P.* (1962), the 'Ladies' Directory' case, which concerned the publication of a booklet containing advertisements paid for by prostitutes, Lord Simonds, many would say against the weight of authority, vigorously proclaimed the existence of a common law offence of conspiracy to corrupt public morals:

'In the sphere of criminal law, I entertain no doubt that there remains in the courts of law a residual power to enforce the supreme and fundamental purpose of the law, to conserve not only the safety and order but also the moral welfare of the State, and that it is their duty to guard it against attacks which may be the more insidious because they are novel and unprepared for' (p.267).

It would be disingenuous to claim that Lord Simonds was here merely reflecting the greater freedom of judges to develop the common law than statute. He was, in effect, asserting that they were entitled, if not bound, to legislate on matters of public morals which fall squarely within the area of public controversy and Parliamentary debate. The fact is that the very phrase 'creative interpretation' is potentially misleading in that 'creative' implies approval. Yet if one rejects the declaratory theory and sees common law principles and statutory wording as existing so to speak in a continuum, capable of bearing a narrow or broad meaning, a literalist approach is also 'creative'.

THE POLITICS OF THE JUDICIARY

The crucial issue remains the nature and extent of the judicial involvement in politics in the broadest sense of the term (see Paterson 1974). Lord Devlin has observed that their 'high powers make the British judiciary more than just a neutral arbitral force' and that 'In the criminal law the judges regard themselves as at least as much concerned as the executive with the preservation of law and order'. But he also sees their role as 'arbitrating between citizens and as holding the balance between the state and the individual'. In his recent book, *The Politics of the Judiciary*, Professor Griffith (1977) describes the judiciary as a political force, in the broad sense of pursuing a definable concept of 'the public interest', which is predetermined by their background, education, training, socialisation and, ultimately, the criteria of their selection.

He perceives a strongly authoritarian political philosophy underlying the judicial perception of 'the public interest', centring on the interests of the state, including its moral welfare, and the preservation of law and order; the protection of property rights and the promotion of certain political views normally associated with the Conservative party, most conspicuously in the spheres of industrial and race relations. He asserts, for example, that:

'It is demonstrable that on every major social issue which has come before the courts during the last 30 years – concerning industrial relations, political protest, race relations, government secrecy, police powers, moral behaviour – the judges have supported the conventional, established, and settled interests' (p.213).

In his book he provides many telling instances from post-1950 cases in support of this otherwise over-generalized claim, arguing that it is only by an unduly restrictive use of language that one can deny the existence of a political element in such judgments.

Certainly the general ethos of Bar and Bench testifies to the strength of an institutional factor calculated to foster and reinforce a striking homogeneity of background and attitudes. Several surveys (Griffith: 24 – 8) have revealed a middle class, public school, and Oxbridge bias, as evidence of an élitism which, though no doubt typical of legal professions generally, seems more pronounced in England than elsewhere. This must at the very least detract from the appearance of impartiality, especially in fields such as labour law. The insularity of life at the Bar has also often been noted. A fairly narrow academic training is followed by pupillage, conceived as an apprentice's initiation into the skills and craft of forensic and drafting expertise. The barrister has only limited and formalized contact with the lay client, by contrast with his constant contact with other barristers, who are predominantly conformist and conservative. Judicial appointment, itself virtually predicated on the holding of 'sound', orthodox opinions, accentuates the insularity through the enforced isolation it imposes. The trappings of judicial office, and the degree of deference it commands, combine with what Sawer (1965) has called the diffuse social influence of absorption into the 'establishment', resulting from regular social and ceremonial contacts (p.91).

It would be naive though to imagine that the broadly conformist ethos described could be substantially different. Whatever their educational background, '...judges will still be of the same type...who do not seriously challenge the status quo' (Devlin 1976a, 8). By and large, people who become judges are not social reformers by temperament and are doubtless even less likely to be so in systems under which they are appointed relatively late in life. Griffith makes this point much more strongly: 'To expect a judge to advocate radical change, albeit legally, is as absurd as it would be to expect an anarchist to speak up in favour of an authoritarian society' (p.215). But to what extent is this *more* than a matter of temperament?

Griffith argues that the overriding importance attached by judges to the preservation of a stable society is incompatible with their commonly asserted commitment to protecting the individual from the power of the state (see p. 196). On the face of it, such a conclusion seems difficult to sustain in view of the increasing readiness of the courts to control administrative discretion (see, for example, *Padfield* v. *Minister of Agriculture, Fisheries and Food* (1968); *Anisminic Ltd* v. *Foreign Compensation Commission* (1969); *Secretary of State for Education and Science* v. *Tameside Metropolitan B.C.* (1976); *Laker Airways Ltd.* v. *Department of Trade* (1977); and *Congreve* v. *Home Office* (1976); see Griffith, Chapter 5). Griffith's explanation of this judicial interventionism is that it is highly selective. If social stability and law and order are not threatened, and especially where the plaintiff can be characterized as a victim of ministerial political policy, the judge feels no sense of obligation to support governmental power. Equally, he claims, the courts are willing to uphold the citizen against the state in respect of property rights, but reluctant to do so in the case of personal human rights. ' ... in the cases arising out of legislation concerned with housing and planning, trade unions, and race relations, the judiciary digs its trenches against what it sees as government not in the public interest' (p.211).

It is difficult to test the validity of such a generalized assertion in the space of a few pages, but brief reference to some of these areas should suffice to suggest that it needs to be qualified. To begin with, it conveys a sense of uniformity of approach which is hardly borne out by an examination of the cases. For a noteworthy feature of several of the cases to which Griffith refers is the degree of disagreement, both between the Court of Appeal and the House of Lords, and often within each court, sometimes culminating in a three to two majority in the House of Lords. We have already described two instances of wide divergence between the Court of Appeal and the House of Lords in the field of race relations. Griffith (1974b) himself has observed in an examination of these cases ' ... that the temper and philosophy of the Court of Appeal and the House of Lords are seldom in accord. A "liberal" Court of Appeal is offset by a "reactionary" House of Lords or vice-versa' (p.734). He goes on to assert that the divergence of opinion in cases such as *Charter* and the *Dockers Labour Club* is explained by the contrast between the 'conservative', individualist philosophy of the House of Lords and the more socially-conscious 'lib-lab' view of the Court of Appeal.

Yet the judges in question had broadly the same backgrounds and were subject to the same institutionalization. It seems difficult to explain such divergences as being consistent with a common judicial conception of 'the public interest' in the rather sweeping form in which Griffith puts it.

There is also a danger of underplaying the extent to which the wording of statutory provisions can impose restraints on judicial activism, even granted the open texture of language. Not all statutory wording is ambiguous. In the final analysis, of course, unduly strained, or controversial, judicial interpretation is liable to prompt nullifying legislation. But short of such a drastic step, there are numerous drafting techniques which can be employed to minimize judicial intervention. Planning law, with its obvious potential for conflict between the demands of administrative policy and of legal regulation, affords several illustrations (Grant 1978). Legislation may, for example, try to exclude or severely limit judicial review of administrative action. It may be so vague in its statement of local authorities' obligations as to effectively preclude judicial enforcement.

'Or an Act may provide an alternative administrative or political remedy as a clear indication to the judges that their intervention would be unnecessary and unwelcomed. Alternatively, discretionary power may be conferred in such a way as to make it clear that the official concerned is to have wide powers in determining the factors relevant to his decision, or in assessing the factual basis upon which he may take action. In addition the statute may attempt to decree some measure of finality for the subsequent decision, or limit judicial review . . . to a specified period. By means both overt and covert parliamentary legislation predicts and attempts to modify judicial intervention' (p.518).

As regards cases involving trade unions, it is certainly not difficult to find evidence of judicial hostility and instances of what most commentators would acknowledge to be law-making (as in *Rookes* v. *Barnard* (1964) which was also an example of a controversial decision precipitating a nullifying statute). Many judges would no doubt plead guilty to an unconscious bias against collective action in principle. In part such a reaction reflects the traditional common law conception of the courts as a forum for resolving disputes between individuals. It is however also reasonable to suppose that judges, who have not experienced any need for the kind of protection afforded by collective action, are unlikely to be sympathetic to claims made in its name, particularly where effective vindication of a claim involves dismissal of an individual employee (as in *Rookes* v. *Barnard* and *Bonsor* v. *Musicians' Union* (1956)). Nor can the question of social background be brushed aside as Lord Scrutton (1923) acknowledged:

' . . . the habits you are trained in, the people with whom you mix, lead to your having a certain class of ideas of such a nature that, when you have to deal with other ideas, you do not give as sound and accurate judgments as you would wish. This is one of the great difficulties at present with Labour. Labour says: ''Where are your impartial Judges? They all move in the same circle as the employers, and they are all educated and nursed in the same ideas as the employers. How can a labour man or a trade unionist get impartial justice?'' It is very difficult sometimes to be sure that you have put yourself into a thoroughly impartial position between two disputants, one of your own class and one not of your class' (p.8).

But in the context of modern industrial relations, when unions, in the assertion of sectional interest, benefit from substantial legal immunities, they are clearly capable of being wrong in law without the need to invoke sinister explanations.

O'Higgins and Partington (1969), in an examination of judicial values in cases involving industrial conflict, concluded: 'Clearly there was less statistical evidence of the influence of judicial bias than might *a priori* have been expected'. But in any event it is doubtful whether there is much to be gained by posing the issue in such a generalized way. For it is always possible to find, even at the highest level, judicial decisions which do not seem to fit into a formula of the kind for which Griffith is arguing. One recent example was *Gouriet* v. *Union of Post Office Workers* (1978): post office workers had refused to handle mail to South Africa, and Gouriet, the leader of the National Association for Freedom, sought either to prosecute the union himself or to ensure that the Attorney-General exercized his authority to do so. Lord Denning delivered a judgment in the Court of Appeal in favour of his claim, which might have been expected to evoke sympathy from a conservative judiciary wedded to individual freedom. But the House of Lords rejected it, Lord Wilberforce observing that executive decisions 'of the type to attract political criticism and controversy showed that they were outside the range of discretionary problems which the courts could resolve'. Similarly, during the steel strike of early 1980, the House of Lords reversed the Court of Appeal's restrictive interpretation of the law on 'secondary picketing' (*Duport Steels Ltd.* v. *Sirs* (1980)).

Analyses of judicial attitudes then do not seem likely to yield fruitful results. Labelling theory can be somewhat crude and facile and attempts to demonstrate cause and effect on the basis of criteria such as social background can be suggestive but not ultimately cogent. This limitation may partly account for the trend towards broader, institutional explanations of the judicial function (for example, Campbell 1974; Paterson 1974), asserting that judicial bias is inherent in the way law itself is characterized and not just a consequence of conditioning and institutionalization. On this view, judges control a source of power because they can persuade the community that the legal interpretation of a situation is the correct one. They use rules to produce 'authoritative' interpretations of reality and the very attachment to rules – legalism as an 'ethical attitude' (Shklar 1964) – fosters a fundamentally conservative approach which is, in the wider sense of the term, political and geared to legitimating the state.

We are not concerned to deny that the overwhelming majority of judges are conservative. But, as does Griffith's thesis, this type of argument understates such elements of independence and variety as are to be found among them. There are, after all, notable examples of 'liberal' judges upholding the rule of law in defiance of totalitarian regimes. Equally, in a country such as the United States, the Supreme Court has at times played an innovative role which would hardly qualify it as an arm of the 'establishment'. In England, though a conservative, formalist approach to interpretation is a distinctive feature of the judicial tradition, many judges display a bluff, no-nonsense pragmatism and a few are conscious social reformers (see Reid 1972).

A COMPARISON WITH THE UNITED STATES

Despite crucial historical and constitutional differences, England and the United States share a common law heritage. Yet, most noticeably at the level of the Supreme Court, one encounters a different approach to the legitimate functions of the legal process. It is reflected in the types of information and analysis deemed relevant: '. . . contemporary American courts are resorting more and more to the method of sociology as a primary decisional tool. They are considering the pragmatic effects of alternative courses of decision . . .' (Aldisert 1977: 41).

The conscious adoption of social engineering as a permissible basis for decision making, coupled with a readiness to incorporate statistical and other social scientific material, has at times made possible a degree of judicial dynamism unthinkable in the English courts. This was particularly pronounced in the Supreme Court under Chief Justice Warren (1953-69), which immediately established a reputation for creative law-making in the momentous school desegregation case of *Brown* v. *Board of Education* (1954). Several landmark decisions affirming individual rights and liberties were to follow on matters such as urban voting rights (*Baker* v. *Carr* (1962)) and the rights of criminal suspects during police interrogation (*Miranda* v. *Arizona* (1966) – though here the Court was sharply divided, 5 to 4). Though the present 'Burger Court' has been more cautious and restrictive in general, it has also effected changes on a substantial scale and in sweeping language, as in its extension of the constitutional right to privacy, to invalidate anti-abortion legislation nationwide (*Roe* v. *Wade* (1973)).

How can one explain this contrast with England in judicial style? In America, the Supreme Court and the inferior federal courts have a power of judicial review of legislation (*Marbury* v. *Madison* (1803)), that is to say, a *constitutional* role which transcends the settlement of the dispute between individual litigants. A state jurisdiction may be called upon to settle major constitutional issues and the terms of its written constitution take precedence over case law. More generally, it has to be appreciated that historically the excessive formalism of the English common law ran counter to the pioneering spirit of the new country, as evidenced in the conscious rejection early on of English precedents.

Such is the diffusion of power among federal and state governments that effective legislation may prove unobtainable on controversial social and political matters. The higher courts have consequently functioned as a kind of supplementary legislature. The very role of constitutional adjudication encourages greater flexibility in handling precedents than is the case in England. The ideological positions of the senior judges are forced further into the open, in a country where they are elected and where the choice of appointment is closely scrutinized by the media.

The sympathy with which the social engineering function of judges is viewed is also rooted in American legal philosophy. Most obviously it is to be found in the works of Pound and the realists. The recognition, in particular, by a number of scholars who were also judges, men such as Cardozo, Holmes, Frank, and Frankfurter, that there *is* such a thing as judicial choice, was to have a profound effect on later generations of judges, practitioners, and academic lawyers.

Conclusions

In this chapter we have considered the question of how legal norms emerge and change, and whose interests they appear to express in doing so. We started by suggesting that such changes could be analysed in terms of a continuum ranging from a consensus model at one extreme, through a pluralist model in the middle to a Marxist, ruling-class one at the other extreme. In practice, the difficulties of deciding what constitutes an 'interest', and to whom it specifically belongs, make it difficult to locate changes in this way. Nevertheless, some general conclusions are possible.

The analysis and case studies at the beginning of this chapter suggest that a flexible pluralist model would be the most generally applicable characterization of legal change. That is, although dominant class interests are frequently the most influential, this is not inconsistent with other sectional or even consensual interests also playing their part. As Carson, Paulus, and Gunningham allow, significant concessions have often been made to both relatively autonomous interests of 'moral entrepreneurs' and to the threat (usually perceived rather than actual) of concerted lower social class opposition.

The fact that such changes have left the fundamental legal structure of private property capitalism unchanged and that the dominant class have usually accommodated to, or even ultimately welcomed them, is not in itself conclusive evidence of anything. Following Renner, we have emphasized that legal forms may express themselves in a variety of ways: just as feudal legal forms long concealed the actual emergence of bourgeois power, so now bourgeois legal forms often conceal the emerging power of the lower social class, as well as other more sectional power sources. As Renner himself illustrates, such emerging power has vastly altered the status of the wage labourer and the real meaning of private property in modern capitalism.

A further complication, however, is that the actual meaning of legal changes very much depends on the nature of the apparatus and procedures instituted for their enforcement. As we saw, Dickson suggests that where special enforcement bureaucracies are set up (as in the case of the Narcotics Bureau in the United States) a kind of Parkinsonian expansionism sets in: the status requirements of such bureaucracies require constant extension of jurisdiction – finding new forms of behaviour to control. This, however, seems to be the case only where those who are to be controlled are powerless and of low status. When the people to be controlled are powerful business men (as in the case of those who are the objects of control of the Factory Inspectorate and Alkali Inspectorate) almost the opposite appears to happen. The control bureaucracies achieve status in a different way – by identifying with those whom they are supposed to control, with a consequent avoidance of formal, legal procedure. This need not *necessarily* lead to less efficient control of the offending behaviour, but examples given by both Carson and Gunningham suggest that it often does. The moral seems to be a rather obvious one: efficient control is in practice difficult to achieve by consensual methods. It seems that enthusiastic and efficient control agencies must, both in their personnel and powers, be conflict-orientated.

The work of both Carson and Paulus illustrates the extent to which legislation is a process in the course of which original interests and issues fade, and new ones appear and assert themselves. This led us to a more detailed consideration of the actual legislative process. Unfortunately, this is a subject on which detailed information is extremely difficult to obtain, not so much because of the usual 'lack of adequate research', but for a reason which is currently of considerable interest in itself: the cloak of official secrecy which hangs over so much of the area.

Nevertheless, one significant feature of contemporary legislation is that it is predominantly government-initiated. Since governments are periodically subjected to general elections, it might be expected that public opinion would be an important influence. Indeed, a study by Hewitt (1974) of a number of post-war political issues suggested that public opinion (as measured by opinion polls) appeared to have had a more important influence on government decision making than had powerful forces such as big business and trade union interests. It would, however, be naive to derive too much from this research. On many, if not most, issues 'public opinion' is not articulated in any direct way. Also, general elections are usually decided on fairly narrow, usually economic criteria. Finally, the legislative process is one of bargaining and trading between interest groups and their representatives which may crucially alter the original government-inspired programme. For reasons such as these, the key to understanding the legislative process has often been considered to be pressure groups and their activities.

The determinants of pressure group success, however, are again rather difficult to ascertain. Certainly there is evidence to suggest that the articulated support of public opinion is one important factor. But it is equally certain, from numerous examples of change which have lacked such support, that it is not the only one. An equally, if not more, important source of success appears to be the extent to which such groups have access to, or representatives and sympathisers among, those who are responsible for government policy and who sit on government committees.

Interestingly, the most readily available examples of pressure group successes which run counter to, or at least lack the general support of, public opinion appear to be liberal-reformist rather than reactionary ones – a fact which is hard to reconcile with a ruling-class model of legal change. The most obvious example was the abolition of capital punishment, but the category would also include homosexual law reform, abortion law reform, and race relations legislation. It is difficult to construe such innovatory changes as reflecting ruling-class interests. Rather, they appear to be examples of autonomous moral entrepreneurship of the kind described by Becker.

More flamboyant and open forms of moral crusading also appear to play their part in pressure group success, as we saw in the case of the NVLA. The crucial element here seems to be the role of the mass media as presumed spokesmen for outraged public opinion. It is perhaps a measure of the elusiveness of 'public opinion' that 'media opinion' is so often what is really meant when that expression is used. Consequently, as we saw, skilful and concerted pressure group lobbying of the media is a potent weapon of change.

In addition to pressure groups, we looked at the significance of advice to governments, in the form of 'official' reports. It would be theoretically possible to portray such forms of consultation prior to legislation as a manifestation of the participatory democratic ideal. However, as we saw, committees often function rather as arenas in which civil servants and the more influential pressure groups take a further opportunity of stating their conflicting positions. Thus the combination of the personnel involved, the framing of committees' terms of reference and the way they conduct their inquiries (especially in this country) tends to produce fairly predictable results, broadly in line with existing government policy. Further, if for some reason they do not do this, the typical response is immediate consignment to the scrap-heap. However, this does not mean that such reports are useless, since they frequently become rallying points and sources of vindication for pressure groups in their continuing battle (this is more evident in the United States where, for reasons which we have outlined, independent committee findings are rather more common).

We concluded by looking at the way in which judicial interpretation may in practice create new law. We accepted the Realists' message that we need to investigate who the judges are and what they do in fact, for what it may tell us about judicial creativity. We saw that judging is neither wholly mechanical nor completely arbitrary. There is a realm of choice about which it is not easy to generalize. Social background by itself is an unreliable pointer. It has to be evaluated in the light of subsequent institutionalization and, at a broader theoretical level, in the light of the reification of law. There are certain internal constraints in the nature of a statute and its particular wording, and in the extent to which the common law on the subject has been clarified. There are also more intangible, but no less real, constraints in the accountability of judges within the hierarchy of the system itself, their need to retain the respect of the legal profession and even, to a degree, their credibility among the population at large.

One can venture the 'judicial hunch' that people temperamentally inclined to 'judging' and who survive the road to high judicial office are likely to be conservative. It would however be naive to single them out as reactionary in so far as their role is the maintenance of a status quo which they have not, in its fundamentals, created. As Friedman (1977) has noted, it would be strange if the courts were immune to the dominant social forces at work in society:

> '*If* the judicial system were highly autonomous, it would produce many "wrong" results, that is, results which went against what major social, economic and political forces saw as their interests ... in the long run, why would society or its rulers tolerate such a system?' (pp.105–06).

Instead, he suggests, it would be challenged, put down by legislation, or bypassed.

To the extent that the judiciary is a creative force, the more we know about its members' preconceptions and criteria of evaluation the better. Their own greater willingness to articulate underlying policies is consequently a healthy sign. Controversy over their 'political' role can be expected to intensify if current proposals for a Bill of Rights, or something akin to one, are eventually implemented.

Suggested Reading

THE EMERGENCE OF LEGAL NORMS

Becker, H. (1963) The Marijuana Tax Act. In H. Becker, *Outsiders: Studies in the Sociology of Deviance*. New York: Free Press.
Carson, W. (1974) The Sociology of Crime and the Emergence of Criminal Laws. In P. Rock and M. McIntosh (eds.), *Deviance and Social Control*. London: Tavistock.
Carson, W. (1974) Symbolic and Instrumental Dimensions of Early

Factory Legislation. In R. Hood (ed.), *Crime, Criminology and Public Policy*. London: Heinemann.

Chambliss, W. (1970) A Sociological Analysis of the Laws of Vagrancy. In W. Carson and P. Wiles (eds.), *Crime and Delinquency in Britain*. London: Martin Robertson.

Dickson, D. (1968) Bureaucracy and Morality: an Organisational Perspective on a Moral Crusade. *Social Problems* **16**: 143.

Gunningham, N. (1974) *Pollution, Social Interest and the Law*. London: Martin Robertson.

Gusfield, J. (1963) *Symbolic Crusade: Status Politics and the American Temperance Movement*. Illinois: University of Illinois Press.

Hall, J. (1952) *Theft, Law and Society*. New York: Bobbs Merrill.

Hay, D., Linebaugh, P., and Thompson, E.P. (eds.) (1975) *Albion's Fatal Tree*. London: Allen Lane.

Paulus, I. (1974) *The Search for Pure Food: a Sociology of Legislation in Britain*. London: Martin Robertson.

Renner, K. (1976) *The Institutions of Private Law and their Social Functions*. London: Routledge and Kegan Paul.

THE LEGISLATIVE PROCESS AND JUDICIAL INTERPRETATION

Cox, A. (1976) *The Supreme Court and the American System of Government*. London: Oxford University Press.

Cross, R. (1976) *Statutory Interpretation*. London: Butterworth.

_____ (1977) *Precedent in English Law* (3rd ed.). Oxford: Clarendon Press.

Devlin, Lord (1979) *The Judge*. London: Oxford University Press.

Farrar, J. (1974) *Law Reform and the Law Commission*. London: Sweet and Maxwell.

Griffith, J. (1977) *The Politics of the Judiciary*. London: Fontana.

Hartley, T. and Griffith, J. (1975) *Government and Law*. London: Weidenfeld and Nicolson.

Hood, R. (1974) Criminology and Penal Change: a Case Study of the Nature and Impact of Some Recent Advice to Governments. In R. Hood (ed.), *Crime, Criminology and Public Policy*. London: Heinemann.

Jaffe, L. (1969) *English and American Judges as Lawmakers*. Oxford: Clarendon Press.

Outer Circle Policy Unit (1977) *An Official Information Act*. London: Outer Circle Policy Unit.

Ryan, M. (1978) *The Acceptable Pressure Group*. London: Saxon House.

de Smith, S. (1977) *Constitutional and Administrative Law* (3rd ed.) Harmondsworth: Penguin.

Walkland, S. (1968) *The Legislative Process*. London: Allen and Unwin.

Wootton, G. (1978) *Pressure Politics in Contemporary Britain*. London: Saxon House.

3
Legal Rules in Operation:
(1) The Criminal Process

Introduction

Having considered the ways in which legal rules come about and change, we now turn to how they are operated and applied. In this chapter we will be concentrating on the criminal law. We will approach it by looking at the various stages of processing that an accused person will pass through on his way to being found guilty and sentenced, or acquitted. Again, the emphasis will be on the way in which the actions of the various personnel involved at each of these stages constitute the 'reality' of the criminal law. As we concluded in Chapter 1, such an approach is necessary not just because there is a 'gap' between what is supposed to happen and what actually happens (although it may sometimes be possible to characterize the process in that way), but also because the formal rules (both substantive and procedural) do not, or indeed cannot, provide a clear-cut unambiguous version of what *is* supposed to happen. In this sense, the reality of the criminal law *can* only be understood through the empirical observation of the way in which 'abstract' rules are 'situationally' interpreted and applied.

With respect to the criminal law, the normal starting point for chronicling this process is the conduct of the police, since they are usually regarded as the 'front line' in its application. Yet this is in fact jumping the gun, for it omits a highly significant prior stage. The point can be illustrated by a simple statistic (see McCabe and Sutcliffe 1978): something like three-quarters of all crimes known to the police become known through the public, in their capacity as victims and observers, reporting them to the police. The 'front line' is thus in reality the general public, for it is *their* interpretations of abstract rules which initially set the parameters of what constitutes crime.

Studies of public opinion and law (see Podgorecki 1973) invariably show a massive conformity to the abstract rules. That is, the vast majority of people express agreement with the formal legal rules. But this is not really very helpful, since people's views on the rules tell us little about how far they act on them in practice. Thus, 'self-report' and 'victim' studies show a very substantial under-reporting of potential criminal offences, even when, in legal terms, they would be considered serious (for a useful summary of such studies see Hood and Sparks 1970). Sometimes, such under-reporting stems from purely practical considerations, but it is also true that people make exceptions, and justify overlooking what they would otherwise regard as being criminal offences because of special circumstances or relationships that are involved. Thus the reality of what actually constitutes 'crimes' consists of the abstract rules, plus the relevant situational considerations that people apply to them. Unfortunately, there is little detailed research available on this subject.

The Police

POLICE DISCRETION

Much more research has been carried out on the significance of the police as creators of the reality of crime. Although, as we have just seen, they are not usually the initiators of this process, they do never-theless act as a highly significant 'filter'. In other words, public definitions of crimes only become official if subsequently accepted by the police, and often they are not. The debate on this issue has been framed in terms of the significance of 'police discretion'. Ranged against a formal view of the police as purely impartial 'appliers' of the law is the argument that they in fact have consider-able discretion both in deciding whether particular acts constitute crimes (and are therefore recorded as such) and in deciding whether particular people are criminals (and therefore should be arrested and charged). Often associated with, or implied in, such arguments is the view that such discretion reflects partiality on the part of the police, and that this in turn reflects the wider power relationships in society (i.e. that the partiality works against poorer and weaker sections of the community – the lower social classes and the ethnic minorities).

However, before looking any further into such issues, perhaps we should first ask whether the 'formal' view of police work mentioned above actually exists – either in the minds of people, or in the realms of possibility. In his study of the Chicago police, K.C. Davis (1975) found that 'The combination of selective enforcement with a comprehensive pretense of full enforcement is deeply established' (p.166). In this country, however, it is now rather more difficult than it used to be to find protagonists of this 'pretence' that the police can and should be full, non-selective enforcers of the law. Thus, for an uncompromising statement of such a view, from the police side, we must go back to Williams (1954). But this does not mean, of course, that the reality of selective enforcement is openly admitted. Whatever the position in relation to admission or concealment, however, it has always been accepted both by the police and by most researchers that full enforcement is an impossible aim even to try to achieve, and that attempts at it would be quite unacceptable to the public at large. There seem to be two general reasons for this.

The first reason is that legislation can never be drafted to cover every conceivable contingency. Consequently, cases will always occur where applying the letter of the law will seem inappropriate or even absurd. This points to an interesting contradiction in our expectations of the police. On the one hand they are expected to be just in the sense of being totally governed by the law, and not to take it into their own hands. Yet at the same time, since such universal enforcement would lead to absurdity and injustice in some cases, the police are also expected to do exactly the opposite, and take into consideration circumstances which have not been recognized by the law. From their point of view the dilemma presents itself as a contradiction between the letter of the law and their common-sense morality. Banton (1964), in his study of the police, notes this point and suggests that the police are ultimately guided by their common-sense morality. This, he says, normally coincides with the strict letter of the law, but when it does not their sense of morality usually wins.

A second reason for discretionary enforcement of the law by the police is a technical one: it is impossible for them to pursue all forms of violation equally relentlessly, or each particular case with equal concern, simply because their resources are obviously limited. Decisions on the allocation of resources are, in effect, the exercise of discretion on enforcement. This is particularly significant in relation to 'victimless' crimes, or crimes which are under-reported (for example, homosexual offences, vice, drug offences, vandalism). The *amount* of behaviour in these areas which actually becomes defined as crime is almost entirely dependent on police activity, and the formation of vice squads or drug squads involves major discretionary decisions which have a crucial effect on enforcement and consequently on the reality of crime. Such decisions are, of course, based on police conceptions of 'seriousness' of particular types of offence – that is, once again, it boils down to their sense of morality (or, as is sometimes the case, pressure exerted on them by other people's sense of morality). For example, the Chief Constable may have a considerable influence on the way particular crimes are enforced in his district. A notable recent instance was the appointment of James Anderton as Chief Constable for the Greater Manchester area. A man known to favour 'flexible policing' (see Kettle 1979), Anderton immediately influenced the nature of law enforcement in Manchester. Thus a policy of 'verbal advice' replaced rigid enforcement of road traffic law and in the year after he took office (1977) convictions declined by 35 per cent. Conversely, searches under the Obscene Publications Act increased five-fold over the same period. Such higher-level policy decisions cannot, however, totally control the policeman's on-the-spot discretion. Anderton himself is quoted as saying that: 'Policing should be flexible enough to allow different enforcement on opposite sides of the same street if conditions dictate it' (Kettle 1979).

For reasons such as these, and also simply because there is a limit to the public's toleration of intervention in its daily life, it has been argued that police discretion is not only inevitable, but necessary. Thus, in the United States, Skolnick (1966) has suggested that the formal model of impartial, bureaucratic efficiency is impossible to achieve simply because police work is a 'human' and not a 'technical' task. That is, it involves such 'human' activities as paying informers, bargaining with suspects, and turning a blind eye. McCabe and Sutcliffe (1978) make a similar point, though rather less dramatically. Bureaucratic organization (typical of complex modern societies) involves a structure whereby:

'decisions are made at the top and a system of rules and instructions ensures that these decisions are reflected in the actions of all subordinates, whose freedom to initiate and amend is very limited . . . Police work is rather different. It is true that legal enactments and force orders set the bounds within which ordinary policemen operate, but the infinite variety of situations about which he is asked to make a judgment prevents the rigid enforcement of bureaucratic procedures. Each policeman stands on his own and exercises a powerful discretion . . . In peace-keeping, in the maintenance of social order, in rejecting or accepting definitions of criminal activity made by the general public, police organisation is not at all bureaucratic.' (pp.36–7).

If the police must and do use discretion in the enforcement of the criminal law the important questions to ask are how do they use it, and with what implications for the reality of the criminal law? For it is obviously true, as critics have pointed out (see C. Williams 1954), that discretion opens up the possibility of bias and partiality. Indeed, it is the very basis of claims that the police operate the law unfavourably with respect to various groups – blacks, the lower social class, adolescents, etc. Thus, the recent findings from 'self-report' studies that people admitting to having committed crimes come from a much broader social class spectrum than those who are arrested, charged, and convicted (who are predominantly lower social class) have been widely interpreted as demonstrating that the police are class-biased in their use of discretion (see, for example, Box 1971).

Before looking at the research evidence on the way in which police use their discretion, it is worth noting that apparent biases need not necessarily reflect the police operating on the basis of stereotypes, or making moral distinctions – they may simply reflect practical considerations. This point has been effectively made by Walmsley (1978) in relation to enforcement of the law on homosexuality – an area especially susceptible to discretion, owing to its 'victimless' status. A curious feature of the 1967 Sexual Offences Act, which was ostensibly aimed at liberalizing the law on homosexuality, was that it was followed by a steady rise in the number of convictions for homosexual offences. As Walmsley notes, this has frequently been interpreted as being the outcome of a discretionary police 'drive' against homosexuals, reflecting a police prejudice against them. While it is obviously true that it reflects a decision on the part of the police to enforce the law (which itself discriminates against homosexuals, relative to heterosexuals), Walmsley's analysis suggests that the increase in offences can be seen primarily as resulting from the fact that the Act both clarified the law relating to homosexuality and, more importantly, made prosecution of the forms of homosexual activity which remained outlawed much simpler for the police (by allowing *summary* trial for indecency between males and by abolishing the need for the consent of the DPP for prosecutions involving offenders over the age of twenty-one).

American Research on Police Discretion

The major English studies (Banton 1964; Lambert 1970; Cain 1973b) of the police tend to rely on American research when dealing specifically with discretion. This is presumably on the assumption that the 'human' problems of handling discretion are likely to be the same here as in the United States and that the findings are open to generalization. Since this is not an entirely satisfactory assumption, we will look only briefly at the findings of the major American studies and use them mainly as a reference point against which to assess the (admittedly limited) evidence relating to this country.

An early study by La Fave (1965) in Michigan suggested various criteria that the police appeared to apply in their decisions on whether to make an arrest or not. The major ones, perhaps not unexpectedly, were their assessment of the likelihood of obtaining a successful conviction (though we will see that this has some important implications) and the seriousness of the offence. In addition, he found that the disposition and demeanour of the victim played an important part, though this was clearly a corollary of the concern with obtaining a successful conviction (i.e. a victim who is both keen to get a conviction and is likely to put up a good performance in court is obviously vitally necessary for this purpose). Finally, he also found that the police were unlikely to take official action, even for quite serious offences, where they felt that the behaviour reflected 'local standards'. This was particularly the case in black ghetto areas where La Fave claimed the police often manifested a 'leave them to it' attitude. Unlike his other criteria, which have been invariably confirmed by other research, this last finding has been rather more controversial, since it runs directly counter to the idea that the police over-enforce the law in relation to the poorer, marginal sections of the community. Indeed La Fave's findings suggest that unfavourable stereotyping of such groups on the part of the police is more likely to lead to *under*-enforcement.

Much the most influential of the American studies of police discretion have been those relating to police encounters with juveniles. Two, in particular, have served as major reference points for studies of police discretion (and have been heavily relied upon in the English studies mentioned earlier): Piliavin and Briar (1964) and Black and Reiss (1970). Since their findings are similar, they can be dealt with together. As in the case of La Fave, both found that the seriousness or triviality of the offence was a major determinant of police discretion – not to take official action being far more likely in the case of trivial offences. However, since the vast majority of encounters were in relation to trivial events, this meant that such discretion was widely used – Black and Reiss found that arrest was used on only 15 per cent of the occasions where the police were called out to deal with juveniles. Hence both studies concluded that the decision to arrest or not was much more likely to be determined by police perceptions of the moral character of the offender than by the nature of, or the facts relating to, the offence. Such moral perceptions tended to be based to some extent on formal criteria such as whether the person concerned had a previous record (if known). But their most influential finding in this respect was of the significance of the juveniles' *demeanour* towards the police in determining whether they were arrested or not (next to the seriousness of the offence and previous record, they concluded that this was probably the most important single determinant). Thus encounters where the juvenile concerned was arrogant, disrespectful, or nonchalant were much more likely to lead to arrest than where he was contrite and respectful (though Black and Reiss also found that an over-respectful demeanour was likely to lead to arrest – presumably because the police interpreted it as ironic and manipulative).

Piliavin and Briar also found that the police used race, dress, known gang membership, and area of residence as indices of moral worthiness. For example, blacks and gang members, particularly in high crime-rate areas, were much more likely to be stopped and questioned for no apparent reason. The police themselves justified such behaviour on the grounds that such people were 'known troublemakers' or that it was known to be a 'bad area'. However, even if these suspicions were correct, as Piliavin and Briar point out, such beliefs and behaviour on the part of the police produce a cyclical, self-fulfilling prophecy: on the basis of such beliefs they police black, lower social class areas more heavily and accost the residents (particularly the young and black) more frequently, which leads to the latter feeling 'picked-on' and consequently exhibiting the kind of demeanour likely to result in their being arrested. This leads to an increase in arrests and thus the statistics confirm that it *is* a high crime area, and that such groups *are* more involved in crime and that the heavier policing is justified (thus completing the circle). It is interesting to note that this conclusion appears at first sight to be incompatible with La Fave's characterization of the policing of black ghetto areas (we will suggest later however that it is not).

Finally, in addition to confirming La Fave's finding that the disposition of the victim was an important determinant of whether official action was taken or not, Black and Reiss found that the disposition of the complainant was similarly important. They also suggested that this was not just a function of the police assessment as to their probable contribution to gaining a successful conviction, but included a moral assessment of *their* worthiness too.

Another factor strongly affecting the police use of discretion has been noted by several American researchers: the extent to which the setting is 'public' or 'private' (Stinchcombe 1963). That is, the police have much more freedom of action in public as opposed to private (e.g. domestic) settings. This has some important implications. Piliavin and Werthman (see Bordua 1967), for example, note that it is a significant aspect of lower social class gang boys' life that much of it is spent on the streets – i.e. in public settings, and it is this in part at least, that makes them particularly vulnerable to discretionary police action.

Bittner (1967) takes this point to an extreme by considering police behaviour on 'skid-row' – the areas inhabited by down-and-outs and alcoholics whose lives are entirely public and whose activities make them potentially arrestable virtually all the time. In this setting, Bittner suggests that the police have virtually total discretion and that the legal rules are almost entirely irrelevant in determining whether official action is taken or not. Arrests are made on an *ad hoc* basis, usually because of failure to co-operate with the police-defined limits of permissible behaviour.

In conclusion, the American studies generally suggest that official legal action is only *one* resource which the police in dealing with potential crimes. This is particularly the case with the mass of trivial cases which constitutes the bulk of their work in the law enforcement area, where there is some pressure to restrict official action since it can so easily clog up the bureaucratic process. In these cases, then, arrest tends to be used for reasons *other* than the fact of, or nature of, the offence. And as we have seen, it is suggested that stereo-typical expectations on the basis of race, class, age, and area of residence play their part in such decisions.

English Research Relating to Police Discretion

As we noted earlier, the major English police studies (Banton 1974; Lambert 1970; and Cain 1973b) tend to rely on the American material, insofar as police discretion is concerned. Unfortunately, there are far fewer equivalent inside studies of the police in action in this country. Although the influence of interactionism and labelling theory in the late 1960s and early 1970s inspired some interest in the police, that interest was mainly in the impact of police work on deviants – observed more from the side of the deviant than of the police. The major and most influential piece of work in this respect was undoubtedly Jock Young's study of the police as 'negotiators of reality' in their enforcement of drug laws in Notting Hill (1971).

Young starts by noting that the police, from the nature of their work (the hours they work, for example) and to some extent as a matter of policy, are relatively isolated from the general public.

This, he argues, makes them particularly prone to stereotyping – especially of those groups they would normally have little to do with (e.g. hippie culture drug-takers of that period). The main source of such stereotypes is the mass media (the latter being another particular interest of the English interactionists). Thus, police action on drug-law enforcement – the people they look for, the way they perceive them and present them in evidence – is determined by these stereotypes. The intensification of such action (e.g. through the formation of drug squads) isolates drug takers from the conventional culture, with two significant consequences: it intensifies their identity as deviants and the significance of drug-taking in their lives, thus *amplifying* their deviant, drug-taking activity, and second, it pushes them into 'living-out' the stereotyped identity created for them (that is, they are transformed from an integrated bohemian community where drug-taking was peripheral, into isolated groups of paranoid deviants amongst whom drug-taking is central).

Thus, according to Young, the whole reality of drug-taking and the meaning of the drug laws is a creation of the police (though originated by the mass media). The fundamental ideas – of both amplification and self-fulfilling stereotypes – were popular themes in the English version of interactionism and labelling theory and Young's account was probably the most radical version of it. However, quite apart from the somewhat anecdotal support for such an extreme theory, it also dealt with an area of deviance which, even at that time, was fairly marginal in the context of police work generally. In addition, there were highly specific features of law enforcement in relation to drugs which made generalization to other forms of deviance highly dubious. The drug-culture of that period was a new phenomenon about which the police had little to go on other than available stereotypes (though, as other observers have noted – see M. Young (1976) – contact with it had the effect of *breaking down* police stereotypes). Secondly, drug offences, being 'victimless', require direct action on the part of the police to be identified as such, and are hence especially susceptible to their stereotypes.

Nevertheless, Young's work on drug-takers illustrates the same sort of potentialities for police stereotypes to be self-fulfilling as do the American studies. Unfortunately, however, no work of the kind carried out by Piliavin and Briar and Black and Reiss is available for this country. Perhaps the nearest equivalent is Owen Gill's study of the relations between police and youths in a 'problem area' of Liverpool (Gill 1976). Once again, though, this was carried out from the standpoint of the youths rather than the police. Relations between the two sides are aptly summed up by the following quotes: 'When you see a gang of youths in that area it usually means trouble.' (PC in court); 'The coppers come round here looking for trouble: it's simple, less coppers, less trouble.' (local youth). (p.321).

Gill echoes the point made in the American studies about the significance of the *public* nature of the life of lower social class youths. This is reflected in the fact that they were typically involved in delinquent acts which were 'nebulous and subjectively defined charges such as causing a disturbance, assault, resisting arrest' – charges that are also particularly susceptible to discretionary interpretation.

The police saw the area as a trouble spot inhabited by anti-social gangs with ring-leaders. Groups on the street were therefore an indication of potential trouble, and the area was relatively heavily policed, so that young people were particularly likely to be stopped and questioned. Perhaps not surprisingly, the local youths saw the police as picking on them and harassing them (and arresting them if they dared to answer back – demeanour playing a similarly important part to that described in the American studies). Gill acknowledges some similarity between his findings and those of Piliavin and Briar and Black and Reiss, but claims that they somewhat oversimplified the complex interaction between police and youths.

Nevertheless, Gill's conclusions are familiar: youthful crime was at least to some extent an outcome of police expectations and actions, the legal definitions being a relatively minor determinant of whether people were arrested or not. Also, the amplification spiral described by Piliavin and Briar is succinctly described by Gill: 'In Luke Street every fresh incident increased the likelihood of further conflict because the boys' action in relation to the police was the product of the beliefs that these incidents supported' (p.334).

As we have already noted, both of the above studies consider the exercise of police discretion from the receiving end, so to speak. Direct studies of the police themselves are few and far between. Recently, however, McCabe and Sutcliffe (1978) carried out a detailed study of police procedures for recording crimes, based on participant observation in two police districts (Oxford and Salford). The main object was to examine the procedures whereby police decide whether or not to record reported incidents as crimes (or whether to change initial decisions), which obviously amounts to a concern with police discretion.

Interestingly, McCabe and Sutcliffe noted that discretionary decisions not to officially record complaints as crimes were recognized by a special police argot term – 'cuffing'. Indeed, they

they suggest that there was a general rule in the police forces they studied that committal to paper was to be avoided wherever possible, so that situations could be more open to on-the-spot discretionary decisions. This meant that there was frequently a marked 'difference between the complainant's view of what should be considered offensive or criminal and the definition of crime made by police officers who dealt with the complaints' (p.82). That is, although people *generally* agree with the police, this does not apply to the usually trivial cases they bring to them themselves. There was some indication, however, that the forcefulness of the complainant concerned could influence matters (as would, presumably, their status and consequent ability to cause trouble if they were dissatisfied).

McCabe and Sutcliffe found that there were two fundamental reasons why the police would use their discretion not to take formal action. First, there were the perceived practical problems of getting an offender to court, persuading witnesses to give evidence, and presenting a credible case. This meant that there were various groups they were particularly loath to take action against: vagrants (because they go away), alcoholics (because they are seen as hopeless cases who simply clutter up the police cells), gypsies (because of special problems they present with identification and obtaining evidence of criminal involvement), and those incidents which the police classify as 'domestics' (see below).

The second reason is related, once again, to the public/private dimension. 'In public places the presence and legal power of the police is unquestioned.' In private, on the other hand, they can only be present at the invitation of the householder, or in other rare circumstances. Thus in public the police are freer to deal with incidents 'on their own merits' – that is, they are more likely to take action, *both* official and unofficial – while in private the incident needs to be much more serious to bring them in, especially to take official action. This problem also is epitomized by 'domestics', a category of the utmost significance in police work. It includes all incidents and potential crimes (of violence, or property) between people known to, or related to each other, in the widest sense (a police definition is 'disputes [between] neighbours, sons, daughters, their families, their fiancés(ées), lodgers, people living together (of the same sex or otherwise), and landlord and tenant', see Calligan (1975: 1345)). Domestics come into both of the problematic categories – practical, because the victims and witnesses are unreliable, being likely to change their minds about wanting a conviction, and in the second category because the incidents characteristically take place in private settings. Thus, official action on the part of the police is comparatively rare even when potentially serious offences are involved (though domestics still account for a substantial proportion of recorded violent offences). McCabe and Sutcliffe found that it was in the case of domestics that 'the gap between citizens' allegations and police response was widest'. Even if a charge was brought, it often bore little relation to what happened. Of twenty-four calls involving domestics that they monitored, only two led to arrests, the remainder being dealt with by reassurance of the victim and a word of warning to the aggressor'.

Finally, in the case of official action taken on police *initiative* (i.e. as opposed to their being called in by the public) it:

' . . . seemed often to have its source in stereotypes of individuals: thieves, known or suspected, or tearaway youths. The events or circumstances giving rise to police action in such cases seemed to be less important than the outward appearance or suspected proclivities of the individual observed' (p.82).

Fortunately, a recent book has provided some insight into these stereotypes, from a rather unexpected source: the police themselves. It is by David Powis, Deputy Assistant Commissioner to the Metropolitan Police and it is called *The Signs of Crime: A Field Manual for Police* (1977). It consists of detailed information, based on Powis's many years of experience as a policeman in the field, on how to spot crime and criminals. Obviously, he cannot be taken as speaking for the police force as a whole, but it is nevertheless of considerable interest as a statement from the police side (it is also endorsed in a Foreword by Sir Robert Mark as virtually the only good book written on police work).

Much of the book consists of practical and technical information, but it also includes, though in a scattered, unsystematic way, much information on what he perceives to be indicators of suspicious characters (who are therefore worth looking into) as against normal, respectable people. As we have seen, such stereotypes are significant not only because they influence the nature of that minority of offences and offenders that become known directly through police initiatives, but also because there is evidence to suggest that they also influence police evaluation of complainants, who are responsible for the majority becoming known.

The following indices of suspiciousness emerge:

young people generally, but especially if in cars (and even more so if in groups in cars);

people in badly-maintained cars, especially if they have a tatty, dog-eared licence;

people of untidy, dirty appearance – especially with dirty shoes (even manual workers, if honest, he says, are clean and tidy);

people who are unduly nervous, confident or servile in police presence (unless they are doctors, who are 'naturally' confident);

people whose appearance is anomalous in some way – e.g. their clothes are not as smart as their car;

people in unusual family circumstances;

political radicals and intellectuals, especially if they 'spout extremist babble', and are in possession of a 'your rights' card (as supplied by the NCCL). These people are also particularly likely to make unjust accusations against the police.

Normal, unsuspicious people are those outside the above categories, especially if they are of smart conventional appearance (which commands natural authority and respect) and even more so if they smoke a pipe.

Powis recognizes that the extra suspicion (and stopping and checking) that he deems appropriate for young people (especially in cars) is likely to be interpreted by them as harassment and to provoke hostility, but regards it as justified since it is for their own good to be prevented from getting involved in more serious crime.

As regards police relations with other professions, he views liberal do-gooders and social scientists as working against police interests (especially since they are seen as soft on police powers). Some lawyers are considered dishonest, but many are seen as being misled by crooks. There is an implicit assumption that all attacks on the integrity of the police are either unfair or dishonest, and a final section shows how to deal with lies and unfair attacks in court.

These points add up to a fairly clear-cut picture; respectable, unsuspicious people conform to extremely conventional middle-aged, middle-class/respectable working-class modes of appearance, lifestyle, and political belief. Anything else is suspicious, and the further it deviates from that model, the more suspicious it becomes. Powis provides an interesting picture of the kind of moral stereotype that may guide the police in their discretionary enforcement of the law. Of course, it would be argued by the police that such stereotypes are *derived from experience* of who the suspicious people are. But as has already been noted several times, since such beliefs guide action they tend to be self-fulfilling whether they are true, partly true, or even untrue.

Some Conclusions on Police Discretion

There are perhaps two over-riding considerations determining the police use of discretion, under which most of the points in the previous discussion can be subsumed. The first of these is 'risk', which incorporates all those factors associated with the police perception of the likelihood of successfully achieving a conviction, and is based on the fact that continued official action which was not successful in this way would be regarded by both police and courts as evidence of poor performance. Obviously, the 'facts of the case' (insofar as they are objectively discoverable) play their part, but as we have seen, other factors also clearly enter into such perceptions of risk. The status and disposition of the participants (whether as offenders, victims, witnesses, or complainants) are relevant since they will influence performance in court. This is most apparent where there is some form of interpersonal relationship between the disputants (epitomized by the 'domestic') which powerfully increases police perceptions of risk in taking formal action. Another important factor is the setting of the incident. As we have seen, public, as opposed to private settings allow much more freedom of action for police, and this in turn has important implications for some groups (such as the young, lower social class) whose life-styles are generally more public.

The second broad cluster of factors influencing police discretion can be subsumed under the term 'control'. An important measure of police work is the visible maintenance of law and order, but the use of official action is one, and only one, way of achieving it. Since the vast majority of incidents the police deal with are relatively minor, there is strong pressure on them not to resort to formal action, to avoid clogging up the criminal justice process with trivia. Conversely, the *seriousness* of acts is an important determinant of official action, as all the studies show. But in the case of the much more numerous minor incidents, the police must find ways of maintaining the image of their authority by other means, using arrest only as a 'fall-back' resource. They must give the impression that matters have been satisfactorily handled by the strength of their personality and presence. Insolence or attempts at manipulation (e.g. by juveniles) are direct challenges and so incline them towards the fall-back resource. Witnesses and complainants must be satisfied that things have been dealt with adequately, although *their* status and disposition are also important in determining how far and in what way this is necessary. Assessment of moral worth is involved and those the policeman favours with discretion, or on whose behalf he takes action, must be seen to be deserving, and it is here that police stereotypes of normality may play their part.

We suggested at the beginning of this section that one of the underlying themes of the concern about police discretion was that it was operated in a way that discriminated against the more powerless and underprivileged sections of the community. Thus, as we saw, it has been used to explain the discrepancy between the marked over-representation of lower social class groups among officially defined offenders, as against their average representation in self-report studies. It has also been claimed that, in some respects at least, such discretion is also used against blacks, especially young blacks. This is very much the argument behind the 'Scrap Sus Campaign', currently supported by the National Council for Civil Liberties (see Boateng 1979). 'Sus' refers to the offence under section 4 of the Vagrancy Act 1824 of 'being a suspected person loitering with intent to commit an arrestable offence'. No warrant is required, only 'reasonable suspicion'. This type of offence is, of course, particularly open to the use of police discretion and the Campaign claims that it has been resurrected in London for use against young blacks (it provides some supporting evidence: of 2,366 'sus' arrests in London in 1977, 44 per cent were black, while blacks only account for 12 per cent of arrests as a whole).

As we have seen, the evidence on police discretion would certainly allow for the possibility of such discrimination. But then again, it is always open to the counter claim that such discrimination, when it does occur, is based on 'real' knowledge of who the likely criminals are. Indeed this is precisely what the police have claimed in relation to their use of 'sus' law and there is some evidence to support them. Rees, Stevens, and Willis (1979) show that official crime rates for blacks are now considerably higher than for whites. While they accept that this could to some extent be explained by greater police watchfulness, they also found that victim reports of assaults revealed eight times as many black assailants as white, proportionate to the population as a whole – a ratio in line with the official statistical pattern. However, even if police stereotypes of 'who the criminals are' have some basis in reality this does not alter the fact that operating in terms of them opens up considerable scope for injustice – a point to which we will be returning later.

The evidence on the consequences of the police using discretion on the basis of unfavourable stereotypes is, in any event, directly contradictory. An important feature of much crime and delinquency is that it tends to be predominantly parochial: that is, the victims and complainants tend to come from the same areas and belong to the same general social groupings as the offenders (unfavourable stereotypes are particularly likely to be associated with areas of cities – see Damer 1976; Armstrong and Wilson 1973). Thus, whereas such stereotyping could well lead to more stopping, questioning, and general harassment, it can equally readily lead to less notice being taken of victims and complainants and the kind of 'leave them to it' approach described by La Fave in the American context. Indeed, it is quite possible for both of these processes to operate simultaneously. We can perhaps illustrate this by looking at the research findings relating to 'criminal areas', which incorporate dimensions of both class and race.

One of the commonest findings in criminology is the extremely uneven distribution of official crime rates in cities. The highest rate areas are invariably the poorest and are stigmatized as 'bad' areas (see Gill 1977; Baldwin and Bottoms 1976). The variations are often enormous – some areas have ten or more times as much recorded crime as others (and this holds for different housing areas of the same general type, eg. council housing – see Baldwin and Bottoms). Are such differences real, or are they the result of stigmatization and police discretion leading to more crime being *recorded*? (Damer, for example, tends to favour the latter explanation.)

There is evidence which suggests that both the processes described earlier operate in such areas. Thus, Gill's evidence on a 'bad' area in Liverpool showed that the local youths saw themselves as being picked on and harassed by the police and that, to some extent at least, they were right. Baldwin (1974), however, comparing high and low rate estates in Sheffield, showed that the general residents of the high rate areas were more likely to complain of *under*-policing than residents in the low rate areas were. For direct evidence on whether or not the police are more likely to take official action in high rate areas, Mawby's work (1978), based on Baldwin and Bottoms' Sheffield housing estate data, is instructive. Mawby looked at the distribution of 'domestics' reported to the police by the public where no crime was recorded or proceeded against. He found that the distribution between high and low estates exactly mirrored the distribution of domestics where official action *was* taken, and concluded that the higher official crime rate in the high areas was *not* due to a greater police readiness to take action. This finding is particularly significant since, as we have seen, 'domestics' include a wide range of crimes which are especially open to discretionary action.

What do these various findings add up to? They seem to suggest the following: police stereotypes of the groups and areas most likely to be involved in crime are probably correct. However, this does not dispose of the problem. It is in the nature of all stereotypes that however well founded they are on the basis of statistical probability, they are still wrong in relation to the majority of individuals incorporated in that stereotype (even in the highest crime rate groups or areas most people are law-abiding). The consequence for police work is that operating on the basis of such stereotypes, however rationally constructed, is likely to lead to harassment and injustice and provoke hostility. Nor is it likely to be especially successful in achieving higher clear-up rates, or, as we have seen, in satisfying the local population. Perhaps it illustrates an important fact about differential crime rates: they are linked with underlying conditions of social and economic deprivation and inequality of opportunity. To expect the police to solve the problem is thus fundamentally to misunderstand its nature.

Given that some degree of police discretion is seemingly inevitable and given that it creates such thorny problems, how can it best be handled? Wilson (1968), surveying the American scene, suggests there are three broad (ideal-type) styles of police work discernible (Cain's work (1973b) in this country suggests that this typology may also to some extent be applicable here).

The first type is what Wilson calls the 'watchman' style. Its main aim is to achieve a general level of control rather than rigorous enforcement of the law. Consequently, only the more serious offences are attended to, minor and trivial occurrences are largely ignored, and as few records as possible are kept. There is an emphasis on the personal approach to police work. This style is predominantly found in lower social class urban districts.

The second is the 'legalistic' style. This is where police work most nearly approximates to the model of bureaucratic, impartial efficiency. There is a much higher level of enforcement, detailed records are kept, the style of police work is more formal, impersonal, and efficient. Movement towards this style inevitably leads to higher recorded crime rates.

The third style Wilson calls the 'service' style. This falls somewhere between the other two as far as level of enforcement is concerned, but its main feature is that it is based on an ethic of service to *the community*, rather than service to 'the law'. That is, the police are sensitive to the views of the community they serve and aim to use their discretion to reflect those views. There is consequently a concern with public relations and self-surveillance. This style, insofar as it is found at all, tends to be found in middle-class districts. Needless to say, Wilson presents it as the ideal form of police work, but clearly it is difficult to achieve since it requires an extraordinarily high degree of openness, self-surveillance, and sensitivity to local feeling (it almost certainly also requires a relatively affluent local community with a low level of criminal activity!).

These sorts of arguments, however, are based on a kind of fatalism as far as police discretion is concerned – that it is inevitable, and hence the most desirable approach is to try and democratize its use (this is the essential feature of the service style). As we will see later in this chapter, there has been an important academic movement towards regarding *all* forms of discretionary administration in the penal process with the deepest suspicion. Such arguments assert that discretion always involves violation of the safeguards provided by due process, and opens up avenues of arbitrariness and partiality, shielded by secrecy. On this view, discretion should be eliminated as far as is humanly possible, and police action should always be governed by rules which are open to public scrutiny.

Perhaps a compromise position is that of K.C. Davis (1975), one of the foremost American critics of the way police discretion is exercised. Davis accepts that police discretion is both inevitable and essential, but argues that 'excessive or unnecessary discretion can and should be eliminated, and that necessary discretion should be properly controlled' (p.141). Davis had indicated the kind of control that he has in mind as follows:

'The police should prepare proposed rules on the basis of staff studies, publish them, invite written comments from any member of the public, revise on the basis of the comments, and then publish the final rules. They should freely amend the rules from time to time to keep up with developing understanding and changing conditions' (p.168).

Such a policy clearly has much in common with Wilson's 'service' style of policing.

In conclusion, however, it is perhaps interesting to note that both Davis's proposals and the service style of policing which would make discretion open to local public scrutiny and regulation, in a sense involve the undermining of discretion. For such openness and regulation would, in effect, make police discretion subject to general (though locally derived) rules – the very negation of discretion. In the end, then, arguments for the recognition of the democratization of discretion tend to merge with those that maintain that police action should always, as far as possible, be subject to clearly defined rules. Davis is rather ambiguous on this point, claiming that 'rules do not neceessarily replace discretion' (p.149). Yet, while it is true that the controls and guidelines he proposes do not aim to *eliminate* discretion, they undoubtedly severely restrict the range of possibilities it can encompass (indeed the prevention of inconsistencies and arbitrariness by such means is precisely Davis's aim).

POLICE POWERS

Two Models of the Criminal Process

Our conclusions on police discretion clearly demonstrate that we cannot fully appreciate its potential without examining the nature and scope of the rules governing police powers. For, as we shall see, the use of discretion is tied up with the vagueness of the rules on proper police procedure and the uncertainty and complexity of the law on such basic questions as what constitutes a valid search or arrest. This lack of clarity in part reflects conflicting social values and public controversy over the proper aims of pre-trial criminal procedure generally.

There are several possible models of the criminal process (see, for example, Griffiths (1970) Berman (1972)), but attention has centred on the contrast drawn by Packer (1968) between 'crime control' and 'due process'. He visualizes these models as ideal types; in practice, the requirements of control and due process need not represent polar opposites. But whereas the former approach grants pride of place to the repression of criminal conduct, the latter pays more regard to possibilities of error and abuse. Packer sees the crime control model as one which places a premium on effective, speedy processing of cases – an 'assembly line' producing conveyor belt justice, in contrast to the 'obstacle course' with which considerations of due process confront the prosecution.

In practice there is a tendency to seek a compromise between the two extremes, partly because of the wide range of people for whom the system has to cater. There is a genuine difficulty in framing a single set of rules appropriate to dealing with sophisticated professional criminals, powerful deviant corporations, marginal, inadequate offenders, and the bulk of the law-abiding population. The appeal to notions of justice, such as the presumption of innocence and the belief that it is better for the guilty to go free than for the innocent to be punished, is a compelling one. Yet at the same time society is entitled to expect effective investigation of crime in the interests of the stability and order which it is a primary function of the law to provide. The institutionalization of policing was intended to reduce lawlessness and prevent resort to self help. These goals necessitate substantial powers, but not to the extent of threatening the substitution of one form of private justice for another.

When recorded crime rates are rising and attract much publicity in the media, the focus of public debate tends to be on the alleged inadequacy of police powers to reduce the level of crime. But criminologists are virtually unanimous in arguing that more efficient investigation, not more severe punishment, is the most effective deterrent (see Chapter 6). Were there not other considerations at stake, increased police powers could plausibly be seen as a desirable adjunct to greater manpower and more technical resources in the 'war against crime'.

The tone of the debate in the 1970s was set by the Eleventh Report of the Criminal Law Revision Committee (CLRC) in 1972 and a televised speech in the following year by the then Commissioner of the Metropolitan Police, Sir Robert Mark. One of the underlying themes of the CLRC Report was that the regulations for police questioning of suspects and the rules of evidence in criminal trials were apt to favour the defence at the expense of ascertaining the truth. This is not to say that the Report was wholly prosecution-minded. But the recommendations which received most publicity would have involved inroads into the accused's right to silence. They would, in certain circumstances, have permitted adverse inferences to be drawn both from the silence of a suspect when questioned and charged by the police and of an accused in court. Some of the views expressed by the Committee were echoed and reinforced in Sir Robert Mark's Dimbleby Lecture (1973), where he argued the case for stronger measures to prevent the acquittal of professional criminals.

There was sharp criticism of the Report from several quarters. In addition, the disclosure of police corruption on a serious scale in the Metropolitan force (at times in 1973 there were thirty CID resignations a week in the London area) and a series of much-publicized cases of mistaken identity, created an atmosphere in which any likelihood of its implementation receded. Eventually a Royal Commission on Criminal Procedure was established (1977) to consider all the circumstances of police investigation, the prosecution system, and related aspects of criminal trials. (The setting up of this Commission coincided with the publication of findings severely critical of police conduct – in the Fisher Report (1977)). Within a matter of months the new Metropolitan Police Commissioner, Sir David McNee, had submitted a lengthy memorandum to the Commission calling for greater powers to search persons and property, question and detain suspects, obtain fingerprints, if need be by force, and set up road blocks. These demands in turn evoked responses similar to those which followed the 1972 Report.

This tendency for the discussion of police powers to degenerate into a battle of slogans is a salutary reminder that research findings can have only a limited effect in such an emotive area. Governmental policy has to accommodate the claims both of the protagonists of 'law and order' and of civil libertarians; it has to 'weigh' the presumption of innocence and the right to trial by jury against waning police morale and signs of public anxiety. The results of isolated studies on the granting of police bail or the incidence of plea-bargaining cannot be expected to have much direct influence on policy. But the growing body of work on criminal procedure does nevertheless serve several valuable purposes. Empirical investigation has highlighted the bureaucratic demands, routinization, and pressures of police work, which combined with mundane yet rational motives of suspects help to account for the high incidence of guilty pleas (in 1977, almost nine out of ten in magistrates' courts and about two thirds in the Crown Court (Home Office 1978a)). Contrary to popular belief, the contested trial is a statistical rarity. The real 'trial' normally takes place at the police station where the police have almost total control over the pre-trial process, as well as technical resources unavailable to the defence. The dominance of the policeman as an authority figure, trained in interrogation, over an anxious suspect with little grasp of his rights, is accentuated by the low visibility of their encounters. In the magistrates' court, the obscure legal jargon, the ritualistic nature of the proceedings, and the structural setting of the court itself foster an impression of processing (see pp.122–24). The very emphasis of such research on *processing* conveys a sense of the fatalism of many defendants and the cumulative effect of their successive encounters with authority. It also enables us to appreciate that the early stages of the accused's experience can have repercussions which vitally affect both later stages and the ultimate result of his case.

The general thrust of much of this research has been that we have a system, or at least a set of procedures, paying lip-service to due process but operationally geared to crime control. And these two models appear to be antithetical. However, as we saw in Chapter 1, McBarnet (1978) has suggested that the formal rule structure, due process *as officially conceived*, is itself tilted in favour of crime control. On this view, despite the superficial appearance of restraints on police powers contained in the rules, despite the 'right to silence', the prosecution's need to prove its case beyond reasonable doubt, the inadmissibility in evidence of previous convictions, and so on, the rules themselves provide so much opportunity for the exercise of discretion by policeman and judge alike that 'due process is for crime control'.

We have argued that this view tends to oversimplify the position. Instead of concluding that the extensive discretion built into the rule structure can only mean that 'due process is for crime control', one might equally plausibly argue that the rules do not and have never *even purported* to provide a full-blooded due process model. Rather they may simply reflect a belief that a set of regulations exclusively concerned with informing suspects of their rights would, given the exigencies of police investigation, merely increase the ever present temptation for the police to bend the rules and, in the words of the Metropolitan Police Commissioner, to commit 'pious perjury'. On this analysis, the legal framework deliberately sets out to accommodate the ideals of due process to realities of police work. What then actually are the powers of the police?

Police Powers Prior to a Suspect Being at the Police Station

The police have certain powers to stop and search individuals and vehicles, to search premises, seize property, and, of course, to make arrests. As we shall see, the law is surprisingly vague about the limits of these powers. Though entitled at common law to search arrested persons, the police have no general authority to stop and search a suspect with a view to possible arrest, unless he consents. Some statutes, however, do permit this. One such provision was introduced in 1967, to permit search where there are 'reasonable grounds' to suspect that someone is in possession of unauthorized drugs (see now, Misuse of Drugs Act 1971, s.23). 'Reasonable grounds' has not been comprehensively defined and the incidence of negative searches has at times occasioned protests about discriminatory or arbitrary conduct by the police. Admittedly it would be difficult to provide an exhaustive list of legitimate grounds, but such a broadly expressed provision almost invites abuse. It is interesting that a Home Office Advisory Committee (1970) felt obliged to state specifically that 'particular modes of dress or hairstyle should never by themselves or together constitute reasonable grounds to stop and search' (para.155v; see also Leigh (1975) pp.134–40). The difficulty of knowing the precise extent of police powers to stop and search is further exacerbated by the existence of numerous, often obscure, statutes granting such powers in different localities. These cover a wide variety of offences, such as suspected possession of stolen property (as under the Metropolitan Police Act 1839, s.66).

Entry and Search of Premises

Entry on private property without authority, or the consent of the occupier, is unlawful (*Entick* v. *Carrington* (1765)). The police may however enter premises, by force if necessary, to stop a breach of the peace, or prevent one they reasonably believe is likely to occur (*Thomas* v. *Sawkins*, (1935)); to effect a lawful arrest (Criminal Law Act 1967, s.2(6)), or to execute a search warrant issued by a magistrate, for example to seize pornographic literature or unauthorized drugs. The premises on which someone has been arrested may be searched and any evidence which may be relevant to a charge against him or anyone else may be taken away (*Elias* v. *Pasmore* (1934)). But when lawful entry is not incidental to arrest, the police may (lawfully) take only articles relating to the crime in respect of which they entered, or which show the suspect to be implicated in some other crime. They have no right to 'ransack anyone's house, or to search for some crime or other' (*Ghani* v. *Jones* (1970)).

In principle, abuse of the above powers entitles the citizen to redress. Wrongful search of persons is a battery; wrongful entry or search of property is a trespass; wrongful seizure justifies an action for recovery of property. But these are largely academic points, almost devoid of substance. The limits on police rights of search remain obscure, couched in vague terms allowing considerable leeway. Such limits as do exist are in any event seriously undermined by the principle that evidence unlawfully obtained normally remains admissible at the court's discretion. In the recent case of *Jeffrey* v. *Black* (1978), Black was arrested and charged with stealing a ham sandwich from a public house and causing criminal damage to a policeman's uniform. The arresting officers told him that they intended, despite his lack of consent, to search his home. There they found some cannabis and charged him with possession of it. The Divisional Court said that the entry and search were unlawful, but admitted the evidence on the ground that this was not a case where the police were guilty of trickery, misleading someone or behaving in a morally reprehensible manner. Yet it appears from a very recent decision of the House of Lords involving an *agent provocateur*, (*R.* v. *Sang* (1979)), that even when the police have acted in such a way, the judge does not always have a discretion to refuse to admit the evidence.

Thus, although the formal rules reflect the importance historically attached to notions of privacy and respect for property – the Englishman's home as his castle – the operational reality is somewhat different. Vaguely worded rules are supplemented by case law so obscure that its precise effects cannot be stated with confidence by legal experts; while unlawful conduct is in effect condoned by the broad discretion as to the admissibility of evidence. The danger of granting too high a priority to the undoubted public interest in efficient law enforcement is well illustrated by reference to police practice in obtaining search warrants. As Street observes (1975):

' . . . those in the know have long been aware that the police abuse the warrant system by taking doubtful cases to a magistrate whom they know to be lax or accommodating in the signing of warrants. Only when an influential person, like Lady Diana Duff Cooper, became a victim in 1968 was it found necessary to do anything about it. The only information on which the police procured a warrant to search her home for drugs was an anonymous phone call. The Home Office has since issued a directive to police and magistrates about anonymous complaints, but in other respects the system's defects remain' (p.16).

Powers of Arrest

There can be few legal areas where the need for certainty seems more compelling than that of the power to arrest. Yet the scope of the relevant law is even more obscure than that relating to search and equally bedevilled by discrepancies between theory and practice. There is substantial reliance on the ignorance of people generally about their rights and some degree of police malpractice is acknowledged even within the police force itself (see Sir David McNee, Metropolitan Police Commissioner: Evidence to the Royal Commission on Criminal Procedure, 1978). Again, the formal framework suggests that deprivation of liberty is not to be regarded lightly. The legality of detention may be challenged by the time-honoured writ of habeas corpus. Illegal imprisonment constitutes both the crime and civil wrong of false imprisonment. But in practice habeas corpus has often proved to be an ineffective remedy and it is very rarely used in cases of police detention (Gifford and O'Connor 1979). In recent years it has been interpreted in a restrictive manner, most notably in deportation appeals; while false imprisonment is notoriously difficult to establish.

An arrest occurs when someone is compulsorily deprived of his liberty. This may take the form of a verbal intimation, or the use of reasonable force. Alternatively it may be implicit, as when a person under interrogation at a police station would not in fact have been permitted to leave of his own free will (*R*. v. *Bass* (1953)), though it is not clear that the police have any duty to inform him that this is the case. The Criminal Law Act 1967 (s.2) draws a distinction between arrestable and non-arrestable offences. For the latter, minor offences, the accused is directed to appear before the court by a summons. Arrestable offences are those for which the penalty is fixed or where, by statute, the maximum penalty is a sentence of five years or more. A policeman may arrest without warrant anyone whom he has reasonable cause to believe has committed, or is about to commit, an arrestable offence. He has similar powers with respect to breach of the peace and under a variety of statutes. Reference has already been made to the broad powers of arrest under the Vagrancy Act 1824 (see p.92). Contrary to popular belief, there is no general compulsory power of detention short of arrest, though it is permitted for certain specified purposes, such as a search for drugs, detention for breathalyzing and under the Prevention of Terrorism (Temporary Provisions) Act 1974. But this bare description is incapable of conveying the degree of academic controversy which continues to surround the precise requirements of a valid arrest in some quite commonplace circumstances (see further *R. v. Brown* (1977); Telling 1978; Lidstone 1978).

It is clear that the police have no general power to detain someone purely for the purpose of questioning him (*R. v. Lemsatef* (1977)) and he has only a moral and social, not legal, duty to answer police questions (*Rice v. Connolly* (1966)). A citizen cannot legally be required to accompany a policeman to the police station without being arrested and informed of the reason. Yet it is common knowledge that the police frequently take suspects to the station for questioning. In those cases where the policeman anticipates reluctance (and the same holds true for requests to search without a warrant) it requires little ingenuity on his part to ensure compliance, either by tone of voice or an ambiguously phrased 'request' (such as 'I must ask you to accompany me to the police station') conveying the impression of legitimate authority where none exists. Innocent or guilty, in this face-to-face encounter only the exceptionally intrepid or foolhardy will resist, given the powerful social and psychological pressures to avoid giving offence and the instinct for self-justification. In addition, should the case come before a jury, it would need a lot of convincing that an uncooperative man had nothing to hide.

At the Police Station: Detention for Questioning

It is important to stress what happens at the police station because it is here that the fate of most defendants is determined, typically through a confession or oral admission (Bottoms and McClean 1976:230). What is the legal position of someone who has agreed to go to the police station 'to help the police with their enquiries'?

Again we have the familiar pattern of obscurely framed legal rules compounded by popular misconceptions and a debatable use of police powers. It is widely believed that a suspect who has been arrested and held at the police station must be brought before a court within twenty-four hours. There is in fact no such 'twenty-four-hour rule' (Munro 1975), merely a requirement that an arrested person must be brought before the court 'as soon as is practicable' (Magistrates' Courts Act 1952 s.38(4)). The precise meaning of this provision is unclear, but there have been several much-publicized instances of detention for several days before any charge was laid (as for example in the London car bombings of 1973), or access to a solicitor permitted. In practice this conduct is very difficult to impugn. Though allegedly excessive delay can be tested by a writ of habeas corpus, the courts, as we have noted, do not currently seem favourably disposed towards granting such applications.

In many cases the police justification for delay is the simple assertion that the suspect is voluntarily helping with inquiries and has not been arrested. The tactical advantages of this claim are plain, as until his arrest there is no obligation to bring the accused before a court 'as soon as is practicable', and he has no 'right' of access to a solicitor. The so-called right to contact a lawyer involves a further misconception. Its true status is that of an unenforceable administrative direction to the police from the Home Office to permit a suspect to telephone a solicitor 'provided that no hindrance is reasonably likely to be caused to the processes of investigation or the administration of justice' (Home Office Circular No.89/1978b). This qualified right is also laid down in the Judges' Rules, a code of fair practice for the police, which equally does not have the full force of law. In court, evidence obtained in contravention of the Rules is liable to be excluded at the judge's discretion (*R.* v. *Lemsatef* (1977)). But it is the judge's assessment of the overall reliability of such evidence which is normally decisive. Only very rarely (as in *R.* v. *Allen* (1977) has it been excluded because of denial of access to a solicitor.

The police, then, should inform a suspect of his qualified right to legal advice. They should also draw his attention to a notice, conspicuously displayed, referring to this and other safeguards. In practice it seems this is often not done until *after* he is questioned and charged, if at all. Baldwin and McConville (1979a), in their study of 500 contested trials at Birmingham Crown Court, found that approximately two-thirds of defendants made no request for access to a solicitor and that of those who did 77 per cent said that it was denied them (the equivalent figure in Zander's study (1972) was 74 per cent). Under the Criminal Law Act 1977, s.62, anyone who has been arrested has the right to communicate this fact to a named person with no more delay than 'necessary'. But no remedy is provided if the right is denied, so that this new provision does not constitute a significant change.

In view of the uncertainty surrounding so much of what occurs at the police station, and since proof of guilt normally depends on statements made there by the suspect, confessions need to be scrutinized with great care. There is a cardinal principle that confessions not made voluntarily, that is, 'obtained by fear of prejudice or hope of advantage exercised or held out by a person in authority', are inadmissible in evidence (*R*. v. *Prager* (1972)). It is for the prosecution to prove that a confession is voluntary. There is an additional, if very limited, safeguard for the accused in the Judges' Rules. Under the Rules, as soon as a police officer has (legally admissible) evidence giving reasonable grounds for suspecting that a person has committed an offence, he must caution him as to his right to remain silent before questioning him further. Once the accused is charged he must be cautioned a second time, after which, questions, preceded by a further caution may be put to him only in exceptional circumstances, for example, to clear up an ambiguity in a previous statement.

At the Police Station: Identification Procedures

(a) *Fingerprinting* The police may take the fingerprints of any person who consents and in the case of persons charged with a crime may obtain a court order to take them without consent (Magistrates' Courts Act 1952, s.40, as amended by the Criminal Justice Act 1967, s.33). In fact fingerprints are taken almost as a matter of routine. Most suspects agree either from ignorance, the wish to comply or appear compliant, or fear of repercussions such as the denial of bail. In the event of a police application, the decision whether to grant an order is entirely at the magistrates' discretion. Some disquiet has been voiced about the taking of fingerprints not subsequently adduced in evidence. A common police rationale for fingerprinting is that taking prints prevents suspects from concealing their criminal record by supplying false information. If the person is not convicted the prints must be destroyed. But in a technological society, when prints are computerized, there is also a danger of them being sought for recording purposes rather than crime detection.

(b) *Identity Parades* In recent years controversy has surrounded procedures used for visual identification, in particular at identity parades. When the wrong person is convicted mistaken evidence of identification is commonly to blame. Many psychological experiments (see pp.120−22) have exposed both the serious limitations of the accuracy of human observation and the tendency for many observers to become increasingly convinced of the accuracy of their mistaken beliefs. As a result of several cases which attracted public attention (the most notable being that of Peter Hain, 1976) a committee was set up under Lord Devlin (1976b) which made proposals aimed at improving identification procedures and the rules on identification evidence. Within two months the Court of Appeal had incorporated some of these proposals in guidelines for judges on instructing the jury in cases where visual identification formed a substantial part of the prosecution case (*R*. v. *Turnbull* (1976)).

A suspect cannot demand an identity parade, but the police will normally agree to one if it is requested. Conversely, the police cannot demand one either, but a suspect's refusal will usually mean that they will arrange a confrontation with the witness. A Home Office circular recently revised in the light of the Devlin Committee's recommendations (Home Office Circular No. 109/1978c), provides guidance to the police on the proper way to conduct parades. Under the revised regulations, all suspects are to be given a leaflet describing the object and nature of the parade and their rights in respect of it. A comprehensive record is to be kept of all aspects of the parade and of the circumstances in which photographs are shown to witnesses.

The Circular however is no more binding that the Judges' Rules. The only sanction is that failure to observe its provisions may lead the judge to comment on the evidential reliability of the parade in his summing up. The suggestion of the Devlin Committee that the instructions should have statutory force has not been taken up, pending an assessment of the effect of the Court of Appeal's guidelines in *R*. v. *Turnbull*. These require the judge to warn the jury of the special need for caution before convicting on the strength of visual identification, and to explain why this is so. The Devlin Committee wanted an acquittal to be mandatory in a case based on visual identification, unless the circumstances of the identification were exceptional, or it was supported by substantial evidence of another kind. But the Court of Appeal adopted a more flexible solution, so that where the quality of the identifying evidence is good, the case may be left to the jury without corroboration of other supporting evidence.

The revised Home Office instructions and the guidelines in *R*. v. *Turnbull* seem to provide an acceptable formal framework. But it is difficult to guarantee fairness of procedure when so much depends on the organization 'on the ground' of an encounter fraught with emotion (see Clifford 1979a). A suspect who does not have a solicitor present at a parade may be unaware of the various factors relating to dress, demeanour, distinguishing features, position in the line, and so forth, which may cast doubt on the fairness of the proceedings. If there is no parade, he is still liable in some magistrates' courts to be subjected to the manifestly unfair process of identification in the dock, despite judicial disapproval of this practice.

Bail from a Police Station

It is only recently that researchers have begun to show interest in the significance of the decision by the police to grant or withhold bail. But there are good grounds for supposing that it is a decision which often plays a crucial role in the later stages and final outcome of a case. Again, police powers in this respect are ill-defined.

A police inspector or the officer in charge of the station may grant bail, with or without sureties, to someone arrested without a warrant if, in their view, the offence is not 'a serious one' (Magistrates' Courts Act 1952, s.38 (1)). There is no official guidance on how this discretion is to be exercised. As Bottomley (1973:87) has observed, there is a distinct lack of systematic information on how the police decide whether to keep an arrested person in custody overnight, or until his court appearance, or instead release him on bail. One small-scale study (Bottomley 1970) found that twice as many suspects (80 per cent) were remanded overnight in an urban court as in rural ones. Of those kept in police custody, 83 per cent (urban) and 90 per cent (rural) were subsequently remanded in custody on their first appearance before the magistrates; of those released on police bail, fewer than 20 per cent in both areas were later refused bail by the courts. It is a reasonable hypothesis that the magistrates' attitude will sometimes be affected by the prior decision taken by the police.

More importantly, the police decision on bail, if used as a bargaining device, can be the main determinant of the outcome. The recent controversy over plea-bargaining has been mainly concerned with pressures on defendants to plead guilty, often to a reduced charge, on the advice of lawyers. There has been less discussion of the extent of 'bail bargaining' at the police station. Yet it is obvious that the pressures on a suspect to make a confession in return for bail are often very strong. Apart from his natural desire to get away and have the matter settled without being incarcerated, he may feel vulnerable on several grounds. His job, accommodation, and human relationships may all be at risk. He might encounter difficulties in preparing his case adequately while in custody and cannot be certain of obtaining legal aid for representation, always assuming that he is aware of its existence (see Chapter 5). Thus the potential cost of defending a case, even in the event of acquittal, can act as a disincentive, as, of course, can the expectation of a heavier sentence if *found* guilty. Indeed it has been said of the sentencing discount on a guilty plea that: 'there is no other single consideration that so pervades the workings of the whole administration of criminal justice or that so conditions and directs the nature of the choices open to a defendant.' (Baldwin and McConville 1978a:116).

For the police there are also compelling reasons for seeking a guilty plea. It takes only a small increase in the number of contested cases to cause a disproportionate increase in their workload. The point has been graphically made by a detective sergeant, with reference to known criminals (see Laurie 1970):

'I'll willingly do deals if he'll be a man and plead – it saves me days of desk-work, writing reports, doing legal-aid forms, rounding up witnesses, going to court every week until the trial comes up – and I'll not put in the poison about him when I'm asked. This may sound very shocking, but what's more use to society: me tied down for a couple of weeks getting him a couple of months more on his sentence, or the whole thing over in a day, a happy informant, me catching out more thieves, and perhaps a string of arrests in the future?' (p.217).

As Laurie observes, a guilty plea not only acts as a source of legitimation for the police, and a mark of their professional competence, but it removes all the imponderable factors associated with a contested trial, such as ineffective witnesses, possible judicial criticism of police conduct, and the unpredictability of juries.

Hard data on the incidence of bail-bargaining is obviously difficult to obtain. But Bottoms and McClean, in a detailed study (1976), claim to have found numerous instances of it and specific complaints, not prompted by direct questioning, in 7 per cent of the cases they examined.

Conclusions

We have not attempted to provide a comprehensive account of the events which precede a criminal trial. Many technical details must be sought elsewhere (for example, Leigh (1975)). But certain patterns seem to emerge. Much of the relevant law is uncertain and obscure; much of it is characterized by discretion. This fortifies the operational control of the police and helps to explain the vital importance of what happens 'on the ground', particularly in the early stages of the process. The experience of practitioners and researchers alike, reinforced by the findings of the occasional official inquiry into miscarriages of justice (such as the Fisher Report, 1977), bear out Professor Street's contention: 'The evidence that the police regularly break the law in handling suspects is overwhelming' (1975: 33).

An apparently obvious gap in the system is the fact that most defendants do not see a lawyer, if at all, before their first appearance in court. The Fisher Report suggested that the current provision for legal advice could be effective only if each police station had a list of solicitors willing to make their services available. In fact by early 1977, seventy-nine duty solicitor schemes had been set up, under which private solicitors give early-morning interviews on a rota basis to defendants, advising on a variety of matters, such as pleas, applications for bail or legal aid, and mitigation (see King 1976). Valuable though this development is, it would be ingenuous to imagine that the mere setting up of such a scheme could guarantee the necessary safeguards. Experience in Cardiff, for example, where the system ostensibly operates round the clock, has shown (Thomas and Smith 1978) that in practice the police seldom contact solicitors until the morning after the suspect has been arrested. Also there is the risk that rigorous enforcement of a provision for access to solicitors might tempt the police to bend the rules at an earlier stage of the proceedings, before the suspect is handed over to the charge unit officers, or after the formal interrogation (Baldwin and McConville 1979a). Thomas and Smith therefore suggest that consideration be given to the weighting of statements, depending on whether or not they were made in the presence of a solicitor, or at least by a suspect aware of his rights.

The central issue concerning questioning remains the authenticity of statements made to the police. Access to a solicitor at the station is one way of helping to ensure their validity, but an imperfect one. The most obvious alternative means would be electronic recording of interrogation, as far as practicable wherever it takes place. This idea has always met with resistance within the police force. But tape-recording (which was recommended by the Fisher Report, 1977), and ultimately videotape, seem likely to be introduced eventually. The arguments against their introduction do not seem to stand up very well to close examination (Williams 1979). As Williams concludes: 'One cannot help wondering whether the real objection of the police to tape-recording (though it is never avowed) is their fear of the consequences of public inspection of what happens in the interviewing of suspects' (1979: 22).

Plainly there are many disturbing features of the pre-trial process and there is a case for introducing a statutory code spelling out police powers in more detail and leaving less room for discretion.

Pre-trial Processes

THE PROSECUTING AGENCY

If called upon to devise a system of criminal procedure from scratch, one would not, on a rational view of the matter, be disposed to entrust to the same people responsibility both for investigating crime and exercising control over its prosecution. Yet, at least in minor cases, it is standard practice for the police to conduct the case for the prosecution. In magistrates' courts, the arresting officer will commonly question the accused, be consulted on the question of bail, decide on the charge and evidence to be brought, as well as conduct the prosecution, for which he is himself a witness. All this is in marked contrast to the Scottish system, in which a public prosecution service operates independently of the police, both as regards the decision to prosecute and the conduct of the case.

In England, a relatively limited number of serious crimes are prosecuted by the Director of Public Prosecutions and a growing number of mainly regulatory offences are dealt with by Government Departments and various public bodies. It is also open to the ordinary citizen to institute criminal proceedings, though this rarely happens in practice. In magistrates' courts the vast majority of prosecutions are undertaken by the police. Some two thirds of police forces employ prosecuting solicitors and the rest engage local solicitors for cases of apparent complexity; but ultimate responsibility for the decision to prosecute rests with the Chief Constable of the force in question. He, as the 'client', is entitled to ignore advice not to institute or continue proceedings.

Not only is the system unique in this respect, but it seems strangely at odds with the rhetoric of justice. It is part of the ethic of our legal system that the Crown does not 'win' or 'lose' cases. In other words it is no part of the prosecution's duty to press for a conviction. On the contrary, it is under an obligation to provide the defence with information it possesses favourable to the accused. In principle, of course, there is no reason why the police should not conform to this ethic and, conversely, no guarantee that a differently constituted prosecuting body always would. But it seems plain that in practice there is more danger of the police misconstruing the prosecutorial role, whether through lack of training and expertise, or because of various pressures unrelated to the proper conduct of the case in hand. Criticism of the extent of police involvement in the prosecution process has come from a number of disparate sources, among them the Magistrates' Association, the Royal Commission on the Police (1962) and *Justice* (1970). The issue is currently under consideration by the Royal Commission on Criminal Procedure.

The essence of the criticism is simply that the qualities needed for effective investigation of crime are different from, if not actually incompatible with, those required for its proper prosecution. A police officer who has arrested someone can hardly be blamed if he is psychologically disposed towards successfully prosecuting him. It is unreasonable to expect him to offer a wholly disinterested view as to the propriety of launching a prosecution. His position is all the more invidious where he has personal knowledge of a suspect's criminal antecedents, or possesses other legally inadmissible evidence. The Chief Constable may also not be sufficiently detached from extrinsic considerations, such as the morale of individual officers or the prospect of provoking public criticism for instigating and then dropping a case. Though some degree of uniformity in police practice is achieved through general advice from the Director of Public Prosecutions, it is questionable whether such broad discretion on the decision to prosecute should be vested in a Chief Constable.

Supporters of the existing system, such as Wilcox (1972), raise the spectre of 'a distant official reading files in his office', 'insensitive to local opinion'. But given the already extensive network of local prosecuting solicitors, it ought not to be impracticable to establish, as *Justice* recommended, a centralized Department based on the Director of Public Prosecutions, with regional and local offices, akin to the Scottish system. Though such a change would hardly eradicate bureaucratic pressures and routinization, these are already conspicuous features of the present arrangements. At least one might anticipate a more dispassionate and informed assessment of the strength of cases and the appropriateness of launching proceedings, as well as more efficient and detached court presentation. At the same time it would enable the police to devote themselves more fully to the work for which they have been trained.

BAIL AND THE COURTS

When a court refuses to grant bail, between 5 per cent and 10 per cent of those deprived of their liberty in this way are not subsequently convicted, and approximately 40 per cent of those remanded in custody and convicted do not receive a custodial sentence. In other words, almost half the people remanded in custody, sometimes spending several months in prison, are not ultimately given a prison sentence. This does not mean that the refusal of bail was *necessarily* unjustified. The reasons for it may have been unconnected with the considerations appropriate to the sentence, as where the defendant has a previous history of 'jumping bail'. But the consequences of this temporary loss of liberty can be far-reaching, even in the event of an acquittal.

It would be still more disturbing if the decision not to grant bail were itself a significant indicator of the outcome of a case. Research is inconclusive on this question, though there is some evidence of a correlation. A higher proportion of those defendants who have been refused bail are subsequently convicted and imprisoned (see Davies 1971a; Bottomley 1970). Given the extra difficulty of adequately preparing a defence while in custody, this link may also have a causal element. Yet bail applications have commonly been dealt with in a perfunctory manner, often taking a mere two or three minutes (Zander 1971).

Refusal of bail also exacerbates the already serious problem of overcrowding in prisons. It is all too easy when producing an academic catalogue of the defects in the criminal process to become submerged in a plethora of niceties about the Judges' Rules and to overlook what in many prisons has amounted to a breakdown in civilized standards, not just for defendants remanded in custody, but for *all* prisoners. In the middle of 1975, there were nearly 4,000 unconvicted persons in custody and 2,000 who had been convicted but not yet sentenced – roughly 15 per cent of the total prison population. In October 1976, the number of people in prison reached the level of 42,000, which the former Home Secretary, Roy Jenkins, had previously said would be intolerable and require drastic action. The pressing need to reduce overcrowding played its part in a shift towards greater readiness to grant bail, which in fact was apparent several years before it was formalized in the Bail Act 1976.

Prior to the 1976 Act there was no general presumption in favour of granting bail. It could be granted only on the application of the defendant. In some courts unrepresented defendants were not always asked whether they wished to apply and even when asked they might have only a hazy grasp of the implications. Though the law provided criteria on the bail decision – substantially similar to those that now obtain – it has always been seen as a question for the magistrates' discretion. Frequently the nature of the charge and the police view have been decisive, without any systematic investigation of the merits of the case. Police awareness of this strengthens their position in court and acts as an incentive for them to engage in bail-bargaining earlier on.

Bail has sometimes been initially refused and subsequently granted in cases where it was difficult to discern any change of circumstances (as in the case of the former MP, John Stonehouse – refused seven times, then granted). This inevitably raises suspicions of abuse – of defendants being remanded in custody to give them a taste of prison. The suspicion is reinforced when one realizes that a third or more of the applications to a High Court judge to review the decision are granted, at least in the case of applicants privately represented at the hearing (King 1971; others will find that legal aid is not in practice available for such an application. They can only apply by letter when the success rate has been as low as one in twelve). Under the 1976 Act, the provision for legal aid for unrepresented defendants has been improved, but does not extend to applications for review, nor to the first court appearance.

THE CURRENT LAW ON BAIL

The Bail Act 1976 created a general presumption in favour of granting bail, even if it has not been applied for, when a person has been charged with, or convicted of, an 'imprisonable offence'. (For practical purposes this covers all but the most trivial offences where the question of bail will rarely arise.) The three most common reasons for which bail may be refused are: where there are substantial grounds for believing that, if released, the defendant would abscond, commit another offence, or otherwise interfere with the course of justice. He may also be remanded in custody for his own protection, or if he has already been arrested for absconding in relation to the proceedings. More importantly, bail can be refused when lack of time has made it impracticable to obtain sufficient information to justify his release. Factors such as the nature of the offence, character, community ties, past record, and the strength of the evidence against the accused may also be considered, but only as secondary evidential matters, not as reasons in themselves. A court which refuses bail, or imposes conditions on it, now has to record its reasons. These are available to the defendant, who must be informed of his right to apply for a review of the decision. The practice of asking an accused for a recognizance (a personal guarantee of a sum to be forfeited if he does not surrender for trial) has been replaced by a duty to surrender, enforced by creating a new offence of 'absconding'. The court still has a discretion to require the accused to provide sureties and the Act specifies criteria as to their suitability.

The right to refuse bail for insufficiency of information highlights a major limitation in the Act, which could have been avoided by adopting a scheme along the lines of the Manhattan Bail project, begun in 1961 and now operating in several American cities. Based on a simple points sytem, the aim is to establish the strength of the defendant's community ties. Before his appearance in court, the defendant is interviewed and a questionnaire completed. The prognosis is then available as a guide for judges. It has been claimed that in addition to the benefits of consistency as between courts, four times as many defendants have been released on bail using this system, yet the overall absconding rate was reduced from 3 per cent to 1.6 per cent (see Davies 1969). Though, of course, this means that *in absolute terms* there were almost twice as many abscIn this country a survey in 1967 (Zander 1971; see also Bottomley 1970) indicated that in half the cases of unrepresented defendants where there were police objections to bail, the court had no information whatever about home, family, and employment circumstances. Despite Home Office approval and recommendation, a London experiment along these lines encountered much opposition from the police and Magistrates' Association and has not been developed.

Though it is too early to evaluate the effects of the new Act (it was not fully operational until 17 April 1978), it has not been universally welcomed. Magistrates complain of being inundated with paperwork to record reasons for withholding bail or imposing conditions. Intended to aid defendants and the courts, as well as serving as a monitoring device, a plethora of forms has been causing serious delays in some courts. Policemen have voiced fears that a more lenient view of bail presages an increase in crime and unnecessary risk to the public.

We would argue that if there is real substance in these claims, a points system would do much to alleviate the problems. But it would be surprising if the criticisms signified much beyond the predictable reactions of opponents of a more liberal and considered approach to the bail decision. Stripped of its rhetoric, the Act does little more than encourage magistrates to treat the question of bail seriously. The criteria are broadly the same as before; the discretionary element is still substantial. How it is operated remains to be seen (White 1977), but a one-day survey carried out in London Magistrates' Courts six months after the Act came into force (Zander 1979) did not point to any dramatic change in the proportion of cases in which bail was granted. There was some evidence of a decline in the proportion of police objections and of greater readiness on the part of magistrates to overrule such objections. It also appears that courts are now imposing conditions on bail more frequently.

PLEA BARGAINING

We have seen that in the early phases of the criminal process external pressures on the police and accused alike may result in a case being resolved by a guilty plea rather than a contested trial of the issues. The popular misconception of the full-scale trial as the typical culmination of a criminal charge is further falsified by the existence of 'plea bargaining' – out-of-court negotiations involving the legal profession, immediately prior to or during the trial.

Plea bargaining is not easy to define with precision. In essence, it is 'the practice whereby the defendant enters a plea of guilty in return for which he will be given some consideration that results in a sentence concession' (Baldwin and McConville 1977: 19). He may, for example, be persuaded to plead guilty on one charge in exchange for a promise that he will not be prosecuted on a more serious one, or on the understanding that a guilty plea will mean a lighter sentence. Such an arrangement may be the result of discussions between prosecution and defence lawyers, as is common in America, advice from the defendant's lawyers, or even consultation between counsel and the judge.

In the United States plea bargaining is an openly recognized part of the system, so much so that it has been asserted that: 'The essence of the criminal justice process is not the trial stage but the negotiation for a guilty plea between the prosecutor and defence counsel' (Nagel 1976; see also Chief Justice Burger's statement in *Santobello* v. *New York* (1971) that it was 'an essential component of the administration of justice'). Apart from the sheer pressure of the caseload, certain features of the American legal system help to explain why this should be so. Many offences carry harsh mandatory sentences, the severity of which can be avoided by negotiating pleas of guilty to reduced charges. (Newman (1956) has shown that the incidence of guilty pleas in different states varies in proportion to the degree of judicial discretion in determining sentence.) The prosecutor may make specific recommendations on sentence, thereby almost encouraging judicial bargaining, added to which, his status as a paid official in practice gives him extensive control over the level of the charge. In England, only murder carries a mandatory sentence, and judges normally have considerable discretion in sentencing. The prosecution may not recommend specific sentences and, at least in the higher courts, do not have the same freedom to accept reduction in the charge (*R*. v. Coe (1969)).

The Official Model

(a) *Advising the Client* Some indication of the view taken of plea bargaining by the English legal profession may be gathered from the following outline of the Bar's submission on the topic to the Royal Commission on Legal Services (Taylor 1978). If the defendant wishes to deny any or all of the charges, or merely seek advice about his plea, his counsel has a duty to tell him not to plead guilty simply through fear of a harsher sentence if convicted, or of the ordeal of a full trial. But if counsel considers the Crown's case very strong and the defence highly implausible, he is obliged to say so. He may then, forcefully if need be, explain why and point out possible advantages of pleading guilty – a sentencing discount, the lesser impact of the bare recital of prosecution evidence, the greater impact of a plea in mitigation after an admission of guilt, reduced charges, and avoidance of an ordeal. But counsel's persuasion 'should never become duress'.

(b) *Discussion with Prosecution Counsel* Before a defendant finally decides on his plea, it is often helpful and in the interests of justice for his counsel to have a 'without prejudice' discussion with counsel for the Crown. Where, for example, it is doubtful whether the evidence is strong enough to merit the more serious of two possible charges, the prosecution may indicate that they would accept a plea of guilty to the lesser charge.

(c) *Discussion with the Judge* If it is felt that the views of the trial judge on a lesser charge would be helpful, as where prosecuting counsel is unsure about accepting it, both counsel may ask to see him. In such circumstances the question of sentencing is not normally discussed. Plea bargaining proper, as understood by the Bar – that is, when sentencing is discussed by counsel and the judge – may take place under the following conditions: both counsel must be present, and the defendant's solicitor if he wishes; the judge may not say anything which would constitute pressure on the defendant; he should never indicate the precise form of sentence (e.g. prison or a fine) he has in mind, except if he feels that it can only take a certain form, having regard to all the circumstances. If conducted along these lines, plea bargaining, it is argued, is 'a realistic and constructive process resulting in a just and expeditious disposal of criminal cases'.

The Reality of Plea Bargaining

Clearly, the Bar readily acknowledges the existence of negotiation over pleas and argues its merits under certain conditions, even if it cannot quite bring itself to use the term 'plea bargaining' except in a severely limited sense. But the Court of Appeal, in a series of recent cases, has made strenuous efforts to deny that plea bargaining occurs at all (e.g. in 1978 in *R. v. Bird, R. v. Atkinson, R. v. Howell, R. v. Ryan, R. v. Llewellyn*. See Baldwin and McConville 1978c). Thus in *R. v. Atkinson*, where the trial judge told counsel before the trial: 'We can dispose of it all today, and he would be out in the sunshine', the Court of Appeal observed:

'Although the learned judge had no intention of making a bargain with the defence as to plea, it may well have appeared to the appellant that he was being offered the relief from a sentence of immediate imprisonment if he should decide to plead guilty' (p.461).

The Court went on to say that 'Plea bargaining has no place in the English criminal law'. As Baldwin and McConville (1978b) point out: 'This seems absurdly unrealistic, at variance with both common observation and substantial research evidence.' The standard technique of the Court of Appeal in these cases – to allow the appeal on the ground that the judge might have given the impression that pressure was being exerted on the defendant – is some indication of judicial fears that open acknowledgement of plea bargaining is incompatible with the rhetoric of justice. Indeed, the maxim 'justice must be seen to be done' is expressly invoked in the denial of the practice.

The extent to which plea bargaining, in whatever sense, takes place in this country is unknown, but there is a growing body of research which suggests that it is more common than has often been supposed (McCabe and Purves 1972a; Davies 1971b; Dell 1971; Bottoms and McClean 1976; Baldwin and McConville 1977). The practice is of low visibility and the whole issue an emotive one. Just how emotive can be gauged by the degree of controversy aroused over a book entitled *Negotiated Justice* (Baldwin and McConville 1977). The senate of the bar tried to prevent publication of this book on the ground that it 'would be directly contrary to the public 'interest'.

The book was based on a study of 150 Crown Court cases in which the defendants 'having initially expressed an intention to plead not guilty, subsequently changed their plea to guilty, very often only on the day of the trial itself and commonly to a lesser count in the indict-ment' (p.3). On the basis of interviews with 121 of these defendants, the authors concluded that almost three-quarters were involved in some form of 'negotiated justice'. Twenty-two claimed they took part in a genuine plea bargain, that is, a bargain struck by their barrister with the judge or prosecution; sixteen said they understood some sort of deal was made on their behalf, and thirty-eight said that they pleaded guilty 'in response to advice or pressure from their own barrister'.

Most of the criticism of these findings centred on the authors' reliance on defendants' accounts, which they have conceded must be 'treated with caution' and which 'hardly provides an unchallenge-able basis for ready generalization or extrapolation' (1978a). In the absence of cooperation from the Bar, they sought an independent check on whether the cases revealed sufficient evidence to warrant a guilty plea. All the committal papers (i.e. after the initial presentation of the prosecution case before the magistrates) were examined by a retired Justices' Clerk and a retired Chief Constable who then tried to forecast the result. On the strength of this admittedly limited evidence, the assessors expressed either uncer-tainty or a feeling that acquittal was likely in 21 per cent of the cases. The authors came to the conclusion that a small number of defendants who may well have been innocent were persuaded to plead guilty; that 'unfair or coercive conduct' by lawyers occurred in 'only a small number of cases', and that a few of the judges concerned were willing to involve themselves in specific bargains, hinting to counsel at the sentence to be expected on a plea of guilty.

Though it is not possible to establish how much plea bargaining takes place, there are good grounds for supposing that its incidence is higher at the Crown Court level (see Heberling 1973). This is primarily because the vast majority of defendants there are legally represented, whereas only roughly a quarter are represented at the magistrates' courts, where in any event the pressures towards pleading guilty often make the need for bargaining superfluous. Also, in cases tried on indictment, the prosecution case and any alibi defence will have been disclosed at the committal stage, so that unlike the position at the magistrates' court, there is considerable evidence available to form the basis for negotiation.

The Case for and against Plea Bargaining

Whatever one's misgivings about the very notion of negotiating justice, for the most part those directly involved and the public as a whole stand to gain from it. The defendant avoids publicity, delay, strain – for family and friends as well as for himself – and the risk of more severe punishment if *found* guilty. The prosecution is saved from having to rely on possibly inconclusive evidence or inadequate witnesses and an unpredictable jury. Society as a whole benefits in so far as the administration of justice is speeded up and the expense of protracted trials avoided, important considerations when the pressure of cases is increasing, and is threatening the ability of the police, courts, and prison service to cope. Also, the bargain itself may often represent a realistic appraisal of the appropriate result, in the light of the actual strength of the case against the defendant (Purves 1971). Why then is the practice regarded in some circles as almost a taboo subject?

Presumably the crucial argument for many opponents of plea bargaining is that nothing could be more subversive of the fundamental ethic of the legal system, at least as popularly conceived, than the notion of trading in justice. Even if we are becoming accustomed, if only through the influence of television, to the reality of deals being done between the police and the petty criminal, the idea that when a case has come to court a similar process is engaged in by the legal profession, at times even at the instigation of the judge, is less easily accommodated.

Unless one is willing to give a very high priority to administrative considerations, it is difficult to justify a system in which even a small proportion of innocent defendants feel pressurized into pleading guilty. On what scale this occurs is unknown, but the risk is undoubtedly increased by a state of affairs in which, according to one random sample of higher court criminal cases, 79 per cent of those pleading not guilty saw their barrister for the first time on the morning of the trial (Bottoms and McClean 1976: 158). Advice to change your plea at this stage from the person about to represent you in court is hard to resist.

But the drawbacks of a system in which plea bargaining is condoned on a large scale, as the American experience suggests, go beyond possible injustice in individual cases. The very nature of the legal process is transformed. The adversary model is altered to an office model of routinization where bureaucratic criteria reign supreme. There develops what Sudnow (1965) has described as a 'normalcy' concept of charge reduction, dependent on the perceptions of moral blameworthiness accepted by the controlling officials. We are almost back to the pitfalls of police discretion, with the semblance of 'individualized' justice masking a penal policy based on stereo-typing. Nor can our confidence in plea negotiation be enhanced by the realization that its main beneficiaries seem to be experienced recidivists (Purves 1971; Baldwin and McConville 1977, confirming Newman 1956), due to their greater awareness of the 'best buy' and greater vulnerability to inducements because of their previous record.

Finally, the much vaunted saving in administrative convenience, money, and expedition has to be set against the wasted time, effort, and money when last-minute changes of plea disrupt the court's working schedule. It is of interest that some American States which have recently experimented with virtual bans on plea bargaining have reported no, or no significant, backlog of criminal cases – because most defendants continue to plead guilty in any event.

Court Processes

THE TRIAL

The emphasis on the fact that the vast majority of cases are to all intents and purposes settled before they reach the court seems almost to have brought us to the point of seeing court processes as virtually irrelevant. This of course is far from the truth. First, all convicted defendants are sentenced there (although the determinants of actual sentences are rather more complicated than that alone suggests, as we will see later when we look at the special issues involved). Second, although only a tiny minority of cases actually go to trial, the trial process nevertheless acts as a crucial reference point for all that happens in pre-trial negotiations. To this extent, it still has some claim to being the centre piece of the criminal justice process.

The pre-eminence of the trial process in popular conceptions of criminal justice is almost certainly due to the strong dramaturgical qualities inherent in it, and their effective exploitation by all branches of the mass media. All the constituents of drama are there – not just those associated with tension and the stirring of the emotions, but also, by the very nature of the setting, language, and costume, the elements of absurdity and satirization (as exploited, for example, in N.F.Simpson's play *One Way Pendulum*). Perhaps not surprisingly, in view of such competition, sociologists seem to have been rather reluctant to take up the challenge. When they have, as we shall see, it is these qualities which seem to have impressed them too.

Yet the trial is also presented as the very paradigm of due process. Chambliss and Seidman (1971) claim that:

' . . . the adversary system largely works according to the norms laid down for its conduct. In this case, the law in action on the whole matches the law in the books because of the unique characteristic that here the bureaucratic pressures reinforce rather than undercut the norms' (p.416).

They add, however: 'The question that arises is whether due process as practised in this one area of the criminal process realizes its ostensible goal?' Ironically, despite its dramaturgical qualities and potentiality for absurdity, the ostensible goal of the trial is the most rational of all goals: the discovery of the truth. The adversary system, epitomized in this context by cross-examination, has been hailed as 'the greatest legal engine ever invented for the discovery of truth' (see Chambliss and Seidman 1971: 425). It is by this most sober and rational intention, then, that the trial process must be judged.

If sociologists of law have been wary of taking on this task, others have not. Criticism of the adversary trial process was central, for example, to the legal realists – especially Frank. Frank (1963) argued that far from ensuring that all the relevant facts are developed for the jury's consideration the system encouraged their concealment – for example by the reliance of lawyers on surprise tactics to bewilder and discredit honest witnesses. As he graphically puts it:

' . . . the lawyer aims at winning the fight, not at aiding the court to discover facts. He does not want the trial court to reach a sound educated guess if it is likely to be contrary to his client's interests. Our present trial method is thus the equivalent of throwing pepper in the eyes of a surgeon when he is performing an operation' (p.85).

Psychological and social psychological research on the reliability of testimony has lent some support to Frank's pessimistic conclusions. A useful summary of such studies by Greer (1971) includes several which conclude that cross-examination is perhaps the least reliable method of eliciting evidence (as compared, for example, with 'free narration' and 'direct examination'). Clifford (1979b) concludes that most early studies found that 'interrogative' methods of eliciting evidence increased the amount of evidence, but decreased its reliability. But he also concludes that both old and new research show that 'leading' or 'suggestive' questions (i.e. as used in cross-examination) decrease accuracy – particularly with juvenile witnesses. Indeed, Dent and Stephenson (1979) suggest that juveniles' accuracy of recall is adversely affected by any prompting whatsoever on the part of the interrogator, especially when concerned with the description of people. However, the overall findings of research in this area point to the general unreliability of witnesses' evidence, regardless of the method by which it is elicited.

The sort of experimental evidence compiled by Greer is now fairly well known: an event is 'staged' in front of an experimental audience without their prior knowledge. They are then asked to recount, in various ways, what they saw – identifying the participants, describing the actions, attributing the actions, and so on. The advantages of such experiments are that, unlike real life, where the 'facts' are lost forever, they can be carefully structured so that all facts are known and consequently the accuracy of the witnesses' evidence can be objectively tested.

The findings have almost always been chastening. Identification evidence, for example, which had long been regarded as virtually conclusive when coming from a source judged to be honest, has been revealed as particularly suspect (and is now treated with greater caution even within the legal system itself, see pp.104–06). Generally, the experimental evidence has shown that even honestly-given evidence is subject to a variety of perceptual distortions resulting from physical factors (such as distance, lighting, and duration) and psychological factors (such as emotion, interest, expectation, and prejudice on the part of the perceiver). Clifford concludes that the error-free report of a witnessed incident is an exception and that the more information a person reports, the more errors there are likely to be. Nor does the certainty of a witness bear any relation to his accuracy. Bull (1979) suggests that people's stereotypes distort their perceptions. That is, people who are unfavourably stereotyped are more likely to have 'bad' actions wrongly attributed to them, and vice versa. Sometimes, the conclusions reverse conventional legal assumptions. Greer notes, for example, that in some common law jurisdictions (more so than in this country) statements resulting from spontaneous, emotional responses to events are considered particularly reliable, on the ground that their very spontaneity precludes distortion. Yet experimental evidence suggests precisely the opposite – that intense emotion has a marked distorting effect on perception and makes it highly unreliable. The significance of this point is further highlighted by Dent and Stephenson: legal settings such as courts and identity parades are especially anxiety-producing, and hence are intrinsically unsuited to the production of reliable evidence – again especially where juveniles are concerned.

As was noted earlier, such findings are not just applicable to the adversarial system, but to any system which relies on witnesses' evidence, which is often the only kind available (other than confessions which, as we saw earlier, p.104, raise equally serious problems). It is clear, however, that the adversarial system cannot make any special claim to rationality in this respect – indeed, there is some evidence to support Frank's conclusion that it is particularly ill-suited to this task. But, more generally, the evidence suggests that we should have only limited expectations of any form of trial process.

Recent sociological studies have taken a different kind of approach to the trial process, though with similar debunking conclusions as far as the formal aims are concerned. Carlen (1976) attempts a descriptive account of the way 'justice' is produced in Magistrates' Courts – that is, she seeks to describe 'the attributed and negotiated meanings of magistrates' justice'. Her approach is committed to both Marxism and phenomenology, though the former consists mainly of a largely unexplored assertion that magistrates' justice is somehow reflective of the underlying values of exploitative capitalist society and that the possibility of justice is consequently a myth. The commitment to phenomenology, on the other hand, produces the somewhat paradoxical result that while a key point in the book's argument is that the court uses baffling and misleading language, the language used to assert this is itself often impenetrable.

Carlen considers the production of magistrates' justice in three parts. First, there are 'the materials of control'. An analogy is drawn between the court and the theatre of the absurd where the 'stage set', props, and timing of events are portrayed as conspiring to confuse and bewilder the accused. In the second part, 'the machinery of control', she analyses the relationships between court personnel in terms of games theory (the accused being in the role of 'dummy player'). The different players (police, magistrates, court officials, social workers) are portrayed as having various different interests in the proceedings, each supported by a 'self-justifying rhetoric', which are reconciled in conspiratorial fashion, usually without any reference to the accused's self-defined interests.

Finally, she looks at the 'modes of control', that is the techniques used to control defendants who come into conflict with the practices of the court. It is here that it is claimed that the process supports the underlying values of capitalism, and that justice is consequently an impossible myth. In practice, however, most of the ineradicable problems confronting the accused stem from his ultimate inequality in the process, and it is difficult to see how this could be otherwise under any system of control, capitalist or non-capitalist. Perhaps a more important question is how far 'justice', in any sense, is achievable given that basic limitation. On the other hand, many of the problems confronting the accused which Carlen highlights are technical, and potentially quite simple to eliminate even in a capitalist society (e.g. bad acoustics).

However, Carlen's study illustrates well the confusions, contradictions and degradations experienced by the accused in the trial process, and these certainly have important implications for the official portrayal of its rationality of aim and procedure. Similar conclusions are reached by King (1978) in his summary of various studies of Magistrates' Courts (including Carlen's). He too sees the whole process of court appearance as conspiring to baffle and disadvantage the accused. Thus, the physical arrangements of the court distance him from everyone, including his own lawyer, and isolate him both physically and symbolically. The language used consists of an 'exaggerated politeness' which conceals real relations, cues, and meanings from him, making *his* language appear unreasonably aggressive by contrast. The use of technical terms confuses him and reduces him to silence, reinforcing a court stereotype of defendant's stupidity. The rules of procedure, on the other hand, assume he is responsible and can understand what is happening and consequently leave him to make important decisions affecting his future position often unaided (for example, whether to consent to summary trial or not: King quotes Bottoms and McClean (1976) who found that 27 per cent of defendants who consented to summary trial had not even understood that there was an alternative). Thus the trial process is based on the assumption of powers of rationality and competence of the defendant, yet it simultaneously conspires to reduce both.

In addition, then, to the inherent problems surrounding reliable evidence and the particular problems of the adversary procedure in eliciting it, studies such as these show that the key participant in the proceedings is systematically disadvantaged. However an important qualification needs to be made. This disadvantaging is much more a feature of the Magistrates' Court than of the less 'conveyor-belt' proceedings in the Crown Court, where the accused is normally represented by counsel. Indeed, when this is the case, the unreliability of evidence is effectively exploited by both sides in the adversary process and consequently produces some discrediting of prosecution witnesses, to the advantage of the defendant. Indeed, giving the 'benefit of the doubt' to the defendant means that he tends to be favoured by the creation of chaos and confusion in the evidence. And granted the kind of human frailty and self-contradiction that the witness research has revealed, it is clearly not necessarily very difficult for the defence to achieve this result.

Nonetheless, all things considered, Frank's likening of the process to throwing pepper in a surgeon's eyes when he is performing an operation takes on real meaning. We now turn to the people who, for the small minority of cases that come before the higher courts, have the pepper thrown in their eyes – the jury.

THE JURY

'We couldn't make head or tail of the case or follow all the messing around all the lawyers did. None of us believed the witnesses on either side anyway, so we made up our minds to disregard the evidence on both sides and decide the case on its merits'

(A juror, quoted by Jerome Frank).

If the reliability of adversary trial as a means of establishing guilt is as tenuous as has been suggested, it might seem fitting that its culmination should be the unexplained verdict of an ill-assorted, more or less randomly chosen gathering of ordinary citizens. In fact jury trial occurs in less than 2 per cent of criminal cases. The fact that the jury nevertheless looms so large in discussion of the criminal justice system gives some indication of the symbolic significance attaching to this resilient Anglo-Saxon institution. The extravagant terms in which it has been paraded as a bastion of our liberties, 'the lamp that shows that freedom lives' (Devlin 1956), have to be qualified by the uneasy suspicion that our legal system has become stuck with a mysterious, antiquated, and irrational mode of decision making, scarcely fulfilling the reasonable expectations of contemporary society.

Legal Provisions

To qualify for jury service one must now be over eighteen and under sixty-five years of age. The property qualification, which in the past had excluded many women, lower social class and young people, has been abolished and inclusion on the electoral register now suffices. Certain categories of people, such as lawyers and clergymen, are ineligible and others, such as doctors, are entitled to be excused from serving. A prospective juror may also be released by the judge on grounds of physical disability or inadequate understanding of English.

A defendant is entitled to object to up to three prospective jurors without giving any reason (prior to 1977 he could exercise this right of peremptory challenge seven times). He may then challenge only for cause. This very rarely happens, especially as since 1973 the defence has not been permitted to question jurors or to know their occupations. The prosecution *technically* has no right of challenge except for cause, but effectively it has an unlimited right of challenge without giving reasons, since it may ask any prospective juror to 'stand by for the Crown'. This means that he goes to the end of the panel and will be called upon again only in the unlikely event of the panel being exhausted.

Though the prosecution rarely invokes this power, it creates the potential for abuse in cases with political implications, especially when allied to the recently revealed practice of jury vetting on 'exceptional cases of public importance' (see Harman and Griffith 1979). In the notorious 'Colonel B' Official Secrets trial in 1978 (*Att-Gen* v. *Leveller Magazine Ltd* (1978)) the prosecution was given permission to vet potential jurors for 'loyalty' (though the fact that the foreman was an ex-Special Air Services officer who had worked on security matters was not deemed to render him ineligible). It transpired from 'Guidelines on Jury Checks' released by the Attorney-General in October 1978 that checks had been authorized twenty-five times since August 1975, most frequently in cases involving the IRA. It emerged from a subsequent Crown Court decision that both judges and defence counsel could ask for juries to be vetted in a wide range of cases outside those covered by the guidelines; though the Court of Appeal was to express serious doubts about the whole practice of jury-vetting, whether by prosecution or defence (*R.* v. *Sheffield Crown Court, ex p. Brownlow* (1980)). That the practice of evading random selection may be widespread is suggested by Baldwin and McConville (1979b) who discovered that in Birmingham, informal selection procedures adopted by summoning officers had resulted in under-representation of women and ethnic minorities. These inroads into the principle of random selection and the rules on challenge are not the only ways in which the traditional concept of the jury has been undermined in recent years. Until 1967 jury verdicts had to be unanimous. But now, a jury which has deliberated for at least two hours without returning a verdict may be authorized by the judge to reach a decision by a majority of no less than ten to two. Also, a considerable amount of criminal work previously dealt with by juries is now handled by the Magistrates' Courts.

Broadly speaking, trial by jury is reserved for serious crimes, those tried on indictment at the Crown Court, as distinct from the summary proceedings brought before the magistrates. Certain offences are triable either summarily or on indictment, though several formerly in this hybrid category have recently (Criminal Law Act

1977) been made triable summarily only, partly with a view to reducing congestion in the Crown Court. But it is a measure of the lingering attachment to the idea of the right of trial by jury that a proposal in the Criminal Law Bill 1977 to dispense with it in cases of minor offences of theft was vehemently opposed in Parliament and the press and subsequently withdrawn.

Jury Research

Since jury deliberations take place in secret it is impossible to study them at first hand. Apart from impressionistic accounts (Devons 1965; *New Law Journal* 1973; Legal Action Group Bulletin 1979), such information as we have about them comes predominantly from simulated jury analysis. However carefully constructed, an experiment of this kind can never be wholly authentic, since it cannot reproduce conditions in which the 'jurors' form a truly integral part of the proceedings, actually responsible for the verdict. This said, it is interesting that what emerges from research findings – in contrast to the highly critical observations on magistrates' justice – suggests a degree of rationality, responsibility, and a sense of relevance far removed from the picture of unreasoning prejudice painted by many critics, and, for that matter, by many jurors themselves. The LSE jury project (Sealy and Cornish 1973) involved a series of experiments with mock juries who listened to verbatim transcripts of trials. The general conclusion was that the participants had approached their task seriously and had rejected specious arguments. Those who had previously been on real juries felt that the simulated one was true to life. Similar findings were recorded in the Oxford Penal Research Unit's study (McCabe and Purves 1972b), in which members of the public eligible for jury service were recruited to form thirty shadow juries, to listen to thirty actual trials, after which they were asked to retire and consider their 'verdict'. In three-quarters of the cases it proved to be the same as that of the real jury – in nine out of thirteen guilty verdicts and nine out of twelve not guilty. In the remaining five cases the shadow jury could not reach agreement, but in four of them the majority reached the same conclusion as the real jury. This high degree of consistency could be seen as casting doubt on the view that juries are often unpredictable. Similarly, in an exhaustive American study (Kalven and Zeisel 1966), it was found that in 75 per cent of cases the jury's decision accorded with what the judge would have decided and in only 30 per cent of the remaining cases did the judge consider the decision to have been made arbitrarily. The impressionistic view of the former Lord Chief

Justice, Lord Parker, that there was even greater conformity between English judges and juries, finds support in the most recent English research (Baldwin and McConville, 1979c) which revealed 85 per cent agreement.

Baldwin and McConville investigated jury trials in the Birmingham Crown Court during 1975 – 76. They sought the views of the judge, solicitors, and police officers involved and classified as 'questionable' those decisions where the judge and at least one other respondent disagreed with the jury's verdict. On this criterion they found that 36 per cent of the acquittals and 5 per cent of the convictions were questionable. These figures are not as disturbing as they appear, as we shall see.

Jury Acquittals

None of the research, in the nature of things, can tell us about the *correctness* of the decisions juries reach. One of the main reasons put forward, both by the Criminal Law Revision Committee and Sir Robert Mark, for further restrictions on the rights of the accused, was the claim that, in trial by jury, too many guilty people, especially professional criminals, are able to avoid conviction. This view has been challenged by, among others, the Bar Council and the organization *Justice* (see also Sanders 1979) but, if true, clearly has serious implications both for the criminal process in general and the role of the jury in particular.

However, as Zander has observed: 'The question whether too many criminals are acquitted is in itself a meaningless one . . . The feeling that [the acquittal rate] is too high is simply a political-social value judgment reflecting some inarticulate sense that the system is tipped too far in favour of the defence' (1974: 60). Sir Robert Mark (1973) put what he called the 'failure rate' – the phrase is not without significance – at around 50 per cent (p.62). But though he began by making it clear that he was referring to *contested* trials only, later references to 'a failure rate of one in two' and 'an increase . . . to about 50 per cent in acquittals' could easily convey a false impression, especially in the context of a televised public lecture. It is essential to distinguish clearly between defendants who *plead* guilty and those who are *found* guilty. Thus in 1977, for example, of every 100 defendants in the Crown Courts, sixty-six pleaded guilty, nineteen were found guilty by the jury, six were acquitted on the direction of the judge and only nine acquitted by the jury. It seems reasonable then to assume that the overall acquittal rate is approximately 15 per cent and the *jury* acquittal rate around 10 per cent.

Two pieces of research (Zander 1974; McCabe and Purves 1972b), based in one case on discussion with the judges, police, and lawyers involved and in the other on interviews with counsel on both sides, point to only a very small proportion of decisions overall (8.8 and 6 per cent respectively) which could be described as perverse, or wholly against the weight of the evidence. The bulk of acquittals were explicable on rational grounds. Even allowing for the problematic nature of conviction rates, one still ends up with a true rate in the region of 10 per cent, amounting to about 1 per cent of all cases *tried* in the higher courts.

What proportion of these acquittals are secured by 'professional criminals'? Uncertainty over the meaning of this term complicates the issue. Zander (1974) defines the 'professional criminal' as an offender with 'a substantial criminal record'. He points out that most acquittals are for relatively minor offences and that approximately two-fifths of those acquitted have no previous criminal record. Someone with a prior record is considerably more likely to be convicted and the worse the record the greater the likelihood of conviction. He therefore concludes that professional criminals constitute only a small proportion of those acquitted by juries.

But the criterion of 'a substantial criminal record' as the mark of professionalism is open to criticism. As Mack (1976) has argued, it both includes many relatively minor habitual offenders and leaves out of account those criminals whose very professionalism helps them to avoid conviction. Some people, after all, are better at their job than others in all walks of life. Using as his criterion the full-time major, skilled operator, as identified by the police on the basis of their criminal intelligence, he found that 'professionals' escaped conviction in a much higher proportion of all the charges brought against them than other criminals. On the other hand, Baldwin and McConville (1979c), basing their findings on structured questionnaires submitted to the police, which incorporated details of criminal records and police assessment of 'professionalism', concluded that jury acquittal of professional criminals was comparatively rare and only exceptionally questionable (Chapter 7).

In the nature of things precise figures are unattainable. We would regard Mack's hypothesis as eminently reasonable and the particular concern of the police to catch the 'professional criminal' as they define him wholly understandable. But increasing police powers to facilitate capture of the 'professionals' would inevitably endanger the overwhelming majority of suspects, who do not come into this category.

The Jury Assessed

Nonetheless, denigration of juries persists, usually focussing on their lack of expertise, ignorance, presumed irresponsibility, and susceptibility to forensic guile. Implicit in such attacks is the call for a more professionalized and scientific approach, reminiscent of Frank's strictures on the vagaries of the trial process and jury system alike. Bankowski and Mungham (1976b) have provided an account of jury deliberations in three relatively short trials which they observed, the bulk of which were recorded in shorthand by one of the jurors. They point to the dangers of considering the jury's deliberations in isolation from the total context of the trial itself and in particular from the influence exerted by the judge, both in his express guidance and own demeanour. They saw the judge's directions as of central importance in structuring the approach of the jury, who, they claim, were mainly concerned to 'divine the content of the judge's mind'. Given the elements of irrationality in the adversary process itself, it is, in their view, hardly a cause for much surprise if ' . . . the style of disputation which the jurors slipped into [was] simply the mirror-image of the courtroom arguments they had earlier watched and listened to' (p.212).

But the plea for a more rational, scientific approach to decision making is liable to understate the extent to which arguments about guilt and innocence are value-laden. In the end, there has to be reliance on *someone*'s judgment of the case against the defendant and there is no guarantee that the relative insularity of judicial training and outlook would produce more accurate results. Curiously enough, in a period when the scope of jury trial is in general diminishing, the judges have to a limited extent been eroding the traditional division of function in criminal law, in which questions of *law* are for the judge to decide and questions of *fact* for the jury. In *Brutus* v. *Cozens* (1973), the House of Lords held that the meaning of ordinary words in a statute was a question of fact, not law. The words in issue were 'insulting behaviour'. A subsequent case applied the same principle to the concept of 'dishonesty' for the purposes of defining theft (*R*. v. *Feely* (1973)). The result is that the jury is given an explicitly evaluative role, becoming in a sense 'creators' of law for the instant case (jury decisions do not set precedents). It is true that a measure of evaluation by juries is inescapable, as for example, in grappling with notions such as 'intention' and 'provocation'. On the other hand it is sometimes argued that the Delphic nature of the jury's verdict, which contrasts with the reasoned decision making taken to be the hallmark of judicial behaviour, makes it an unsuitable body to entrust with complex moral evaluation. Jury verdicts are very difficult to impugn and appeals in criminal cases are overwhelmingly concerned with points of procedure.

Depending on one's viewpoint, this blurring of the distinction between law and fact signifies either an abdication of judicial responsibility or an acknowledgement that judicial definitions are apt to lose touch with contemporary standards. Whatever misgivings one might have about the capacity of juries to make these evaluative judgments, the principle in *Brutus* v. *Cozens* adds a concrete dimension to the argument that the jury is an important symbol of participatory democracy (see Damaska 1975). The use of juries is an affirmation in practice as well as theory of the ideal that the criminal law should be broadly intelligible to the layman and that he has a civic role in the administration of justice. In these respects the jury could be seen as an ideological weapon, legitimating the law and legal institutions. On the other hand, the jury's power to 'defy' the judge and substitute its own version of equity also makes it a potentially subversive, or corrective, device which has, over the centuries, earned the gratitude of poacher, petty thief, and dangerous motorist alike (see also Kadish and Kadish 1973).

SENTENCING

If guilt-*finding* and jury work are, numerically, insignificant court activities sentencing certainly is not. All offenders proceeded against in this country receive their sentences in the court setting, although as we will see, this is often only within very broad parameters – the specific sentence ultimately being determined by administrative discretion. Sentencing is perhaps the major area of discrepancy and confusion between formal intention and actual practice in the criminal process. To a considerable extent this is due to the fact that whereas in guilt finding, for example, the aim is fairly clear (however difficult it may be to realize), in sentencing it is not. Several different, sometimes contradictory, aims and intentions are built into both sentencing tradition and available sentences. It is possible to distinguish at least four such aims, although in practice they are often variously intertwined in particular sentences.

First, there is retribution. That is, punishing the offender in proportion to the seriousness of his wrongdoing. In its pure form retribution is not concerned with the effects of punishment for achieving particular ends (such as altering the offender's future behaviour, or preventing potential offences): it is backward looking, focussing on the nature of the offence for its justification. Its most primitive form is the biblical 'eye for an eye', which has as its modern counterpart the 'tariff system'. The available punishments are notionally arranged in order of severity, the offence is similarly located on a scale of seriousness (adjusted for mitigating circumstances) and is 'read off' against the appropriate punishment.

Retribution has been discredited in penal reformist circles as being irrationally revenge-seeking, and harshly punitive. This, however, is not necessarily implicit. Retribution does not require any specific *level* of punishment – it can express itself as easily in different amounts of fines as in different amounts of corporal punishment. Indeed, the most punitive period in the history of our penal system (the first half of the last century) was based on elimination rather than retribution (i.e. hanging and transportation) and retributive arguments were used *against* this policy. For all its apparent irrationality retribution has one very important feature: it demands that although the offender must be *sufficiently* punished for his wrongdoing, the punishment must not *out-run* the seriousness of the offence. The significance of this aspect of retribution will become apparent later.

The second possible aim of sentencing is deterrence, which is usually divided into two sub-types: individual deterrence and general deterrence. Individual deterrence, like retribution, is concerned with punishing the offender, but the aim here is a forward-looking, instrumental one – to dissuade him from committing further offences in the future. General deterrence is similarly instrumental, but is concerned with dissuading *potential* offenders. Thus, while the success of an individual deterrent is measured by the extent to which it stops particular offenders committing *further* offences, general deterrents are measured by the extent to which they keep the general *rate* of crime in check (i.e. including first offences).

Retributive and deterrent aims are usually very difficult to distinguish from each other. This is because they both demand punishment and because it is often simply assumed that the retributively appropriate punishment will also be the most effective deterrent (this conflation is particularly apparent, for example, in arguments in favour of capital punishment). It should be noted, however, that neither individual nor general deterrence is necessarily compatible with retribution, nor is either necessarily compatible with the other. There is much evidence to suggest, for example, that murderers are unlikely to commit similar offences again, regardless of the punishment and that the severity of the punishment has little effect on the murder rate. Yet, in retributive terms, murder is regarded as the most serious crime and consequently merits the most punishment. Also, general deterrence is often manifested in 'exemplary' sentences. That is, the offender is given a particularly severe punishment in order to deter potential offenders. This would obviously require him to receive more severe punishment than would be retributively appropriate, or necessary for purely individual deterrence.

Rehabilitation, like deterrence, is a forward-looking and instrumental aim. It is concerned to prevent offenders from committing further offences (though it ignores the problem of general deterrence). Unlike individual deterrence, however, it does not aim to achieve this through punishing the offender and simply frightening him off. It has a more ambitious aim: to make the offender not *want* to commit further offences, by 'curing' him of his criminal desires, or by altering his environmental opportunities. Although rehabilitation precludes punishment as a formal aim, the rehabilitation process may obviously unintentionally involve punishment from the offender's point of view. Again, the significance of this will become apparent later.

Finally, there is restitution. This involves the offender paying for his offence, though not in the retributive sense of being made to suffer for it. Rather, it involves him making amends in some way either to the offender or the society that he has harmed. The Community Service Order, for example, embodies at least in part the idea that the offender should do some good to make up for the harm he has done.

All of these aims play their part in differing combinations and to different degrees in the contemporary penal system. Thus, fines involve retribution and deterrence; prison and other institutional treatments a mixture of retribution, deterrence, and rehabilitation; probation is largely rehabilitative, and community service involves a mixture of rehabilitation and restitution, while, overall, this array of treatments and punishments is arranged within some sort of retributive tariff system. Perhaps it is not surprising then that accusations of inconsistency and bias have frequently been levelled at sentencers. Yet the very plurality of possible aims built into the system make such accusations difficult to sustain: an apparent inconsistency could always be explained by the fact that the critic holds different assumptions about the aims of sentencing from those of the sentencer.

One kind of inconsistency, however, has attracted particular attention and inspired some research – apparent inconsistency *between* sentences in different parts of the country. Some attempts have been made to ascertain the *basis* of this variation (such as differences in personality, social background, etc. of the sentencers). Such research as there is has concentrated on magistrates. This is not unreasonable, since 98 per cent of sentences are handed out by them. Also, it is perhaps assumed that there is greater consistency for the tiny minority sentenced by Judges and Recorders, if only because they constitute a much smaller and more cohesive group, more aware of each other's sentencing practice, reinforced via the appellate system. A recent Home Office study (Tarling, 1979) showed wide variations between different magistrates' courts around the country: use of fines varied from 46 per cent to 76 per cent of total cases, imprisonment from 3 per cent to 19 per cent and probation from 1 per cent to 12 per cent. Although local conditions such as police use of cautions, resources for probation and social and economic conditions (which influenced the use of fines) accounted for some of the variation, Tarling concluded that considerable discrepancies still remained unexplained. He suggested that the more extensive use of recommended penalties (or tariff guidelines) would reduce them.

One of the most systematic attempts to examine the sources of such apparently arbitrary variation was the study carried out by Hood (1972) of magistrates' sentencing of motoring offenders. 500 magistrates were given transcripts of actual cases of eight different types of motoring offence to evaluate (thus avoiding the problem that variation between sentences may be due to the different types of case they confront). The magistrates' decisions were then related to (i) their personal and social attributes (age, class, etc.), (ii) their perceptions of, and attitudes towards motoring offences and offenders, (iii) the 'bench effect' – that is, the tendency for particular magistrates' benches to develop their own special policies, based on some informally developed criteria of basic penalties and tariffs.

Hood confirmed that there was considerable variation in both the amounts of fines and the use of disqualification between the different magistrates for the same offences. The findings on what kinds of factors seemed to account for this were perhaps rather surprising. First, differences in the personal and social attributes of the magistrates seemed to make little difference except in some specific types of offence – for example, older magistrates were relatively more severe on young reckless drivers. Differences in magistrates' perception and ratings of the relative seriousness of different types of offences and offenders also accounted for only a small proportion of the variation. By far the most important factor was the 'bench effect'. Under the influence of clerks and senior magistrates, different benches apparently developed their own traditions about basic penalties and tariffs, and new magistrates were socialized into them. Thus, most of the variation was between magistrates on different benches, while magistrates on the same benches were much more uniform, despite variations in personal and social attributes.

A more recent study by Lemon (1974), using simulated cases over a wider range of types of offence, again found that personal characteristics of magistrates did not seem to be important as sources of variation in sentencing practice. He looked at sentencers' differing attitudes towards justice, punishment, and types of offences and found that they seemed to have little effect on the outcome (interestingly, punitive attitudes were not necessarily associated with punitive sentences). However, Lemon found that one personality trait *was* relevant – the extent to which magistrates were 'concrete' rather than 'abstract'. 'Concrete' magistrates tended to be dictatorial, inflexible, anti-democratic, were prone to see things in black and white, and generally held strong opinions. They were inclined to be more severe, though not in all types of case. Lemon also found that the first year's experience and training as a magistrate tended to make them more severe in their sentencing practice.

Unfortunately there is no systematic data on variations in sentencing practice in more complex areas, as in the case of juvenile offenders, when more sophisticated demands are made of the sentencer. Nor is there, as we have already noted, much research on sentencing practice for the more serious offences dealt with by the higher courts. However, detailed compilations of appellate decisions (see Thomas 1979) disclose a high level of consistency because of the presumption in favour of a notional retributive tariff.

In view of the ambiguity and complexity of the sentencing process, it is perhaps not surprising that the sentencers themselves have come under attack. There are two rather different sources of criticism. First, there are those who point out the narrow 'establishment' social background of both judges (see Blom-Cooper and Drewry 1972) and magistrates (see Bartlett and Walker 1978). Such criticisms are presumably based on the assumption that those who do the sentencing should be more democratically selected. Whatever the arguments in favour of this view, what evidence there is suggests, as we have seen, that it would probably make little difference to the decisions made.

The other type of criticism is rather different. It is associated with the emergence of rehabilitation as a key aim of the penal system. This requires, it is argued, decisions that are based on expert knowledge of the causes and treatment of crime – knowledge that is almost totally lacking in existing sentencers (see Wootton 1963). They either have no special qualifications at all, as in the case of magistrates, or purely legal qualifications, as in the case of judges whose training, if anything, disposes them towards the establishment of a retributive tariff, which is entirely irrelevant to rehabilitation. The dismissive attitude of many judges towards the very idea that systematic instruction on sentencing might be valuable is well illustrated in the Report of a recent Working Party (*Judicial Studies and Information* 1978). Many judges even objected to the phrase 'judicial training'. One view was that 'common sense and forensic experience [were] the sole legitimate sources of wisdom', and a judge's 'robust common sense' was 'liable to be distorted or impaired if he is required to study the learning and opinions of experts in subjects other than his own'. It is sentiments such as these that have led some proponents of rehabilitation to conclude that sentencing can be properly carried out only by panels of 'experts'.

Yet, in practice, and despite the formal retention of sentencing decisions by magistrates and the judiciary, there has already been a steady trend towards the reality of sentencing being taken away from them and placed in the hands of precisely such experts. For example, sentencers are frequently aided by social information provided by social workers and probation officers (such information is *required* in the case of juveniles). This usually includes sentence recommendations from these 'experts', which is extremely likely to be accepted (see Hine, McWilliams, and Pease 1978). More significantly, custodial sentences now usually lay down only the broad limits of the type and duration of the sentence, that is, they are mostly 'indeterminate'. Again, this is especially marked in the case of juveniles (under the age of seventeen), particularly since the Children and Young Persons Act 1969. The main institutional treatment for them is the Care Order. The magistrate makes the order, but the type of institution the offender goes to (or, indeed, whether he goes to one at all) and the length of time he spends there are entirely determined by Local Authority social workers and treatment personnel in the institutions concerned. Similarly for young adults between seventeen and twenty-one, Borstal has always been an indeterminate sentence. The offender is merely sentenced to 'Borstal Training', the length of stay (up to a maximum of two years) is determined by treatment personnel. Equally significant, the introduction of parole in 1967, for prison sentences, means that the offender may serve anything between a third and the full term of the sentence set by the Court, the actual duration being determined by the Parole Board, assisted by Local Review Committees comprising prison staff and probation officers as well as magistrates. More importantly, parole and release from all the indeterminate institutional sentences mentioned, are not based on retributive criteria (i.e. as a reward for good behaviour) but on rehabilitative ones (that the offender is 'cured' of his criminal tendencies and is hence safe to release). Finally, the recent report by the Advisory Council on the Penal System (The Younger Report 1974) proposed a further extension of the indeterminate sentence in relation to young adult offenders. It recommended replacing the present Borstal, prison, and detention centre sentences with a general 'custody and control order' which would set broad limits under which once again, the actual type and length of stay would be determined by treatment personnel on treatment criteria.

Traditionally in academic and penal reformist circles, any advance in the rehabilitative approach at the expense of retribution has usually been regarded as a triumph of humanity and rationality. In recent years, however, there has been a significant turn of the tide. Starting in those countries where the rehabilitative approach had progressed furthest (the United States – see the American Friends Service Committee 1971, and Scandinavia – see Christie 1974) this reversal of opinion is beginning to establish itself in this country (see Bean 1976; Hood 1978; Taylor, Lacey, and Bracken 1980). This new movement essentially resurrects a retributive model of the penal process and uses it as a weapon to attack what it sees as the excessive interventionism facilitated by the rehabilitative approach. To understand this debate, it is necessary to spell out the positions of the two sides in a little more detail.

We have already noted that the retributive approach has some important restraints built into it. These are particularly associated with the emphasis on justice and due process which it is seen as containing. There are three elements in particular which have been used in the attack on rehabilitation. First, and perhaps rather strangely, there is the emphasis on punishment. It may seem rather odd that this should be seen as a virtue. But it is the 'honesty' of retribution in this respect which is important: as we will see, a major criticism of the rehabilitative approach is that it maintains the pretence that because punishment is not intended it does not occur.

The second element is allied to this: retribution implies *justice* – in two senses. First, that the punishment should be proportional to the wrongdoing which, as we have already noted, includes the principle that it should not *out-run* what is justified by the offence, and this applies whether the *intention* is to punish or not. In addition, it implies that similar offences and offenders should be similarly punished. The only considerations which should count are the seriousness of the offence and the existence or non-existence of mitigating factors which alter its moral gravity. Other differences in the circumstances and background of offenders should be irrelevant.

The third element is the emphasis on due process. That is, that there should be recognized and standardized procedures for determining sentence as well as guilt, which are open to public scrutiny. Although this is not necessarily implied in retribution as are the other two elements, it is readily associated with it. This is because, as we have already seen, retribution accepts that the intention of the penal process is ultimately to punish, and therefore harm the offender. This makes it more difficult to justify if the process is not as open and fair as possible (more so, that is, than when the process is seen as being for both society's and the offender's own good).

There is perhaps one final aspect of retribution which has made it attractive by comparison with rehabilitation. This is its view of man as being free, responsible and self-determining. Retribution is based on the contention that man can choose between 'right' and 'wrong', for it is this which justifies his being punished when he chooses wrong. As we noted in Chapter 1, traditional criminology's opposite, deterministic conception of man was one of the principle targets of the 'new deviance' of the 1960s which helped give rise to the revival of interest in the sociology of law.

The rehabilitative approach differs on nearly all of these points. First, it abandons the idea of punishment altogether in favour of treatment tailored to the individual needs of the offender. It is based on a deterministic theory of the causes of crime: crime is seen as a form of individual pathology, usually reflecting psychological problems generated by trouble of some kind in the family background (for example, the White Paper *Children in Trouble* 1968, which preceded the Children and Young Persons Act 1969, stated unequivocally that delinquency was an index of trouble in the home).

The treatment of such problems clearly requires experts (psychologists, psychiatrists, social workers) to assess what is needed. Sentencers have none of the appropriate qualifications. The whole paraphernalia of due process of law is irrelevant to rehabilitation and is often seen as simply getting in the way. The offence is not particularly important in assessing the offender's needs. Indeed if he has problems which need treating, it is not even particularly important whether he committed one or not (in the United States, the Gluecks (1950), perhaps the foremost proponents of the treatment ideology, developed 'prediction tables' so that potential delinquents could be detected and treated *before* they committed their offences. However, although President Nixon is known to have toyed with such an idea, no such programme was ever formally instituted). It is of course possible both in this country and the United States to be compulsorily detained in institutions without having committed a criminal offence, under mental health legislation and care proceedings for juveniles.

In addition to excluding punishment, treatment programmes must also be indeterminate. That is, treatment would obviously be terminated when the offender had been 'cured' or rehabilitated. Since it cannot be known in advance how long this will take, it does not make sense to predetermine its duration. Thus, just as the type of treatment must be decided by the experts, so must its termination date. This requirement for indeterminacy is the crucial and most criticized feature of the rehabilitative approach.

The rehabilitative approach has been most extensively instituted for the treatment of juvenile offenders. Indeed, in those countries where it has been taken farthest, it has involved the abandonment of formal 'criminal' proceedings altogether in favour of some kind of treatment panel. This is the case, for example, in Scandinavia and also Scotland. In Scotland juvenile offenders are brought before 'children's hearings' whose sole function is to determine treatment measures appropriate to the child's needs. In England and most of the United States, the juvenile courts represent something of a compromise between an informal hearing and a formal court (partly, as we have seen, through the withdrawal from them of the most important treatment decisions, and also because of a modification of formal due process in their proceedings).

What is it then, about this apparently humane and well-intentioned approach which has incurred such concentrated opposition in the United States, Scandinavia, and now here? Traditionally, it has been opposed in conservative quarters as being 'too soft' on criminals. Yet now the opposition is coming from precisely those more liberal and radical quarters where it traditionally would have expected to find support. To explain this, we need, as so often, to look at how things have worked out in reality – in those countries where the process has been carried farthest.

First, even if it is not intended, rehabilitative treatments *do* involve punishment, especially when they keep people in institutions. Indeed, since rehabilitation requires indeterminate sentences, it allows for offenders to be kept in institutions for greater periods than would be justifiable on a retributive basis. In the United States Lerman (1970) has shown how the approach has meant that juveniles are more likely to get longer periods of incarceration than adults for equivalent offences, while the American Friends Service Committee (1971) demonstrates that the advanced system of indeterminate prison sentences operated in California has led to more, and longer prison sentences. The Committee's conclusion is that the approach has simply led to gross injustice, in retributive terms, facilitated by a sleight of hand which redefines punishment as 'treatment' for the recipient's 'own good'. They suggest a simple test of whether or not treatment is really punishment: can the subject take it or leave it? If he takes it can he leave it any time he wants to? If the answer to either question is 'no' then 'the wolf is still under sheepskin' (p.24).

Second, in its enthusiasm for treatment and moving away from punishing and 'criminalizing' offenders (especially when they are juveniles), the rehabilitative approach has tended to regard due process of law as irrelevant and an obstacle. The counterclaim is that the abandonment of due process simply leads to the denial of defendants' rights, as epitomized in the case of Gerald Gault in Arizona in 1967. Gault, aged fifteen, was sentenced to indeterminate detention in a training school, for allegedly making a lewd telephone call to a neighbour. On appeal, the case eventually went to the Supreme Court. Ironically, the retributively disproportionate sentence for such a minor offence was not in issue, since the rehabilitative approach quite clearly allowed this if it was thought to be what he 'needed'. What was in issue, however, was the denial of due process in the finding of guilt. The enquiry revealed an extremely rough-shod approach: no prior notice was given for preparation of a defence, no legal representation was allowed, nor any right to cross-examine witnesses – all, of course, perfectly consistent with the court's primary concern of helping him according to his needs, for which such 'criminal' processes were irrelevant. In a historic decision, the Supreme Court reversed the finding – a decision which subsequently had some influence on juvenile court procedure.

Third, the removal of the most important treatment decisions from the formal legal process in favour of discretionary decisions made by experts is wide open to all sorts of bias – political and social. Accusations of bias, however, are difficult to sustain since rehabilitation obviously does not require that like offenders should be treated alike, as their 'needs' may be entirely different. It does not require 'justice' in this conventional sense. Nor can such discretionary decisions be open to public scrutiny, since they are made by 'experts', on grounds which cannot be expected to be fully understood by laymen. Indeed, it is precisely its qualities of private, discretionary indeterminacy which make rehabilitation ideally suited to disguise political repression. It is no accident that in the USSR it has often been found preferable to deal with political dissidents under compulsory mental health procedures – for it is these which provide the most extreme version of the rehabilitative approach (its excesses in the mental health context in the USSR are notorious. But see also Szasz 1974). Nor has the rehabilitative approach in the penal system escaped accusations of political bias in the West. A much publicized case in the United States was that of George Jackson, the black revolutionary writer, who achieved his revolutionary consciousness while serving a 'one year-to-life' sentence for driving the getaway car in a $70 robbery. He was eventually shot trying to escape after serving more than ten years. This quite disproportionate sentence for the original offence was, of course, allowed for by the indeterminate nature of the sentence under California's rehabilitative system. Jackson's resistance to the racism and degradation of Soledad prison, together with his political consciousness which developed from this, were clearly crucial as indicators of his failure to be rehabilitated (see Jackson 1971).

In addition to political bias, the approach is equally open to class bias. This is particularly likely in relation to juveniles, since there is a heavy reliance on family background characteristics as indicators of treatment need, which themselves are likely to be class-related. But even if this is not the case, the use of different family backgrounds as justification for treating similar offenders differently is obviously objectionable in terms of retributive justice, whatever good sense it makes in treatment terms. This ambiguity is neatly captured in the following quotation, describing how the Children's Hearings system operates in Scotland (Morris, McIsaac, and Gallacher 1973):

'The contrast between a court and a hearing is ...between a system which rested mainly on the idea of crime-responsibility-punishment and one proceeding mainly on the principle of treatment. The following two case histories highlight the effect of this change in emphasis.

Two girls, both 14, defaced a wall with black paint. The Reporter felt that a children's hearing might encourage them to undertake more worthwhile pursuits. One girl was disruptive in school and there was tension between her and her mother and between the parents. The social worker felt that the girl's general discontent was a result of family relationships and recommended supervision. Extreme, long-standing family problems were subsequently revealed in the discussion at the children's hearing and the child was removed from home to an institution to let her get the emotional support to allow her to develop normally.

The other girl came from a stable home where the disclipline was strict, but the social worker felt that the parents were not providing sufficient help and understanding with her adolescent difficulties. The social worker recommended supervision, but the decision at the hearing was that the girl should work in a children's home in her free time. She was later discharged after encouraging reports from the children's home.

Thus, although the offence was the same, the girls were dealt with differently by the system according to their individual needs. This would rarely have occurred in the court system . . . ' (p.280).

This one example encapsulates almost all of the problems raised by the rehabilitative approach. First, there is the disproportionate sentence: rephrased in the language of retribution, one of the girls was 'put away' for drawing on a wall. Second, there is the unfairness: her partner was scarcely 'punished' at all, despite her offence being identical.

But the example best illustrates the third, and perhaps most damning criticism of the rehabilitative approach. The needs of the first girl, it is stated, were such that she 'was removed from home to an institution to let her get the emotional support to allow her to develop normally'. This assumes, as does the rehabilitative approach generally, that we (or rather 'the experts') are both able to diagnose need, and to apply appropriate (and effective) treatments for these needs. The plain fact is that this is simply not the case. Empirical evidence has shown, over and over again, that no treatment or punishment is any more (or less) effective than any other (a useful summary of the research is to be found in Lipton, Martinson, and Wilks 1975). Admittedly such findings are limited by methodological problems and perhaps also by the paucity of adequately funded and supported treatment programmes. But that hardly alters the point at this stage: the justification for programmes of treatment which involve either more punishment or at least more intervention in the lives of offenders than would otherwise be the case, is simply not there. Even if it were, there would still be the problems of injustice and inequality in retributive terms. This conclusion raises another even more contentious issue: could the answer be to establish much more radical treatment programmes using drugs and advanced forms of 'reconditioning' techniques (i.e. what is more loosely referred to as 'brainwashing')? It may well be that for treatment programmes to be truly effective this is precisely what they will have to do (still one of the better sources of the moral dilemmas involved here is Anthony Burgess's novel *A Clockwork Orange*).

However, putting such dramatic implications to one side, what stage has the rehabilitative approach reached in this country? We have already noted its progress in relation to juvenile offenders. Certainly the potential for injustice and disproportionate punishment are there. Yet, ironically, most of the criticism has been in the other direction – that it has involved relatively less use of institutional measures, for example, and on the whole has led to greater leniency. It is not clear, however, insofar as this is true, to what extent it has resulted from inadequate resources as opposed to policy. In the case of young adult and adult offenders the use of indeterminate sentences is much more circumscribed here than, for example, in the case of California. Borstal has a set maximum of two years, and parole allows only for the deduction of up to two-thirds of a prison sentence which is intended to be set by the normal retributive considerations (although this cannot, of course, rule out the possibility of sentencers giving longer sentences to 'allow for' parole). On the other hand, parole in particular facilitates injustice through unequal treatment (in retributive terms) and has met with considerable opposition on these grounds, particularly from prisoners themselves (see Fitzgerald 1977). But what is perhaps of most concern here is the apparently uncritical acceptance of the rehabilitative approach and its myths in 'official' circles (see the already mentioned Younger Report 1974) at a time when it has come increasingly under attack in those countries where it has advanced farthest.

The anti-rehabilitation argument does, of course, have its difficulties too. Not least is the tendency for it to be confused with reactionary demands for a return to draconian penal regimes. But also, there always seems to be some residue of truly 'dangerous' offenders for whom some form of indeterminacy of sentence does seem to make sense in the interests of 'public protection', even if it does violate retributive justice (Hood (1978) pp.298 and 307, for example, makes precisely such an exception). This is, of course, not justified on the grounds that this particular group *can* be treated and cured, but simply that it is beneficial to keep them out of circulation for indeterminate periods of time. Yet the same problem arises: unless indeterminate literally means 'for ever', some release date has to be decided upon. What could be the basis of such a decision? How could it avoid arbitrariness any more than any other indeterminate sentence? Or do such problems not matter so much when the offender is 'dangerous' (whatever that may be taken to mean)?

Perhaps a more consistent conclusion is that of the American Friends Service Committee (1971) which accepts the logic of going the whole way: the elimination of discretionary justice at all levels, a return to (humane) retributive justice where the parameters of punishment are set by the offence with the inclusion of treatment only on a genuinely voluntary basis. Similar views, in relation to the treatment of juveniles, are now being expressed in this country (see Taylor, Lacey, and Bracken 1980, Chapter 4).

Suggested Reading

THE POLICE AND THE PROSECUTION PROCESS

Davis, K.C. (1975) *Police Discretion*. Minnesota: West Publishing Co.
Gill, O. (1976) Urban Stereotypes and Delinquent Incidents. *British Journal of Criminology* **16**: 321.
Justice (1970) *The Prosecution Process in England and Wales*. London: Justice Educational Research Trust.
Leigh, L. (1975) *Police Powers in England and Wales*. London: Butterworth.
McCabe, S. and Sutcliffe, F. (1978) *Defining Crime*. Oxford: Blackwell.
Powis, D. (1977) *The Signs of Crime: a Field Manual for Police*. London: McGraw Hill.
Street, H. (1975) *Freedom, the Individual and the Law*. Harmondsworth: Penguin.
Wilcox, A. (1972) *The Decision to Prosecute*. London: Butterworth.
Young, J. (1971) The Role of the Police as Amplifiers of Deviancy. In S. Cohen (ed.) *Images of Deviance*. Harmondsworth: Penguin.

THE TRIAL, THE JURY, AND SENTENCING

Baldwin, J. and McConville, S. (1979) *Jury Trials*. London: Oxford University Press.
Bean, P. (1976) *Rehabilitation and Deviance*. London: Routledge and Kegan Paul.
Cornish, W. (1971) *The Jury*. Harmondsworth: Penguin.
Damaska, M. (1975) Structures of Authority and Comparative Criminal Procedure. *Yale Law Journal* **84**: 480.
Frank, J. (1963) *Courts on Trial*. New York: Atheneum.
Hood, R. (1972) *Sentencing the Motoring Offender*. New York: Heinemann.

Hood, R. (1978) Tolerance and the Tariff: Some Reflections on Fixing the Time Prisoners Serve in Custody. In J. Baldwin and A. Bottomley, *Criminal Justice: Selected Readings*. London: Martin Robertson.

King, M. (1978) A Status Passage Analysis of the Defendants' Progress through the Magistrates' Court. *Warwick Law Working Papers No. 3*. University of Warwick.

Taylor, L., Lacey, R., and Bracken, D. (1980) *In Whose Best Interests? The Unjust Treatment of Children in Courts and Institutions*. London: Cobden Trust.

Thomas, D. (1979) *Principles of Sentencing* (2nd ed.). London: Heinemann.

4

Legal Rules in Operation: (2) The Settlement of Disputes in Civil Law

Introduction

We have seen that the conventional image of criminal justice, as a process culminating in a full-scale adversarial trial, does not correspond with reality in the vast majority of cases. At all stages extraneous considerations present themselves and are frequently decisive. The constraints of operating a *system* of general application are not fully compatible with formal notions of individualized justice. Police discretion is inevitable. Policeman and accused alike actively seek to have cases disposed of with a minimum of formality and delay. Judges too wish to avoid long trials. In the circumstances, it should not surprise us that techniques more appropriate to office management loom so large.

In this chapter we turn our attention to the civil law. In contrast to the pronounced *public* element in criminal law, the bulk of civil law is concerned with *private* rights and obligations. It provides a framework within which people may arrange their affairs and a mechanism whereby an aggrieved individual may seek a remedy. It covers a broad and disparate range of topics, such as the transfer of land, the making of contracts and wills, matrimonial disputes, and accident claims.

This diversity of civil law and its lack of the public dimension crucial to criminal law require us to approach it in a rather different and more selective manner. Not only do many civil law transactions take place without any reference to the possibility of court action, but the institution of civil proceedings is for most purposes a voluntary matter. Unlike the position in criminal law, only the injured person may sue in respect of a civil wrong and he is free to discontinue his action at any time, or to agree to some compromise solution. It is true that in certain civil matters, which are deemed to have a public aspect, some court involvement is obligatory. But the degree of involvement is often minimal as we shall see in the case of divorce.

Our concern then will not be with the details of civil procedure, but with how certain features which we identified in the criminal sphere – such as bureaucratic processing, bargaining, and the importance of extra-legal goals – are also prominent in certain areas of civil law. Here too the operative reality is often very different from the 'law in the books'.

Of course, when resort to the courts is voluntary it should come as no surprise that the formal system is frequently by-passed, or not utilized to the full. A variety of compelling reasons deters most people from ever contemplating going to law. The spectre of inordinate cost and delay, the unpredictability of the outcome, and fear of, or distaste for, public confrontation, are powerful disincentives. In addition there is the very real problem of the accessibility of legal services, which we will consider in the next chapter.

Given that the law is just one among several mechanisms of social control, it would be odd for people to make use of it of their own volition if they could find more congenial and less destructive or hazardous ways of resolving their differences. This is especially true where the parties have some long-term interest which transcends any particular dispute, as in the case of businessmen anxious not to jeopardize their future commercial relationship. The existence of continuing relationships, as occur also in the matrimonial and industrial spheres, for example, is a further distinguishing feature of many civil disputes which raises important questions about appropriate modes of dispute settlement. We will examine this issue more generally in the second part of this chapter. First we propose to consider three areas – personal injury claims, contracts between businessmen, and the divorce laws – which display a wide divergence between theory and practice.

Personal Injury Claims

The branch of English civil law concerned with the rights of an injured person to compensation is known as the law of torts. The civil wrong, or tort, which provides the legal basis for the vast majority of personal injury claims is negligence, defined as the breach of a legal duty to take care resulting in damage. Nearly 90 per cent of negligence cases are accounted for by injuries at work and road accidents. Yet of some 250,000 personal injury claims a year *only 1 per cent actually reach the courts* (see the Peason Report 1978).

It is worth dwelling on this last point because it immediately highlights the impracticability of litigating fully all but a tiny fraction of such cases, without causing the entire civil process to grind to a halt. They already constitute over half the entire workload of the Queen's Bench Division of the High Court. Even if there were no other compelling reasons – and there are several – administrative considerations alone would dictate other solutions. In fact, just under 90 per cent of all personal injury claims are dealt with by insurers. In other words there are pressures towards bargaining and the routinized processing of cases similar to those that we have seen at work in the 'negotiated justice' of the criminal law.

But before examining the contrast between the formal model of a tort action and the ways in which negligence cases are typically handled, it is necessary to sketch in the total context of accident compensation. For the shortcomings of the tort action have been partially concealed by the existence of other potential sources of aid. Many injured people will be eligible for industrial injury or other social security benefits, as well as being entitled to medical treatment under the National Health Service. The circumstances of the injury may justify payment by the State under the criminal injuries compensation scheme. Provision for sick pay by employers, occupational pensions, personal insurance, and financial help from trade unions and charities, family and friends, *may* be available to an accident victim.

As a broad generalization however, someone who has to rely totally on one or other of these sources will be considerably worse off than if he is able to obtain tort damages as an additional or alternative form of compensation. If he is wholly reliant on the Social Security system much will depend on the cause of his disability and the circumstances of its occurrence. If he is injured on the way to work, for example, he will not be entitled to industrial injuries benefit. Disability caused by accidents at work will be substantially better compensated for than the same degree of disablement due to accidents in the home, which account for over a million accidents a year, a third of the total number. People disabled either from birth or through illness or disease – who comprise the vast majority of the permanently handicapped – are in the main defendent on means-tested supplementary benefit. A bewildering variety of complex rules governs the level of state benefits and the somewhat haphazard way the 'system' has developed has created many anomalies. As was pointed out in the recent *Royal Commission on Civil Liability and Compensation for Personal Injury* (Pearson): '122 leaflets are issued to explain different aspects of the social security scheme' (p.37). Its unifying feature is that benefit is available as of right, according to the criterion of *need*. To obtain tort damages however one needs to prove that another party was at *fault*. As between two severely injured accident victims, then, the level of compensation may differ considerably for reasons of pure chance, such as the presence of a reliable witness at the scene of the accident.

We shall consider the various criticisms which have been made of the tort approach shortly. At this stage we need only note that dissatisfaction with the negligence action has led to its abandonment in New Zealand, in favour of a social insurance scheme, while in England the Pearson Report recommended a further shift of emphasis towards the social security model of compensation and called for more effective co-ordination between it and the tort system.

The fact that only 1 per cent of personal injury claims are resolved by the courts obviously means that a realistic account of how such claims are handled requires us to divert our gaze from the principles of liability and compensation to be found in the standard tort textbooks and to focus on the process of negotiation leading up to a settlement. Yet even this very necessary change of perspective does not fully convey the extent of the departure in practice from the formal model. This is because it presumes a degree of awareness of their rights on the part of accident victims which is often not borne out by the facts. In the nature of things, it is not possible to ascertain with certainty how many injured people are unaware of the right to bring an action for negligence. But survey findings point to a significant lack of 'claims consciousness' (Harris 1965; Abel-Smith, Zander and Brooke 1973; and see Atiyah, pp.203–06). The most recent information comes from the Pearson Commission's personal injury survey (1978) which found that ' . . . of those who thought that their injury had been caused by something another person had done or failed to do, some two thirds took no steps towards making a claim for tort compensation. Of these, about a fifth either did not know that they could claim or did not know how to go about it' (p.62).

Let us now assume that the accident victim is aware in general terms of the possibility of making a legal claim. He must still overcome what for many people are deeply entrenched cultural inhibitions about any contact with the law, as well as fears of excessive costs. Harris and Hartz, and Abel-Smith, Zander, and Brooke found respectively that 46 per cent and 43 per cent of the accident victims they questioned had not even heard of the legal aid scheme. It must also be borne in mind that the prospect of a court case is especially daunting for someone with no prior experience of court procedures, who may still be suffering from the effects of an accident. Ironically, the layman's very identification of the law with court resolutions of disputes is an additional hindrance. Much of his anxiety would be allayed if he appreciated that a trial was the remotest of possibilities.

But if he perseveres, and in many cases of accidents at work a trade union will provide legal services to members, he or his legal advisors must obtain evidence of fault. In practice, this can pose problems of access not unlike those which face someone accused of a crime who lacks the facilities to conduct a proper investigation. In an industrial accident the employers' insurers will be able to carry out their investigation on the spot, with access to records and technical expertise. The plaintiff may not have an opportunity to inspect the site of the injury for some time (if at all), when machinery may have been removed or replaced and witnesses are no longer available. In the case of road accidents the plaintiff is able to obtain the police report and witnesses' statements, but as we have noted, much will still depend on chance. Some drivers will fail to stop, either deliberately or unaware that they have caused an accident. Witnesses may be non-existent, unwilling to cooperate or ultimately unreliable, and the accident victim is seldom ideally placed to detain them. Even leaving aside such fortuitous factors, it may be intrinsically difficult to establish fault to the satisfaction of the court. It may be far from easy to prove causation in the case of a split-second car crash or a disease allegedly attributable to an industrial process. Even a marginal failure to do so could prove a very costly and long drawn-out exercise.

Another highly relevant feature of industrial accidents and, as we shall see, of many business contracts, is that they involve continuing relationships. Potential witnesses may be reluctant to testify against their employer, a foreman may be unduly influenced by the implications for him of a finding of negligence. The observation in the Pearson Report (p.64) that the adversary system is bad for industrial relations provides an instance of the crucial role of non-legal considerations when the parties have to look to the future. Even in an appreciable number of road accidents the parties in dispute have a pre-existing relationship, such that the prospect of litigation appears distasteful.

Considerations such as these inevitably point to out-of-court settlements in which it is clear that insurance companies typically exert extensive control, dictating the pace and often the outcome of negotiations. What takes place is a process of bargaining akin to business negotiations in which the methods and practices of particular insurance companies assume a central importance, and in which the insurance assessor is a key figure. How does he perceive his role and how does he achieve his objectives? To demonstrate his own efficiency in 'clearing the books' and saving the company money, he may try to persuade a claimant to agree to a quick settlement before he has received legal advice to hold out for a higher sum. The assessor's technical expertise and facility in creating the impression that the claim warrants only a small amount of compensation may meet with little resistance from the uninitiated accident victim who wants his money as soon as possible. There is an obvious parallel here with some aspects of bargaining at the police station to which we have already referred.

Naturally insurance company practice will vary. Most companies respond to an initial letter by or on behalf of a claimant with a stock denial of liability and a request for further evidence. But whereas the more responsible firms will often settle small claims in a reasonable manner, a few will put every obstacle they can in the way of reaching accommodation and employ delaying tactics as a matter of routine (Winn Report 1968, pp.25, 162–63).

In any event, the negotiations will often resemble a 'phoney war', if only because while there is every expectation of a settlement, the possibility of a court hearing cannot be ruled out. This fact of life points to a further gap between the formal model and the operative reality. The rules of civil procedure are geared to the possibility of an eventual confrontation in court. Apart from certain provisions about costs, they provide relatively few positive aids to settlement. Instead, particularly in the High Court where the more substantial cases are heard, the procedure consists of elaborate preparatory stages which supposedly 'clear the decks' for a (usually non-existent) trial. Despite rules that pay formal lip-service to a policy of 'cards on the table', in practice each side typically proceeds with the minimum of disclosure required, both to preserve its bargaining position and in case a trial should materialize. Yet the knowledge that a trial is unlikely also acts as a disincentive to building up costs by requesting detailed particulars of the opposing side's case. The very intricacy of the procedure gives an advantage to the party who can best afford both the time and money to exploit the rules to the full.

This is not to say that the rules of procedure totally disregard the likelihood that the parties will settle. In particular, if a defendant makes an offer of settlement by way of 'payment into court', the plaintiff will have to pay all the costs subsequently incurred if he refuses the offer, continues the action, and is awarded no more than the amount paid in. He is often well advised to accept, as the costs of the trial usually represent the bulk of the total costs. There is a further rule as to costs which provides a powerful incentive for parties to settle in most actions. Though the normal order made by the judge is that the loser pays the winner's costs as well as his own, this will not in practice cover the whole of the winner's expenditure. It is only his reasonably necessary or 'proper' costs that the loser must pay – those *necessarily* incurred after the writ has been issued. But prudent preparation of a case will involve more expenditure than this and successful litigants frequently have to pay anything up to a third of their total costs themselves (and may still face the prospect of losing on appeal quite apart from the risk of losing in the first place). As we shall see in the next chapter, the scope of legal aid has been too limited to make substantial inroads into these difficulties.

In principle the resolution of legal conflict without the parties having to go to court is socially desirable, as well as administratively unavoidable. A settlement can be a victory for commonsense and reasonableness; an impending court action can engender much bitterness more especially in an adversary system where law suits – particularly in the higher courts – have all the characteristics of a battle between the parties, in which the judge does not descend into the arena to take on the role of investigator, still less that of conciliator.

But ultimately it is the *fairness* of settlements which should concern us, rather than their volume. The greatest indictment of the common law negligence action is that it provides only an elaborate process for compensating adequately the few who succeed in what has been appropriately called 'the forensic lottery' (Ison 1967). Moreover it does this at great administrative expense:

> ' . . . the total costs of operating the tort system represent about 85% of the value of tort compensation payments, or about 45% of the combined total of compensation and operating costs. These are high figures by any standards, and more so in comparison with the figures of about 11 and 10%, respectively, which apply to social security compensation for the injured'
>
> (Pearson (1978): 64–5).

Accidents, many of which may signify little more than momentary inadvertence, are now commonplace in factories and on the roads. The tort action, designed for an earlier age, before the introduction of insurance, could at one time be more plausibly defended for its deterrent effect. It also still accords with most people's expectations that the person responsible for the injury should be formally accountable, even if he seldom actually pays. But the arguments for its retention seem inadequate when set against the various defects we have outlined. The truth is that the formal law envisages an unsuitable, protracted process which occurs in only a minute fraction of cases. It thus conveys an image of dispute resolution which distorts reality, *except* to the extent that decisions of appeal courts influence settlements. Both points are forcefully put by Atiyah:

'To stress that cases which are settled by negotiation are tort claims; that how negotiations are carried on is part of tort law; that the behaviour of insurance adjusters is important to tort law in the same way as the behaviour of judges is important to tort law; and that the levels of compensation which are agreed in settlements are a part of tort law in the same way that the levels of compensation awarded by judges are part of tort law; to stress all these things is not to suggest that what happens in appeal courts is not a very central and important part of the tort system. Naturally the way in which settlements are negotiated is profoundly influenced by what happens in courts; settlements are arrived at because of what the parties think would happen if their case ever got into court. Nevertheless, the process of settling claims by negotiation has as much right to be regarded as part of the tort system as the process of settling claims by trial' (p.227).

The Non-Use of Contract

The basic principles of the law of contract, as delineated in standard textbooks, evoke a world of laissez-faire economics peopled by litigious businessmen. The formal model has a pleasing, almost architectural quality. The student is led along a closely structured path in which he is shown first the various elements which combine to produce a binding agreement and then how misunderstandings, misconduct, or events beyond the control of the parties, may serve to destroy it. He is instructed in the remedies available in the event of a breach of contract and is thus equipped to pronounce on the respective rights and obligations of the parties. What he has not been taught, however, is how business activities are *actually* conducted.

In his Wisconsin study of non-contractual relations in business, Macaulay (1963) interviewed a number of businessmen (mainly manufacturers) and lawyers. His object was to discover how much use was made of the law in the planning of contracts and the extent to which sanctions were invoked to induce performance or compensate for non-performance. He found that while rational planning was characteristic of large-scale agreements for expensive or complicated machinery, in *routine* transactions large companies attached little significance to legal formalities, preferring to trust to a 'gentleman's agreement' and the proverbial handshake. There was widespread use of standard form agreements, many of which were not in fact 'contracts' in the full legal sense, and therefore not legally enforceable, because order forms and acknowledgement-of-order forms often contained mutually inconsistent conditions. The parties were either unaware of the anomaly or aware but unconcerned. They were far more concerned about the common understanding reached, and the terms customary in the trade.

Disputes were often settled without reference to the contract or to legal sanctions. It was common, for example, to accept the cancellation of orders without making a (legally sustainable) demand for loss of profit. Both buyers and sellers saw delivery dates as targets rather than firm promises, and there was a very marked reluctance to have disputes resolved in the courts.

A small-scale study of English engineering manufacturers by Beale and Dugdale (1975) broadly confirms Macaulay's major findings. They did however encounter more awareness of the technical failure to make a contract and some evidence of a tightening up of procedures to ensure that legally enforceable agreements were made. There was a tendency towards careful planning on *particular* issues – such as special payment terms – if the risk was seen as justifying it, while little attention might be paid to the rest of the arrangements. Beale and Dugdale's general explanations for the use or non-use of contract law were very similar to Macaulay's. Much of the aversion for legal measures stemmed from a fear of jeopardizing continued commercial relationships. Detailed planning was often deemed unnecessary where the parties regularly traded with one another and wished to retain flexibility in their dealings. Where there was a high level of common understanding about appropriate conduct, the cost of such planning was often felt to outweigh any risks associated with the transaction. Even where contracts did contain detailed provisions for various contingencies, such as defective performance, reliance on legal rights was less common than informal settlement of disputes. A company's natural wish to do business in the future and maintain its general reputation in the business community would often take priority over any desire to vindicate itself in respect of a particular transaction.

The importance of human interaction in determining the nature of agreements between businessmen is reinforced by the extent of their personal contacts, especially if these are social as well as commercial. The personal goals of those concerned in the actual process of negotiation and the pressures on them may have a conspicuous effect on the strategies they adopt. The salesman under pressure to meet his target, or the engineer engrossed in the problems of production may pay scant attention to legal niceties. Macaulay pointed to the importance of the balance of power in some firms between thrusting sales departments and more legalistic accounting departments as one determinant of policy on contractual planning and the use of remedies.

In addition to the fear that legalism and litigation can sour commercial relationships, many companies are inhibited by the cost and delay involved in taking legal advice and the nature of court proceedings, with the attendant publicity and exposure of the company's affairs. High level staff do not relish the prospect of spending valuable time away from their work during court hours or of having to submit themselves to the indignities of cross-examination. Thus Beale and Dugdale found that disputes over defective machinery or inadequate performance, indeed over all matters apart from simple non-payment, were overwhelmingly resolved by a negotiated settlement, often conducted informally by representatives over the telephone.

They also showed how the nature of the settlements usually arrived at reflected the primacy of continuing good relationships in the minds of the disputants. Rarely would there be direct money payments. More commonly a credit note would be given for spare parts, or any losses suffered would be taken into account in the next contract to be negotiated.

Firms not wishing either to negotiate a very detailed, formal contract, or to rely entirely on mutual understanding, may, of course, adopt various other strategies to minimize the risk of loss. Sellers might seek references, obtain a credit-rating, and/or take out bad-debt insurance; buyers will plan schedules to accommodate late delivery and diversify their orders.

Beale and Dugdale found that planning was most evident in regard to time of payment and that it was in the event of non-payment, especially in 'one-off' transactions, that legal procedures were most commonly invoked. This is partly attributable to the relative cheapness, speed, and simplicity of court proceedings in an action for a liquidated debt. Also, of course, where there is a serious bad-debt problem, there is correspondingly less incentive for the seller to wish to renew the relationship. It is interesting in this context to note the similarity in technique between this routine use of the county court and the bureaucratic office model of magistrates' court processing. For it is not adversarial dispute settlement which the court is providing here, but, in effect, the services of a debt collecting agency (see Abel-Smith and Stevens 1968). In 1978, over one and a quarter million (some 80 per cent) of the cases commenced in the county courts were for debts of various kinds (*Judicial Statistics* for 1978). Indeed, such a service was expressly envisaged by the original County Courts Act 1846, which was entitled 'An Act for the more easy Recovery of Small Debts and Demands in England'.

The Divorce Process

There are few areas in which the 'gap' between legal formalism and social reality is more pronounced than in the law relating to divorce. Because of the intimate and emotionally charged nature of marriage and family relationships, any legal framework, however much it aspired to accord with prevalent social attitudes, would be bound to encounter difficulties. The problems are particularly acute now that traditional conceptions of the family and the status of marriage are increasingly being questioned.

Within the last decade the law relating to divorce and the division of matrimonial property has undergone substantial change, reflecting alteration both in the moral climate and in the position of women (see Eekelaar 1978). But the social transition from a model of the family based on the concept of duty and rooted in religion to one increasingly concerned with the fulfillment of personal relationships is not without its tensions. Deep-seated traditional attitudes have found powerful expression in the ceremonial aspects of marriage and divorce, which have underlined the law's role of symbolic affirmation.

Even though, as we shall see, the recently introduced 'special procedure' ('divorce-by-post') provisions have considerably weakened the law's symbolic significance in the divorce process, the legal status conferred by marriage may still be crucial in determining rights of nationality, citizenship, inheritance, and maintenance. The perceived public interest in the status of marriage and the family, with all its ramifications, therefore prevents certain issues from being resolved without recourse to the courts. In matrimonial disputes the courts cannot be by-passed – as they can generally in contract or tort – except in the limited sense of *de facto* separation of the parties.

Yet many instances of marital conflict are classic examples of disputes between parties with a continuing relationship, the very situation where court resolution is arguably least suitable. Certainly where there are children, or where the parties have been married for a long time, the continuation of some kind of relationship after divorce is to be expected and, ideally, the law should encourage adjustment to the changed circumstances. But the very notion of 'divorce' in its root sense all but precludes this. In particular, the model of adversary trial is peculiarly inimical to the conciliation which, failing reconciliation, seems an appropriate objective for the law. For while it is true that the vast majority of cases are undefended, when the parties need not attend the hearing (in fact in 1978 of 153,720 divorce decrees, 148,765 were granted under the special procedure (*Judicial Statistics* for 1978)), the earlier stages of the process are often for tactical reasons conducted in a very hostile manner, with the protagonists sometimes impelled to adopt a more antagonistic stance than is justified by the circumstances. Granted that the decision to initiate proceedings frequently – though by no means invariably – argues a serious breakdown in the relationship, any prospect of salvaging it by reconciliation or post-divorce conciliation and adjustment is seriously impeded by the legal framework itself. Outraged solicitors' letters and pleadings replete with allegations and counter-allegations reinforce such hostility as the parties bear towards one another.

It is true that in many cases legal formulae do little more than reproduce in rather artificial terms the basic attitudes of the respective spouses. The 'gap' between form and reality may not be pronounced; the formalization of the hostility may even act as a safety valve for some spouses at certain stages of the proceedings. But where the gap has, of course, been a glaring one, is in the high incidence of rigged divorces, where those officially operating the formal system felt obliged to turn a blind eye to collusion, as in the trumped-up cases of hotel-room adultery prior to the Divorce Reform Act 1969. While today the reality of divorce given the liberal way in which 'unreasonable behaviour' (formerly 'cruelty') is interpreted is almost tantamount to divorce on demand.

A word or two of explanation is necessary about the law of divorce before and after the 1969 Act and it should be stressed that we can only provide here a bare outline of these developments, fully conscious of the possibilities of distortion in isolating the divorce process from the concomitant problems relating to children and financial arrangements.

Subject only to minor exceptions, until the 1969 Act the law of divorce was based on the concept of *fault*. The petitioner was normally required to prove that the respondent had committed a matrimonial 'offence', namely adultery, desertion for three years or

more, or cruelty (incurable insanity was an exception to the requirement of matrimonial misconduct. A wife could plead the additional
ground of unnatural offences by the husband). The petitioner's
(mis)conduct could also be relevant in that if, for example, he/she
had condoned the respondent's cruelty or encouraged adultery, a
decree of divorce would be denied. The rationale of this *fault* criterion was not unlike that in tort, it being seen as having the virtues of
accountability and deterrence, however misguided this may seem.

The Divorce Reform Act 1969, introduced in 1971, represented an
attempt to break away from the often destructive framework of
'guilty' and 'innocent' parties and replace it by one less calculated to
embitter future relations between the husband and wife and parents
and children. 'Irretrievable breakdown' became the sole ground of
divorce, to be established in one of five ways, including divorce by
mutual consent after two years' separation and unilaterally after five
years' separation (subject in *theory* to safeguards based on
hardship). But in practice there has been only a partial abandonment
of the fault approach. The old offence grounds of adultery, cruelty
(recast as unreasonable behaviour) and desertion, with minor modifications, remain as conditions entitling the court to find irretrievable breakdown. The number of divorces has risen dramatically
since the Act, but the offence grounds, especially now unreasonable
behaviour, are still the most commonly used. For example, in
England and Wales in 1978, of petitions based on a single condition,
some 34 per cent were for unreasonable behaviour, 27 per cent for
adultery, 25 per cent based on two years' separation, 9 per cent based
on five years', and 5 per cent based on desertion. One important
reason for the continuance of such a high proportion of fault-based
divorces is that blame remains a relevant consideration when appor-
tionment of property and future financial provisions are dealt with.
Under s.25 of the Matrimonial Causes Act 1973, judicial powers are
to be exercised 'having regard to [the parties'] conduct'. Though in
theory only 'obvious and gross' misconduct should be taken into
account, a 1974 study showed that a third of registrars took conduct
into consideration as a matter of course.

It is clear that the offence conditions also remain popular because
they do not require a two or five year waiting period. But it is equally
obvious that a couple who wish to end their marriage consensually
without that delay have a strong incentive to circumvent the system
by collusion. It is hardly surprising that many succumb to this temptation when the divorce process itself is typically little more than a
charade. In an investigation of 763 undefended divorces in 1973,
Elston, Fuller, and Murch (1975) found that where a barrister

represented the petitioner he or she had usually met him for the first time a few minutes before the hearing; 85 per cent of the cases took less than ten minutes and the judge asked no questions about the marriage in 73 per cent of the cases. The proceedings were often perceived as a mere formality if not a 'farce', and an expensive formality at that, costing from £100 to £200. Criticism was mounting as well at the large proportion of legal aid funds (80 per cent or so) that was being spent on matrimonial matters and in 1973 the Matrimonial Causes Rules were altered and a new special procedure introduced which by 1977 was to apply to all undefended divorces. In 1978, 97% of divorces were dealt with in this way, as against 66 per cent in the previous year (*Judicial Statistics* for 1978).

Eekelaar (1978) has described the current practice as follows:

'Under this procedure the divorce file is examined by a registrar and, if he is satisfied that the conditions for divorce are made out, he issues a certificate. The file is thereupon forwarded to the judge who must pronounce a decree *nisi* in open court. Neither party need attend. The function of the judge is reduced to performing an empty ritual. He may simply say, "I pronounce decree *nisi* in cases 1 to 50."' (p.143).

The pretence of carrying out a proper investigation into the conditions required by the substantive law for irretrievable breakdown are in effect cast aside. Legal *aid* is no longer available for divorce, though legal advice is available for the proper preparation of the documents. Cheap Do-it-Yourself divorce is fast becoming the order of the day:

'Essentially divorce has become an administrative process. Sentiment is satisfied by the solemn pronouncement of decree by a judge in a (possibly empty) courtroom. The choice of 'grounds' by the parties is simply part of the ritual. It has not the slightest relevance to the social or legal processes that take place' (p.144).

This last point was brought out in research by Eekelaar and Clive (1977) which revealed significant regional and culturally determined variation in the choice of conditions. So again we can see the importance of process and the objectives of litigants in determining how the substantive law is operated, or, to all intents and purposes, side-tracked. How one reacts to all of this depends on one's view of the appropriate role of the law in matrimonial affairs. Social interests may be as ill-served by the law abdicating *all* effective control, as by the intrusive, often bitter, and protracted defended divorce. Neither of these attitudes looks to the future. Both have destructive implications. The adversary model is apt to aggravate the wounds. The Do-it-Yourself model on its own may be too impersonal, mechanical, and abrupt to allow for the adjustment of the parties to their new situation.

It is true that the 1969 Act expressly provides for legal advisers to inform their clients of facilities for attempted reconciliation, but it seems clear that this is a dead letter – lip-service paid by the reformers to those opponents of the breakdown principle who feared that the institution of marriage was threatened by the proposed new law. Solicitors accustomed to a partisan role in matrimonial matters do not find it easy and may regard it as invidious to take on a different one for which they have not been trained.

Yet there are signs that the family law of the future will place much greater emphasis on mediation and conciliation. As the matrimonial offence is progressively phased out, so the perceived need for a formal framework of confrontation diminishes. Developments in several Commonwealth countries, notably in South Australia and British Columbia, herald a new characterization of the role of law in family matters, with the courts acting as one social service among many, encouraging client access for a whole range of domestic issues, within a structure of family courts providing a direct liaison to counselling services. The idea of family courts has been mooted in recent years in England, most notably by the Finer Committee on One Parent Families (1974). Though the proposal has not found favour with the Law Commission or Government, largely on financial grounds, it is widely recognized that the existing distribution of family-related matters over a wide variety of civil courts, not to mention the jurisdiction which magistrates exercize over matrimonial disputes falling short of divorce, is irrational. Tentative steps towards rationalization have taken place with the creation of the Family Division of the High Court and the recent Domestic Proceedings and Magistrates' Courts Act 1978 aimed at bringing magistrates' jurisdiction in line with the philosophy of the 1969 Divorce Reform Act. In the 1978 Act, for the first time a duty is placed on *the court* to consider if reconciliation is possible, and there is provision for a spouse who originally sought an offence-based order to change his/her mind and apply for an agreed order.

In the meantime, does empirical research provide any clues as to the most appropriate role for the law in matrimonial disputes? Some indications of client perception of legal processes can be discovered from a study carried out in Bristol (Murch 1977). One of the findings was that while most divorce petitioners (63 per cent) wanted their own solicitor to adopt a partisan stance, 45 per cent also believed that ideally his role should be that of a mediator and conciliator (p.636). Moreover, a surprisingly favourable view of solicitors as counsellors emerged, seemingly related to the absence of stigma in consulting them by comparison with marriage guidance counsellors. Because their perceived role is to advise clients of their rights and not to, as it were, treat them for presumed marital inadequacy, a degree of covert counselling is possible.

However, as Manchester and Whetton point out (1974), the lawyer's adversary stance is inimical to effective counselling, quite apart from the likelihood that he will lack the kind of skills necessary for it, or the time to devote to it. On the other hand, the possibilities of solicitors acting more frequently as a referral agency in matrimonial matters seems more plausible, or at least would do in a system where there was much more liaison and integration between them and appropriate social services, and in which the court was perceived as a forum for mediation rather than confrontation.

Aims and Methods in the Civil Process

CONFLICTING AIMS

Some of the limitations of legal processes for resolving civil disputes are unavoidable. Cost, delay, and inconvenience are inescapable elements of any machinery for settling disputes in a complex, industrial society. But one of the most striking features of the three areas we have looked at is the common failure of the adjudication process to provide the participants either with what they might reasonably expect from it, or with what seems a socially harmonious outcome. Here we wish to consider further the question of competing aims and how they are related to differing conceptions of the civil process.

Reasonable expectations of the legal process are in certain respects mutually inconsistent. We would like the system to operate 'justly' and efficiently and to produce 'just' and socially harmonious results. Up to a point these aims seem to be congruent. Results which are commonly acknowledged to be just should help to promote social harmony; lack of efficiency is almost bound to lead to injustice and social discord. But in various ways, the attempt to satisfy any one of these requirements is liable to undermine others and this remains the case however one tries to define the elusive concept of justice.

Let us assume for the moment that the notion of a 'just' result entails arriving at the *legally* correct, or at least more plausible, solution of a dispute. Quite apart from the sometimes ambiguous nature of both the legal and factual issues, their exhaustive investigation is incompatible with running an efficient system. Even assuming a rough parity of resources as between the parties in preparing a case, we have seen that bureaucratic needs and the interests of efficiency combine to dictate a very high incidence of out-of-court settlement, in which non-legal considerations enter. The elaborate preparation by a solicitor of one case often means delay, neglect, and thus a likelihood of 'injustice' in many others.

We have also seen that, in so far as it is taken to connote an outright 'winner' and an outright 'loser' – itself a highly questionable approach to the concept of justice – a 'just' result may not be in the long-term interests either of the parties or of society at large. A dispute can in other words be *decided* without being truly *resolved*. The legal victory of one spouse or businessman over another, or of a tenant over his landlord, may prove hollow and short-lived. The search for 'truth', or even for a technically correct disposal of the case as presented to the court, need not be seen as the only desirable aims of dispute settlement. Indeed, as we shall see, some important inroads have recently been made into our traditional conception of the civil process. First, in a few areas at least, there has been a shift away from adversarial techniques in the resolution of individual disputes. Second, though the dominant focus of the system is still on *individual* rights and obligations, tentative steps have been taken towards a broader conception of the civil process as a vehicle for achieving broader social and economic ends.

MODES OF DISPUTE SETTLEMENT

There are several models of dispute settlement, in most of which a third party exercises some degree of control over the proceedings. A judge or arbitrator, for example, has authority to impose a solution after hearing the evidence of the parties. A mediator hears both sides, in formal or informal hearings, and expresses a view which they may or may not accept. A conciliator acts rather as an objective negotiator, seeking to persuade both sides to trade and compromise their positions, without himself determining the rights and wrongs of the matter. Alternatively, the disputants may resolve their differences themselves by direct negotiation or bargaining.

In our legal system the classic approach is adversary-style adjudication, found in its purest form in the higher civil and criminal courts. Arbitration has a long tradition in England in commercial matters and a version of it has recently been introduced in the county court small claims procedure. Mediation and conciliation play an important role in industrial relations, notably now through the machinery of the Advisory, Conciliation and Arbitration Services (ACAS); while the institutional framework for combating racial and sex discrimination lays stress on initial efforts to resolve disputes through conciliation. We are here describing models only; it is clear that in practice there is considerable interplay between these various techniques.

THE ADVERSARY SYSTEM

> 'What is going on is a fight, a pitting of strengths and wits against each other, a display of aggression mitigated only by the ritual of a complex set of rules and conventions' (*Justice* 1974: p.18).

The notion of 'trial by battle' is deeply embedded in our history and has persisted from earliest times, when it was a literal reality, to the present day forensic contest, encapsulated in the image of two skilled advocates engaging in a war of words. Historically, the courts provided the public with a spectacle, an oral entertainment, in some ways akin to a sporting contest. The system then is fundamentally an 'adversary' one, conceived of as a gladiatorial contest in which the judge adopts a passive role, taking care not to descend into the arena (see *Jones* v. *National Coal Board* (1957)).

This non-interventionist stance of the judge is reflected in a distinctive feature of the Anglo-American civil law system, namely that the litigation belongs to the parties. It is for them and for them alone to choose the ground on which to fight. In modern terms it is a free enterprise model of dispute settlement. As Rapoport (1975) puts it, in the American context: 'The adversary system is a direct transplant of competitive economics into the apparatus of justice' (p.29). Under such a system, he argues, justice is unattainable, because the ability to win reflects the respective resources of the parties, which are mobilized to advance each side of the case to the limits allowed by the rules. For it is not only the trial which is conducted on the lines of a battle, but all the preliminary skirmishing which leads up to it. Tactical and strategic considerations will be paramount throughout; success may reflect the resources brought to bear and the proficiency of legal advisers as much as the apparent merits of the case.

It should be added that the 'winner takes all' basis of our civil law system, in which the loser nearly always pays the winner's costs, is in one sense difficult to reconcile with a 'just' result. Almost by definition, a dispute which gets as far as the courts for adjudication presupposes an arguable case on each side. To win a civil action it suffices to prove your case on a balance of probabilities. While the result may reflect only a marginal difference in the strength of the respective cases, it can impose a disproportionately large financial burden on the loser, both in terms of the damages awarded and costs. It would of course be naive to imagine that constructing a universally acceptable procedural framework for settling disputes is an easy matter, or that the intricacies of litigation are amenable to some simple formula which could eradicate the shortcomings of the present system. We are here mainly concerned to emphasize that the general ethos of the adversary system is unsympathetic to the view that legal processes might have important purposes besides the vindication of narrowly conceived individual legal rights, in an all-or-nothing fashion.

THE INQUISITORIAL SYSTEM

It seems appropriate at this point to draw attention, again in general terms, to the alternative mode of adjudication which prevails in continental countries, known as the inquisitorial system. Here the underlying theory is interventionist, reflecting a different conception of the purpose of the legal process, as a conscious searching out of the 'truth' rather than a game being played according to the rules. It would be misleading to draw the contrast too sharply. Not only do the lines become blurred in practice, but negotiated justice is a pervasive feature of the Anglo-American and continental systems alike, both in civil and criminal law (see Goldstein and Marcus 1977). Nonetheless, inquisitorial systems do differ markedly from our own in the amount of control they deem it legitimate for the courts and legal officials to exercise.

In France, for example, on the basis of a judicially supervised investigation of the facts, a dossier is compiled which incorporates the examination of parties and witnesses and, where appropriate, the report of expert witnesses appointed by the court itself. The actual trial rarely lasts more than an hour or two, as legal argument is confined to drawing inferences from the facts and law as they appear from the dossier. Unlike the situation in an English trial, there is little opportunity to challenge effectively the version of the facts revealed by the dossier. Such an approach encourages a more loosely-structured and wide-ranging initial investigation, which may be quite protracted. It is less circumscribed by technicalities of procedure and admissibility of evidence. Also, not being constrained by the parties' characterization of the issues, the court is formally entitled to take account of the public interest in reaching its decision.

Moreover, to the extent that judicial supervision displaces the initiative of the parties it can help to counteract the unfair consequences of their differential resources and differential access to legal services. In principle, such official intervention in the early stages of a dispute is more likely to promote an early settlement. On the other hand, there are obvious drawbacks to giving a judge extensive control over the investigation process if he is later to act as an adjudicator. In France, the judge who supervises the investigation is also one of the three judges who constitute the court.

It is interesting that conceptions of the litigation process which are different in important respects could have taken root and survived in societies with broadly similar socio-economic backgrounds. Yet some of the similarities in practice are equally revealing. We have already referred to the prevalence in both systems of negotiated justice, as one of the constraints of operating on a large scale. An additional practical consideration which has led to much of the work of magistrates' and county courts being conducted along what could be loosely described as 'inquisitorial' lines, is the fact that parties there are frequently unrepresented. The practical difficulty of compelling litigants in person to conform to abstruse technical rules of presentation means that, in their daily routine, these lower courts present something of a compromise between an adversarial form and an inquisitorial reality.

This relaxation of the formalistic requirements of adversary procedure has recently been taken a little further, with the introduction of small claims courts; while outside the orthodox court structure there has, over the years, been a substantial increase in the use of tribunals of various kinds to provide more informal means of resolving a vast range of legal disputes. It is to these developments that we now turn.

SMALL CLAIMS COURTS

In 1973, a small claims arbitration system was established in the county courts, as an alternative to normal trial (Administration of Justice Act 1973, s.7). Where the amount in issue does not exceed £200 (or, by agreement of the parties, up to the limit of the county court jurisdiction, currently £2,000) the registrar may order the case to be heard privately and without strict application of the complex rules of evidence and procedure (see Practice Direction [1973] 1 W.L.R. 1178).

It is up to the arbitrator, almost invariably the registrar, to adopt a convenient, informal procedure. He is expected to play an active role on inquisitorial lines. He need not confine himself to the evidence adduced by the parties and may, for example, use his own initiative to call for an expert report on faulty equipment, or help promote a settlement.

The new scheme reflects pressures to provide a cheap and speedy procedure for small-scale disputes over goods, services, and professional fees (see Consumer Council 1970). One of the major problems of small claims is that legal aid is not normally available when the costs of an action are disproportionate to the value of the claim. This in itself means that many litigants would appear in person which, as we have just noted, virtually precludes the court from operating along strict adversary lines. Though legal represent-ation is not excluded, its cost is not usually recoverable for claims under £200, so that litigants are encouraged to appear in person and costs are kept to a minimum. In 1975, when the no-costs rule applied to cases involving claims of £100 or less, they accounted for 91.2 per cent of all cases. 34 per cent of plaintiffs and 8 per cent of defendants were legally represented and in 7 per cent of cases both sides were. But in 36 per cent of cases both sides appeared in person.

The scheme began slowly, partly because a number of registrars were reluctant to operate the law in an inquisitorial manner, and though it has grown steadily the number of arbitration decisions remains relatively small (in 1978 there were 11,911). It is rather early to judge how far the system is achieving its aims. It has been suggested (Applebey 1978) that in cases to which the no-costs rule applies solicitors should be excluded altogether (as they have been in two experimental voluntary schemes set up in London and Manchester), because '[their] presence inhibits informality of the proceedings and may make it more difficult for the registrar to adopt an inquisitorial role'.

Ironically, there are grounds for believing that the scheme, essentially envisaged as an aid to consumers, is more often used by firms as claimants in cases of non-payment – 'consumer cases in reverse'. In 1975, for example, firms were defendants in only 24 per cent of all cases. The small claims court, like its parent the county court, was heralded as a forum for people of modest means. Yet it runs the risk of becoming primarily a debt-collection agency within a debt-collection agency!

TRIBUNALS

We now have a wide range of institutional methods for dealing with disputes in a less expensive and formal way than is provided by the courts. Many of them are voluntary grievance procedures for the investigation of complaints, where mediation is provided but enforcement powers are lacking – as in the case of ACAS, or the Press Council, or the various 'ombudsmen' who investigate allegations of injustice resulting from maladministration by central government departments, the National Health Service and local authorities. By far the most important mechanism however is the tribunal.

There are over 2,000 tribunals deciding more than a million cases a year. Many of them have extensive powers and much more bearing on the lives of most citizens than any courts of law, in matters as vital as health, housing, and financial security. How do they differ from ordinary courts? In particular, is there anything in the nature of certain disputes which makes a tribunal a more appropriate forum for them than the courts? If so, to what extent is this borne out by the actual division of labour between them? Is it an essentially rational one, or rather the result of a combination of historical, social, and administrative factors?

The sheer number and variety of tribunals makes generalization hazardous (see de Smith 1977: 528). They include ordinary court substitutes, such as social security tribunals, policy-oriented bodies, such as planning tribunals, and bodies which deal with questions of professional discipline, such as the General Medical Council. Historically, the growth of tribunals was primarily attributable to the development of the Welfare State, originating in the early part of the century with special bodies set up to handle disputes over health insurance, unemployment benefit, and war pensions, and expanding enormously after the Second World War. On the face of it, disputes of this kind, mainly between the individual and the state, are no less justifiable than those traditionally dealt with by the ordinary courts. But for a number of reasons they came to be treated differently.

First, just as we have seen that the volume of litigation in the courts is severely limited by administrative constraints, so too the large-scale introduction of social welfare legislation necessitated the development of an accessible and relatively cheap and speedy means of processing cases. The judges were on the whole ill-disposed towards this legislation, perceiving it as too overtly political and fundamentally concerned more with social engineering than the resolution of individual disputes. The unhappy experience of highly legalistic adjudication of workers' compensation cases between the Wars also suggests that they were ill-suited to the task. Labour governments in particular feared that judicial supervision would, in a period of marked literal statutory interpretation, obstruct their broad social aims, unless they could retain effective control over tribunals (Bell 1969; McCorquodale 1962). Also, the lack of expertise and flexibility in the ordinary courts in matters of planning, so crucial in the period of post-War reconstruction, pointed to the need for a new approach.

In the Welfare State, then, administrative tribunals became the primary means of deciding disputes between government and citizens. From the point of view of governments which encouraged their growth, there was much to be said for characterizing the work of tribunals as essentially within the realms of administration. And though some fears had been expressed in the 1920s and 1930s about 'administrative lawlessness', it was only after the Report of the Franks Committee (1957) that tribunals were, so to speak, re-characterized 'as machinery, provided by Parliament, for *adjudication* rather than as part of the machinery of administration' (para. 40). 'Openness, fairness and impartiality' were to be the hallmarks of their procedure and they were subjected to stricter supervision by the courts (Tribunals and Inquiries Act 1958).

By 1968, Abel-Smith and Stevens could assert that 'adjudication of a civil dispute by a court rather than a tribunal is more the exception than the rule' (p.221), and that: 'Properly understood tribunals are a more modern form of court' (p.228). The structure and functions of a hybrid such as the Restrictive Practices Court illustrate how the lines of demarcation can become blurred. Technically a part of the High Court and presided over by a judge, it also includes expert lay members and is self-evidently very much concerned with matters of policy. Abel-Smith and Stevens take the argument further, claiming that 'there is no fundamental difference between courts and tribunals', and advocate their merger. Policy-oriented tribunals may normally have more discretion than do courts, but no more, they point out, than the Chancery Division of the High Court in dealing with trusts or what is now the Family Division in its jurisdiction over wards of court. Conversely, some court-substitute tribunals can be as precedent-conscious as the ordinary courts.

On this view then the court/tribunal dichotomy is a non-issue. Decision making ranges from the highly rule-governed to the discretionary. To most lawyers, however, the courts remain distinct from other institutions however similar their functions. It is difficult to avoid the conclusion that the customary perspective of the lawyer on this matter owes more to traditional attachments and reluctance to acknowledge sufficiently the role of the judge as policy maker, than to rational assessment. Certainly to the applicant appearing before a tribunal these esoteric definitional distinctions may be virtually meaningless. Thus Frost and Howard (1977), researching into Supplementary Benefits and National Insurance Appeal Tribunals and Rent Tribunals, stress the 'essentially "conflict-oriented" nature of tribunal appeals', and conclude that:

> Despite attempts to humanise the tribunal setting, to demystify it and to make it more informal, the individual appellant operates from a position of powerlessness and finds himself ranged against powerful bureaucratic and private interests. It cannot legitimately be maintained that case-hearings are simply informal discussions, where the two sides come together on equal terms and the matter is arbitrated by an independent third party . . .
>
> Although the tribunal system constitutes an attempt to avoid the alleged disadvantages of a court system, the adversarial nature of the experience persists. (p.72).

One can find a similar discrepancy between the official portrayal of industrial tribunal procedures and the reality. The description of the process issued by the Department of Employment in 1976 was at pains to project an image which would relieve the anxieties of potential claimants: 'An industrial tribunal is not a court and bears no resemblance to one . . . No one is on "trial" and the general atmosphere is relaxed and informal.' Yet some accounts of actual hearings are at variance with this picture (see, for example, Forester, 1978) and employers and employees alike complain of excessive legalism and delay, not to mention expense.

Paradoxically, measures such as the introduction of 'Do-It-Yourself' divorce and the small claims procedure suggest that the County Courts are acquiring some of the informal characteristics more commonly attributed to tribunals, at a time when the increasing technicality of work in many tribunals is making them appear more and more like ordinary courts (see *Wall's Meat Co.* v. *Khan* (1979) *per* Lord Denning, M.R.: 'If we are not careful, we shall find industrial tribunals bent down under the weight of law books . . . '). If the Pearson Commission's proposals for strengthening the role of social security in accident compensation are implemented, the case for assimilation of functions would seem stronger still.

It is not however the question of the forum as such which matters. In any event, the County Courts as presently constituted can cope with only a minute proportion of the cases over which they currently exercise jurisdiction, and the workload of welfare tribunals alone is enormous and continually growing. What should concern us are issues such as the appropriate balance between the competing claims of rules and discretion in the process of resolving disputes and the closely related one of suitable representation for litigants. Thus despite the increasing technicality of the matters with which many tribunals deal, legal aid is not available in them (with the exception only of the Lands Tribunal and the Employment Appeal Tribunal). There is a large body of opinion which thinks that it should be, but also some apprehension that this might make tribunals even more narrowly legalistic. We consider the various problems associated with the provisions of legal services generally in the next chapter.

THE ROLE OF CONCILIATION

Tribunals, even when flexible, informal, and inquisitorial, are essentially concerned with all-or-nothing adjudication, in the same way as the courts. Whether the dispute involves a social security benefit, compensation for unfair dismissal, the refusal to grant a licence of some kind, or professional misconduct by a doctor, the appropriate tribunal will either uphold or dismiss the applicant's claim. We have seen however that in some contexts, more particularly where parties have a continuing relationship, all-or-nothing determination, far from effectively resolving a dispute, may serve to exacerbate it. To achieve a true 'settlement', or at least an acceptable compromise, techniques of conciliation and mediation can sometimes be more suitable.

In the abstract, procedures of this kind seem more attractive than adjudication. They do not artificially set out to establish one version of events as necessarily 'right' or 'wrong', but rather to encourage the conflicting parties to reach or work towards a mutually acceptable solution. Naturally, not all disputes are equally amenable to such an approach. There may not, for example, be a workable compromise between the granting or withholding of a licence. Nor are attempts at conciliation likely to prove successful unless there is already some measure of common ground, of shared standards, between the parties, as well as a willingness to seek an accommodation. Where such conditions do not obtain, an imposed solution may be the only practicable way of breaking the deadlock.

It seems to follow that the ideal system would have to provide for various styles of dispute settlement in a way which cut across established categories and paid more attention to the realities of any particular controversy. The approach might well vary not only according to the nature of the dispute and the disputants, but also according to the stage which the dispute has reached. We have noted that attempted reconciliation in divorce may prove fruitless in part because it often comes too late and has been undermined by the adversary proceedings which have gone before. It must however be conceded that as soon as one thinks in terms of operating a system, as distinct from focussing on a particular dispute, it becomes very difficult to visualize how the civil process as a whole could be adapted in this way.

In industrial relations, on the other hand, realism itself dictates a major role for conciliation, if only because imposed decisions deemed unacceptable by powerful unions are liable to be disobeyed. Conciliation has thus been a formal feature of the labour law scene since the Conciliation Act 1896 and has been further institutionalized with the statutory establishment of ACAS in 1974. Even earlier in the nineteenth century the Factory Inspectorate was performing a not dissimilar function in respect of breaches of the Factory Acts; while the introduction of the rent officer 'to dispel the atmosphere of litigation and forensic dispute' (Francis Committee 1971) was aimed at encouraging landlord and tenant to settle their differences without resorting to the full tribunal structure.

More recently, legislation on race and sex discrimination has laid stress on conciliation procedures, while at the same time granting certain powers of enforcement to statutory bodies through the medium of the civil law. We shall now take a closer look at this development and its wider implications for the civil process generally.

Racial Discrimination

The decision to invoke the law at all to combat discrimination met with considerable opposition. Legislation in this sphere is liable to be ineffectual and/or to lead to subtle forms of subversion or, in the case of race, even violent backlash. Criminal sanctions were not deemed politic and even civil ones too freely imposed were considered not to be conducive to improving race relations or diminishing sexual prejudice. An exclusively laissez-faire adversary approach is unlikely to make much impact, and is not applicable to certain problems, such as discriminatory advertising where there is no single individual victim. Specific instances of discrimination are also often difficult to prove. Consequently there has been a resort to institutional devices such as the Commission for Racial Equality (CRE) and the Equal Opportunities Commission (EOC) both to monitor the relevant legislation and to act as a catalyst for its implementation. The hope has been that the symbolic and educative effects of the legislation would go some way to obviate the need for direct enforcement measures.

The common law provides little protection against racial discrimination, limited as it was by its essentially passive character, deference to private contractual arrangements, and judicial reluctance to innovate. In the commercial sphere it afforded no protection beyond the narrowly interpreted duty of innkeepers and common carriers not to discriminate unfairly (*Constantine* v. *Imperial Hotels Ltd* (1944)). Indifference was only overcome after race riots had erupted in Notting Hill. The first Race Relations Act, in 1965, did little more than extend the common law duties of innkeepers and carriers. Discrimination was made unlawful only in certain specified places of public resort and though incitement to racial hatred was made criminal, the need to obtain the Attorney-General's consent to prosecute and to prove a specific 'intent to stir up hatred' rendered the provision largely ineffective.

A more comprehensive Race Relations Act was passed in 1968, making discrimination in the provision of goods, facilities, and services unlawful in numerous contexts. But, as we saw in Chapter 2 (pp.59–61), restrictive court decisions undermined the effectiveness of the Act. A Race Relations Board (RRB) was set up to investigate complaints and try to conciliate if it thought that discrimination had taken place, failing which it could take the case to court itself. But the Board lacked power to initiate investigations effectively, or to compel the production of evidence. A law had been passed, but without the institutional back-up to enable it to make any real inroads into the problems.

The 1976 Race Relations Act was designed to close some of the gaps. It reversed some of the more controversial appellate decisions, extended the definition of discrimination, and allowed scope for 'positive discrimination' in training and the creation of job opportunities. Perhaps most importantly, it added teeth to the enforcement machinery. A new Commission for Racial Equality was created to administer the Act, with both policing and investigatory powers and the task of promoting good community relations. The CRE may subpoena witnesses and documents; issue Non-Discrimination Notices and in the event of non-compliance obtain a court injunction. These powers, modelled on equivalent ones vested in the Equal Opportunities Commission under the Sex Discrimination Act 1975, are additional to the civil action for damages which may be instituted directly by the aggrieved individual. The CRE has the *power* (by contrast with the *obligation* of its predecessor, the RRB) to assist him (s.66), if the case raises a question of principle, or is unduly complex, or if it is unreasonable to expect him to deal with it unaided. But it is likely to use this power sparingly, since its prime

function is to launch a strategic attack on discrimination at the institutional level.

Not surprisingly, racial minorities have shown relatively little
interest in using legal machinery to air grievances. In 1976, for
example, there were fewer than 2,000 complaints to the RRB, of
which only 22.6 per cent were upheld. County courts have been loath
to find discrimination, and the same is true of industrial tribunals in
the context of employment cases. Neither venue is well-suited to
uncover the subtleties of much discriminatory practice. The Board
explicitly condemned the use of industrial panels which were
originally created to hear labour disputes and are staffed by
representatives of employers and unions who might be unsympathetic or indifferent to the aims of the legislation. The proceedings
tend to be brief and essentially adversarial.

Now that the individual will normally have to 'go it alone', it
seems even less likely that he will take proceedings (Freeman 1977).
As one commentator has put it: ' . . . the mind boggles at the almost
lunatic kind of courage an ordinary black citizen would need to go
into court on his own against lawyers employed by a large institution
on which his future may depend' (Legum 1977). The powers without
teeth of the RRB have been transferred to the individual, while the
CRE is expected to play the dual role of policeman and community
relations officer.

If the procedural structure is unsatisfactory, it would seem that
conscious modelling of the 1976 Act on the Sex Discrimination Act
1975 is largely responsible. Bureaucratic demands based on administrative convenience led to a facile equation of sex and race discrimination and a costly disruptive reorganization, in which the experience
built up by the RRB was lost and industrial tribunals, unsuited to the
work and already under pressure, were further overloaded: 'In all
this there was not one ounce of ill-will. Everyone was genuinely
striving for better race relations and an effective law enforcement
procedure. We failed because the process of consultation and
research was inadequate, so that the final judgement was half-
baked' (Legum).

We are concerned here primarily with the deployment of the civil
process in an untypical manner by legislative means. Any 'failure' of
the legislation to provide adequate procedural machinery is of
course secondary to the ultimate failure, which as Legum points out,
goes much deeper. It stems from the illusion that legislation to
prevent overt discrimination can prevent racial prejudice, in the
absence of social programmes designed to improve housing, education and job prospects, destroy myths, and overcome distrust built

up over centuries and culturally implanted. Nor can the issue be tackled effectively in isolation from other aspects of race relations such as the adequacy of our immigration laws. Discrimination is still common in employment and housing, though much less so in advertising and in places of public resort (see Chapter 6).

Sex Discrimination

Legal recognition of sexual equality has proceeded slowly (see Sachs and Wilson 1978). Until 1882 a married woman had no right to own property; everything she had belonged to her husband. Despite legislation which changed that rule, the husband usually continued in practice to be the sole owner or tenant of property and the only income was his. The first wave of feminism achieved the vote and some minor improvements. The first anti-discrimination law was passed in 1919, the Sex Disqualification (Removal) Act, which made it unlawful to bar women from public office on grounds of sex. But lacking enforcement procedures, it had little effect. Women were not given the vote on the same terms as men until 1928.

Discrimination, overt or subtle, has remained prevalent socially and has been reinforced by legislative anomalies, especially in taxation and welfare law. The second wave of feminism, equally militant, but more broadly based, was able to draw on sophisticated sociological and psychological explanations of less favourable treatment and we have recently seen, at least in principle, more far-reaching legislative change. The Equal Pay Act 1970 came into force in 1975. It requires equal pay and contractual conditions for men and women where their work has been rated as equivalent under a job evaluation scheme, or where a woman is employed on like work. Disputes and enforcement are within the jurisdiction of industrial tribunals. Also in 1975, the Sex Discrimination Act was passed.

The Act, subject to numerous exceptions, renders discrimination unlawful on the ground of marriage in employment and on the ground of sex in employment and other fields. Discrimination consists of relatively less favourable treatment, or victimization for use of the Act (or of the Equal Pay Act). It may also take an indirect form, when a limiting condition is imposed which in fact will have a discriminatory effect – such as an arbitrary requirement as to height in employment. The employment provisions of the Act are enforced by industrial tribunals. other complaints go to the county courts.

The working of the Acts is monitored by the Equal Opportunities Commission, which has wide-ranging powers to initiate investigations, assist litigants, conduct research, and generally promote equality. As we have just seen, its powers of warning followed by non-discrimination notices enforceable by court injunction were adopted as a model for the CRE.

The statutory role of the EOC includes 'working towards the elimination of discrimination'. But once a Quango such as the EOC is set up, how it interprets its mandate is very much its own affair, which serves to underline how important criteria of personnel selection can be in shaping enforcement policies. If it is too early yet to assess the EOC's achievements, there are already some indications of how it perceives its task. The evidence suggests that it has opted for 'cautious consensus-seeking with the emphasis upon educating attitudes rather than changing them by using its powers of enforcement' (Byrne and Lovenduski 1978: 161). Consequently, its successes have been in the politically less contentious fields – job advertisements, the practices of credit companies and building societies, and in the provision of advice to individuals.

Though the Commission has supported quite a number of *individual* complaints to industrial tribunals, it has made little impact on general patterns of employment, as affecting the lower paid, industrial training and promotion prospects. In these key spheres, the scrupulous political balancing in selecting members – a Labour chairman, Conservative deputy chairman, three TUC and three CBI nominees etc. – has had a predictably stultifying effect. Management is concerned about the cost of furthering sex equality and the unions are worried by the implications for male membership. In a system where industrial grievances are normally resolved through collective bargaining machinery, a case-by-case approach on discrimination is scarcely likely to have much impact.

In its first three years, the EOC issued no non-discrimination notices and conducted only two formal investigations, both as a result of external pressure. Limited resources and cumbersome procedures are partly responsible, though the similarly constituted CRE has been noticeably more active.

If one sets up a framework which combines opportunities for conciliation and enforcement, the role perception of the supervisory body is plainly crucial. It is not only courts which can operate in an active or passive manner in implementing the law. The EOC and the CRE have, in the words of Lord Denning, ' . . . inquisitorial powers of a kind never before known to the law' (*Science Research Council* v. *Nassé*, 1978). Perhaps they need to be far-reaching if real change is to be brought about, though, as in the context of race relations, one cannot expect too much from legislation alone. As the EOC observed in its first annual report (1977):

' When patterns of discrimination and exclusion have persisted for long enough, a self-sustaining cycle is set up in which the failure to provide equal opportunities results in a lack of motivation on the part of women, and this lack of motivation is then produced as a justification for the failure to provide equality of opportunity' (p.3).

But the Commission remains wedded to a policy of gradualism. It is instructive to compare this attitude with the more combative approach in the United States. As well as awarding compensation, courts are entitled to lay down quotas for female employees with which companies must comply at all levels of their corporate structure. There are positive requirements on affirmative action programmes to foster recruitment and promotion of women. The head of the American Equal Employment Opportunity Commission has been reported as saying that: 'No one who is serious about the equality of the sexes would advocate the British system' (Forgan 1978).

CHANGING PERCEPTIONS OF THE CIVIL PROCESS

The philosphy underlying the establishment of agencies like the EOC and the CRE marks a significant departure from the traditional view that our civil process is essentially a vehicle for resolving individual disputes along adversary lines. A comparable development in the consumer law field is to be found in the powers of the Director General of Fair Trading to have restrictive trading agreements investigated by the Restrictive Practices Court (Fair Trading Act 1973, s.35). As Jolowicz (1978) points out: 'The creation of specialised agencies whose powers or duties include the taking of civil proceedings involves the deliberate use of the legislature of the civil process in the pursuit of general social or economic ends' (p.226).

It is true that the use of the civil process to protect the 'public interest' – or even sectional interests – was not previously unknown to English law, but the scope for it has been very limited. As Lord Wilberforce indicated in *Gouriet* v. *Union of Post Office Workers* (1978), it is a 'fundamental principle of English law that private rights can be asserted by individuals, but that public rights can be asserted only by the Attorney-General as representing the public'. Power rests then in the Attorney-General to initiate such proceedings though it is rarely exercised. Individuals or corporate bodies may seek permission to bring actions in his name to protect the 'public interest', but the decision is within his discretion and a successful applicant has to finance the action, for which legal aid is not available. Since 1972, local authorities have had the right to bring proceedings in their own name, where they deem it 'expedient for the promotion or protection of the interests of the inhabitants of their area' (Local Government Act 1972, s.222).

Mention should also be made of the class (or representative) action. One reason for the more vigorous implementation of, for example, anti-discrimination legislation in the United States has been the use, or more importantly the threat, of this procedural technique to encourage compliance with the law by large corporations. By a class action is meant one in which a party seeks to protect a right which he shares with others. Such an action may be brought provided that all concerned have 'the same interest' in the proceedings. In England it has been used as a procedural device only, so that several parties with identical interests can be joined in the action. Its main application has been in enabling minority shareholders in companies to enforce a claim which the company itself will not pursue. More ambitious development of the class action is unlikely in the absence of public funding. Legal aid would hardly ever be available as the means of all members of the class would have to be taken into account (see Chapter 6 for an explanation of the legal aid system). Also, as American experience has shown, the class action can be cumbersome and expensive and can cause considerable administrative difficulty when vast numbers of people, not all of them readily identifiable, are affected by a single judgment.

However, it is also evident from developments in the United States that the class action can be an effective means of asserting group interests and broad social purposes. Seen in this light it:

'provides a method whereby the civil process is used to achieve more than the settlement of private disputes and the compensation of individual victims of unlawful conduct; it becomes part of the armoury of the State – not of the Government or of law enforcement agencies but of society as a whole – for ensuring compliance with the law'   (Jolowicz 1978: 222).

Suggested Reading

Atiyah, P. (1975) *Accidents, Compensation and the Law* (2nd ed.). London: Weidenfeld and Nicolson.

Beale, H. and Dugdale, T. (1975) Contracts between Businessmen: Planning and the Use of Contractual Remedies. *British Journal of Law and Society* 2: 45.

Coussins, J. (1976) *The Equality Report*. London: National Council for Civil Liberties.

Eekelaar, J. (1978) *Family Law and Social Policy*. London: Weidenfeld and Nicolson.

Farmer, J. (1974) *Tribunals and Government*. London: Weidenfeld and Nicolson.

Jolowicz, J. (1978) Some Twentieth Century Developments in Anglo-American Civil Procedure. *Anglo-American Law Review* 7: 163.

Justice (1974) *Going to Law*. London: Stevens.

Lester, A. and Bindman, G. (1972) *Race and Law*. Harmondsworth: Penguin.

Macaulay, S. (1976) Elegant Models, Empirical Pictures, and the Complexities of Contract. *Law and Society Review* 11: 507.

Rapoport, A. (1975) Theories of Conflict Resolution and the Law. In M. Friedland (ed.), *Courts and Trials: a Multi-disciplinary Approach*. Toronto: University of Toronto Press.

Runnymede Trust (1979) *A Review of the Race Relations Act 1976*. London: Runnymede Trust.

5

The Provision of Legal Services

Introduction

It is one thing to have a sophisticated legal system, it is quite another to make it accessible to the vast mass of the population. The biggest single indictment of our civil law – the most glaring gap between the law in the books and the law in action – is the contrast between what the system appears to offer and what it delivers.

We have given some indication of the common reluctance to resort to the law and a pronounced disenchantment with legal processes. Here we wish to examine how the nature and limitations of the services which lawyers offer are inextricably bound up with the organization of the legal profession itself, and what steps have been taken towards ameliorating the situation.

The kind of legal services we have reflects the social significance which we attach to them. The setting up of a Royal Commission on legal services in 1976 seemed, at least at the time, to mark a crucial turning point. Above all it signified that the profession's own conception of the lawyer's role in society was not immune from criticism and that more attention should be paid to the needs and wishes of the consumer. Zander (1978) has pointed to '...the growing recognition that legal services are becoming, or have indeed become, part of the bundle of benefits that modern states are expected to provide' adding that ' ... although there is (and will probably always remain) a great gap between the promise and the fulfilment, states now feel morally committed to applying resources to meeting the need for the services of lawyers' (p.19).

An analogy with medicine, provided it is not pressed too far, is instructive. It is possible to depict the law, at least in some of its functions, as providing a 'health service' to 'cure' social ills. Broken marriages, for example, as well as broken bones, require treatment. By introducing the legal aid scheme in 1949, principally to meet the increased demand for divorce consequent on the War, the government was proclaiming that the philosophy of the welfare state applied in some measure to legal services.

More recently, the development of a public legal sector, with the establishment of a number of state funded law centres, has revealed a previously insufficiently appreciated level of unmet need. In so doing it has prompted questions about the future role of the private profession, which continues to provide the vast bulk of legal services in the country. It is to the existing structure of the legal profession and its capacity to satisfy the general public's requirements which we now turn. But first it is instructive to consider briefly how people become lawyers in the first place.

Legal Education and Training

The process of becoming a lawyer is relevant to the provision of legal services, because it helps to perpetuate certain distinctive features of the profession which reduce its capacity to meet the reasonable expectations of the public. Academic legal education is markedly influenced by the profession's views on what it is appropriate for a budding lawyer to study. Vocational training and professional entry requirements tend in practice to restrict admission to people from a comparatively narrow social range, conspicuously so in the case of the Bar, with its profoundly traditional and conservative ethos.

The legal profession is overwhelmingly a graduate one, increasingly composed of law graduates. By granting partial exemption from professional examinations to graduates who have passed specified 'core' subjects (Constitutional and Administrative Law, Contract, Torts, Criminal Law, Land Law and Trusts), the Law Society and the Bar Council retain a measure of indirect control over academic law courses. We have referred earlier to criticisms of these courses for putting disproportionate emphasis on common law subjects, traditionally conceived, and on a narrowly analytical approach to legal study. We have also noted the recent attempts to broaden legal education. Clearly, teaching the law in context and the development of clinical legal education could help to create a broader conception of the lawyer's social role, especially in so far as such courses focus on the problems of the poor.

Just as tribunals have in practice assumed more importance for most people than the courts, so legal education is beginning to come to grips with previously neglected areas of law with which tribunals are concerned, such as housing, social security, and immigration. But it is very much a beginning. The bulk of academic law teaching reveals an uneasy compromise between a liberal educational ideal and vocational demands. As Zander observes, '... in spite of the undoubted improvements, legal education in most universities and polytechnics is somewhat pedestrian. Worthy, but dull, is probably a not unfair description of the average course' (p.144). The problem is in part one of resources. Within the limits of the standard three-year course it is not easy to impart, over a wide range of subjects, both the necessary analytical skills and a fuller appreciation of the role of law in society.

But quite aside from this difficulty, law departments are not immune from considerations of supply and demand. It would be unrealistic to expect a substantial proportion of intending lawyers to be motivated to apply their skills in fields not conventionally covered in, or at least not central to, private practice, especially on a long-term basis. At Sussex University, for example, one of the pioneers of a contextual approach, the course has, partly in response to student demand, been modified to include the 'core' subjects, thereby inevitably restricting the range of innovative subjects offered.

If there has been reluctance to innovate at the academic stage, vocational training has in the past been notoriously unimaginative and uninspired, demanding little more of the student than a very retentive memory and being largely devoid of exercises to impart practical skills. Several of the worst features of these courses have recently been eliminated, but despite new proposals (as suggested, for example, in the Ormrod Report, 1971) no radical restructuring has taken place.

The cost of becoming a lawyer obviously plays some part in determining the social class composition of the profession. This is notoriously the case at the Bar. The prospective barrister faces considerable expense in qualifying, maintaining himself during the twelve-month period of apprenticeship known as pupillage and often in his early years at the Bar (see the findings of a Bar Students Working Party, in Hazell 1978:76). This of course assumes that he is one of the approximately 50 per cent to be offered a place in a set of barristers' chambers. Practising from chambers is a prerequisite of a career at the Bar, which has the effect of limiting competition. The hazards are such that few will take the risk without access to private means. Solicitors during their apprenticeship as articled clerks face a much less daunting prospect, though their initial remuneration is also relatively modest.

The Organization of the Legal Profession

The most distinctive feature of the English legal profession is its unique and rigid division into two separate branches, and the practical consequences which flow from this. In 1976 there were some 28,000 solicitors and 4,000 barristers in practice. Despite their substantially similar academic qualifications and the similarity of much of their work, whether as advisers, negotiators and advocates, or in drafting documents, barristers and solicitors remain organizationally quite distinct. In general, advocacy and specialization are more characteristic of the Bar and routine office work more common among solicitors. But the differences have been exaggerated (Zander 1976). The majority of barristers do not in fact specialize, at least in the sense of pursuing a very narrow area in depth. Contrary to popular belief, their academic training is, if anything, somewhat less exacting than that of solicitors. Most of them concentrate on acquiring a measure of expertise and general competence in a limited number of broadly defined fields, such as crime, commercial law, matrimonial matters, and personal injury claims, or conveyancing and other property matters. Some rarely, if ever, appear in court. Conversely, a number of solicitors frequently appear as advocates in the magistrates' and county courts. They are not permitted to conduct cases in the High Court or Crown Courts (though since 1972 solicitors for the defence have been able to appear in Crown Courts on committals for sentence, or on appeals from magistrates' courts only). Yet the differences in jurisdiction as between the higher and lower courts are not drawn on functional lines but, broadly speaking, reflect the amount of money at stake in civil cases and the gravity of the offence in criminal ones.

Without impugning the high standards of the bulk of legal practitioners, it is difficult to imagine that someone asked to devise a blueprint for the organization of the legal profession would construct a system which closely resembled the one we now have. A whole network of restrictive practices persists, allegedly to preserve standards but often of seemingly questionable value when measured against the criterion of public interest in more competition and reduced cost. Yet precisely because it is the system we have, advocates of fusion or at least of less rigid separation, and of other reforms, are expected to provide elaborate justifications, while traditionalists need offer little more than dubious rationalizations of the *status quo*, coupled with blunt denials that criticism is well founded (for example, Leggatt (1976): 'The assertion that the two branches are of unequal status is quite simply false: the difference is of function'.)

But there are strong grounds for believing that the organization of the profession in its present form is conducive to, if it does not actively encourage, an inadequate service for the public as regards the preparation, conduct, and cost of cases. The potential for inefficiency is most strikingly exemplified by the high incidence of last minute instruction of counsel. Bottoms and McClean (1976) found that in 96 per cent of uncontested cases and 79 per cent of contested trials in the higher criminal courts, the client saw his barrister for the first time on the morning of the trial. It is not uncommon for unqualified solicitors' clerks with only a cursory knowledge of a case to accompany a client to court and for a barrister to conduct it on the basis of inexpertly gathered information. As Zander (1976) has commented: 'No self-respecting professional could claim that this is a proper way to run a legal service'.

Consider the position of a prospective litigant seeking advice in pursuit of a civil claim. First he must instruct a solicitor because he cannot approach a barrister for his services direct, even though the case may ultimately be conducted by one. Research on the location of solicitors' offices (Foster 1973) has shown marked differences as to their accessibility in various parts of the country. Stringent restrictions on the right of individual firms of solicitors to advertise have in the past made it difficult to find out whether a particular firm is well-suited to handle a given case, though in 1978 local law societies were given permission to publish information about the work undertaken by solicitors in their areas in local newspapers. Let us assume that the prospective client has overcome the initial hurdles and that his case is being dealt with by an able solicitor, well versed in the relevant area of law. Even then, it hardly requires an expert in organization and methods to appreciate the potential for inefficiency in a divided profession, if a barrister needs to be consulted. Since the barrister and solicitor operate from different premises, there is no single centre of operations for the preparation of a case. At the most mundane level, there is needless delay every time a necessary document chances not to be included in the instructions to counsel or an inexperienced, unqualified clerk sends him incomplete information. This is quite apart from the delays of correspondence in general. Also, because the division of labour is not in all respects precise, there being no clear-cut dividing line between fact-gathering and legal analysis, there is the all-too-human tendency for each to assume that a particular matter is being dealt with by the other. The result is occasionally painfully apparent at conferences, held invariably at the barrister's chambers. The absence of continuity and true cooperation in the barrister/solicitor relationship is accentuated by the deferential stance which the latter, however well-informed, is called upon to assume, while the barrister has the consultant's role. The client who by this time may have paid several visits to the solicitor's office, to see 'his' lawyer, is often understandably disconcerted, if not exasperated, by the apparent lack of coordination, the duplication, and the need to reiterate the same information.

As well as its potential for inefficiency, it is difficult to see how such a system can avoid inflating the cost of litigation, at least as a general rule. It is true that the overheads of running a solicitor's office are higher than those of barristers' chambers and that in a fused system more work would be undertaken in the equivalent of solicitors' firms. But it is likely that this would be more than offset by minimizing the existing tendency of solicitors to resort to counsel unnecessarily, with its attendant costs of communication, and by cutting down on the number of cases where two or sometimes three separate fees have to be charged.

What are the main arguments put forward in support of the present division within the profession? It is said to promote detachment in the assessment and conduct of cases. It helps sustain the 'cab rank' rule, according to which barristers must accept any brief offered to them, thus embodying the principle of equal facilities being available to all. It ensures the survival of a separate, independent body of legal practitioners, whose expertise is readily identifiable and who are able to provide a specialist service, including that of skilled advocacy, to all solicitors and hence to the general public. Finally, the existence of a small, close-knit group of practitioners with whom the judiciary has common understanding, facilitates the efficient administration of justice and the maintenance of high professional standards.

These contentions are not without some force, but they are liable to be pressed too far. Detachment, for example, is plainly an essential virtue in the handling of a case, and one which a solicitor's closer involvement with the client may make it more difficult for him to achieve. On the other hand, it can in practice, as we have noted, preclude fruitful collaboration between a client's legal advisers, and convey to the client an impression of lack of concern.

The effectiveness of the 'cab rank' rule is limited in two important respects. First, because a client cannot go straight to a barrister, solicitors can sift out unwelcome clients. Second, the distribution of work in barristers' chambers is controlled to an extent not appreciated by the general public by the chambers' clerk, 'a complicated cross between a theatrical agent, a business manager, an accountant and a trainer . . . ' (Megarry 1962:55). The senior clerk is almost invariably paid on a commission basis. This not only gives him an undesirable interest in the fees which it is his job to negotiate and in the allocation of work within the chambers, but highlights the fact that competition at the Bar is as much between sets of chambers as between individual barristers.

More fundamental is the question of whether the quality of services provided by the Bar would be lowered to an unacceptable degree in the event of fusion. We have noted that the Bar consists of a mere 4,000 or so practitioners, most of whom do not really specialize (indeed over half of all practising barristers are of less than ten years standing). Consequently, much of the work in complex areas such as tax and company matters has either become the province of accountants or is handled by the large City firms of solicitors who have their own specialists. In any event, the significance to be attached to expertise in advisory and forensic matters is partly a function of one's social priorities in the provision of legal services. Undoubtedly the present arrangements result in very high standards in the more complex, elaborate, and expensive law-suits. But these remain overwhelmingly the preserve of institutional and other wealthy litigants. In the bulk of cases, the end result is not determined by highly skilled advocacy or exceptionally expert advice as much as by the merits of the case, as assessed by the judges.

Nor is fusion incompatible with a considerable amount of specialization, as is apparent from the organization of several other legal systems. In fact the use of the term 'fusion' has made this whole issue unnecessarily acrimonious, insofar as it is suggestive of compulsion. There is not, nor could there be, any question of lawyers being required to engage in particular areas of work. The question is rather whether the existing rigid lines of demarcation are on balance beneficial. *Justice* (1977) in a report based on its evidence to the Royal Commission, pointed to the merits of a gradual 'convergence' of functions, beginning with easier transfer between the two branches of the profession. It is in any event unlikely that a very pronounced shift in occupational roles would result from whatever changes took place. However, convergence could help reduce the inefficiency of the present system.

It has been suggested that the controversy over fusion has in any event been unduly concerned with parochial demarcation disputes, thereby concealing possible broader, long-term implications for the very nature of our procedural system. Mann (1977) has argued that the distinctive features of our trial process – the emphasis on orality, the single and continuous hearing, and the heavy responsibility of counsel to place all the relevant legal arguments before the court –

can only flourish given a separate Bar. Fusion, in his view, would entail a move towards the continental reliance on written materials and extensive judicial involvement in the analysis of the legal issues. Such a shift may well, of course, be desirable and we have touched on the differences between these conceptions of the legal process in Chapter 4. But it is far from clear that a dramatic transition would ensue, at least if we are correct in assuming that fusion or limited steps towards it would not unduly affect specialization in practice.

In addition to the division of the profession itself, a number of specific restrictive practices have been the subject of criticism in recent years. Perhaps the most contentious has been the statutory monopoly exercised by solicitors over preparing the instrument of transfer in conveyancing. Lord Devlin (1978) has asserted that: 'The bugbear of landlaw is the ridiculous conveyance, which survives as the only way yet devised of giving solicitors a decent living' (*Observer* 1978). In fact, by 1976 conveyancing fees totalled £300 million, representing one half of the total income of solicitors. It is beyond the scope of this book to examine the technical details of the controversy. Suffice it to say that the complexities of English landlaw are such that the occasional transaction presents difficulties which only a skilled conveyancer can cope with. Much conveyancing however is capable of being and is dealt with by relatively untrained staff. Solicitors' charges for conveyancing have often been attacked as disproportionately high (Prices and Incomes Board 1968; 1971; Joseph 1976; see also Bowles and Phillips 1977) and their monopoly has recently been challenged by the rise of cut-price concerns. Public disquiet was reflected in the specific inclusion of the issue in the terms of reference of the Royal Commission, though in the event it rejected the suggestion that licensed conveyancers should be permitted to set up in competition with qualified solicitors, as has happened in South Australia.

In the case of the Bar, one of the more notorious restrictive practices, the two counsel rule, under which a Queen's Counsel was not permitted to appear in court without a junior barrister, was abolished only in 1977. We have already referred to the monopoly over the rights of audience in the higher courts. There are also several rules relating to fees which have provoked criticism, such as the rule that a barrister may keep the whole of his agreed fee (fixed in advance of the case, except for legal aid work) even if the case is settled.

But our concern is not simply to enumerate restrictive practices and elements of monopoly. It has to be acknowledged that they are common to professions generally. In the legal profession however, it is hard to resist the conclusion that an antiquated and cumbersome structure stands in the way of providing the public with an adequate service. Recent confirmation of this impression can be found in a critical survey of the Bar written, significantly, by a number of barristers (Hazell 1979), which has been described as 'almost the first crack in the determined resistance against change that has been maintained by a small rearguard of practitioners with the supine acquiescence of the great majority of others' (Lord Goodman 1979). But when one is considering the use made of legal services there are far more intractable problems than those to which we have so far referred. The various proposals for the reorganization of the private profession would not significantly increase the small proportion of the population who can afford those services, nor could they mean anything to citizens who are not even in a position to appreciate that they have a problem which may require a lawyer. In the words of the *Justice* Report (1977):

'Lawyers tend to assume rather too readily that the man in the street, even though he will not know what the answers are, will at least be able to frame the right questions. In fact this is not so. The great majority of the population, even today, is ignorant not only of what the law is, but of how it works, what is its scope, what it can do and what it cannot. To most, The Law connotes only the police and the criminal courts, and lawyers are remote and expensive people to be avoided unless one is in serious trouble on a criminal charge. We doubt whether more than a small proportion of any random sample of people in this country would have even the vaguest concept of 'civil law', let alone the difference between that and criminal law' (p.4).

It is to the problems implicit in the above passage and the attempts to deal with them that we now turn.

Unmet Need

Current research into the provision of legal services is centrally concerned with what has become known as 'the problem of unmet need' (Morris, White, and Lewis 1973; Abel-Smith, Zander, and Brooke 1973). This ambiguous phrase has been the source of much confusion. Not only is 'need' clearly a relative notion, but what is described as a need for legal services often, on analysis, dissolves into the much broader concept of 'social need'.

The debate over 'unmet need' is in some respects akin to the general controversy over the appropriate orientation of the sociology of law. The 'problem-solving' liberal reformer is naturally disposed to seek a solution through the provision of more legal services and extending the legal aid system, all broadly within the context of the existing social structure. Others have argued that most of the 'legal' problems of those with least access to the law either are, or at least directly stem from, social problems, and are better treated as such. On this view, only cosmetic solutions are possible in the absence of a restructuring of social institutions, or at least a redirection of social priorities. Linked to this difference in approach is the different degree of emphasis placed on meeting individual and group needs. The legal system is best adapted to settling individualized disputes and ill-suited to satisfying the claims of socially disadvantaged groups. As we shall see, much of the controversy surrounding the development of law centres has concerned the extent to which they see themselves as a force for social change rather than as a more accessible alternative to traditional firms of solicitors for individual citizens.

It is fruitless to look for a consensus on what is meant by 'need' in the abstract. It has been shown (Feldstein 1967:193) for example, that if the number of hospital beds is increased, so is the average length of stay in hospital – 'medical need' is redefined. Similarly, limited national resources severely restrict the amount of money which governments are willing and able to allocate so that people's rights can be more effectively obtained. The individual citizen's perception of his need for legal services is also affected by his own resources, priorities, and expectations. But if there can be no consensus on the level of unmet need, there is considerable agreement on the most common reasons for people's legal rights going by default. Ignorance, apathy, inability to identify the appropriate agency to approach, fear or suspicion of any contact with lawyers and of the possible cost, the inaccessibility of solicitors' firms due to their location, office hours, and uninviting premises, and their unsuitability for dealing with welfare problems – such factors are frequently cited.

This sheer variety of causes calls for imaginative and varied responses. Among these is the dawning realization that a need for legal services is not necessarily to be equated with a need for the services of lawyers, and much attention is now focussing on the potential role of para-legals. The ambiguity of the phrase 'unmet need' is not solely attributable to the elusiveness of the concept of need. One must also consider what is involved in the notion of a need being 'met'. In certain areas of law it is increasingly being argued that adequate help can be provided through the participation of laymen. Nor need this imply a layman effecting a legal solution. Merely because a problem admits of a legal solution, it does not necessarily follow that an alternative approach would not meet someone's need as well or better. Every day of the week social workers, for example, are resolving issues relating to the custody of children, or eviction, without regard to possible legal procedures, either through simple ignorance of the law or a calculated decision on the perceived *needs* of their clients. First, however, let us see what progress has been made to date in the provision of effective legal assistance.

Legal Aid

Until some thirty years ago there was no systematic provision of legal aid by the State. The poor could look only to whatever makeshift charitable services existed. Historically there had been sporadic, half-hearted attempts to make the courts more accessible to them. As far back as 1495, a procedure known as *in forma pauperis* was instituted for civil cases, but it had little impact in practice. Only plaintiffs were eligible and a strict means test was applied. Nor was the procedure extended to the system of County Courts established in the nineteenth century. Heralded as the new poor man's courts, they proved most effective as a convenient means of satisfying the commercial requirements of the middle classes for a cheap debt enforcement agency.

The growing demand for cheaper legal services was reflected at the turn of the century in the development of a number of 'legal aid' societies, which operated on a commission basis. Faced with opposition from the Law Society, they led a precarious existence and proved short-lived. The *in forma pauperis* procedure was replaced by the Poor Persons Rules; in 1925, public funds, controlled by the Law Society, were made available to cover the cost of administration. But the legal work itself was still financed on a charitable basis and the inadequacy of the arrangements became steadily more apparent. Eventually, the combined effect of a relaxation in the divorce laws in 1937, increased demand for divorce with the advent of the War, and a legal profession reduced to almost a third of its strength, impelled the Government to establish a Services Divorce Department employing salaried lawyers. This allocation of public funds for lawyers conducting litigation amounted to official acknowledgement that legal aid should, within limits, be available as of right and not as charity. Against a background of substantial social reform in the immediate postwar years, the Legal Aid and Advice Act 1949 established a state-funded scheme for civil litigation (see Pollock 1975).

Administered by the Law Society, the scheme now covers virtually all courts, though not tribunals. The proposals for legal advice, as distinct from court representation, were not initially implemented, but provision for it was substantially improved in 1972. A further proposal contained in the Legal Advice and Assistance Act 1972 (see now Legal Aid Act 1974) for the setting up of law centres by the Law Society has not been implemented, government funding not having been forthcoming. To qualify for civil legal aid an applicant must satisfy a committee of lawyers that he has a reasonable prospect of success in a case which, in all the circumstances, it is reasonable to pursue. He must also be eligible on financial grounds. Legal aid is provided free for those who have very little by way of disposable income and capital and subject to contributions on a sliding scale for people of moderate means. 'Disposable income' is what remains after tax, national insurance, housing costs, and certain other deductions, including allowances for dependants, are made.

Criminal legal aid was for centuries confined to the system of 'dock briefs', under which an accused, on payment of one guinea, was entitled to representation by any barrister present in court. Needless to say, the absence of any real preparation in such cases made for an inadequate service, quite apart from the fact that many prisoners could not afford the fee. In 1903 the Poor Prisoners' Defence Act made some provision for representation in the higher criminal courts, but only if the accused disclosed his defence. In 1930 this requirement was dispensed with and legal aid was extended to magistrates' hearings. Today criminal legal aid is granted subject to a means test and provided that it serves 'the interests of justice'. Though over 90 per cent of all applicants obtain it, in the magistrates' courts a substantial number of defendants do not apply and, as appears from evidence to the Royal Commission on Legal Services, many courts have adopted an unduly restrictive approach.

Legal advice and assistance, also means-tested, is available under the Green Form Scheme introduced in 1973. It covers up to £25 worth of work by a solicitor (the amount may be increased on application), which may now include written advice, the conduct of negotiations, and perusal of documents. It has been used primarily for matrimonial problems. A voluntary scheme has also been introduced to provide half an hour's advice for £5.

Public expenditure on civil and criminal legal aid has grown to reach a total sum of £81 million for 1977–78. (In 1977 there were 297,000 legal aid orders for proceedings in magistrates' courts and 97,000 for Crown Courts; in 1977–78 149,000 legal aid certificates were issued for civil proceedings, and some 300,000 cases handled by lawyers under the Green Form Scheme). It is now available in virtually all courts and for all types of legal proceedings, with only a few exceptions, most notably defamation. Yet because of limited resources and the effects of inflation, the proportion of the population for whom it has catered steadily decreased until very recently.

Though the scheme was introduced at a time of relative austerity, in 1950 approximately 80 per cent of people were eligible for civil legal aid on grounds of income, more than twice as many as in 1978. It has been estimated that the proportion of households with children who qualified declined between 1964 and 1974 from 64 per cent to 23 per cent. The income limit for free legal aid was until recently only just above the level of supplementary benefits. In all, in 1978, no more than a quarter of the working population was eligible for legal aid.

It is this state of affairs which has often prompted the assertion that only the very rich or the very poor can afford to go to law. The truth has been, if anything, bleaker still. For while the financial limits undoubtedly penalized people of moderate means, the contribution levels of many *within* the scheme equally constituted a disincentive to taking proceedings (Partington 1978). It was widely acknowledged that a substantial allocation of resources was needed to raise the means test levels and reduce contribution levels. The Legal Aid Act 1979 signalled a distinct improvement. As we saw in the previous chapter, now that the special procedure for divorce has been extended, necessary assistance is made available under the Green Form procedure, releasing an estimated £6 million. Under the current provisions some 70 per cent of households with two children are eligible, over 30 per cent of whom need make no contribution, and the financial conditions for the Green Form scheme have also been improved.

Inevitably there are still several features of the scheme which could be improved by more financing. Presumably the underlying rationale of legal aid is that, so far as possible, people should not be prevented from exercising their legal rights through lack of means. The absence of legal aid in tribunals, with their ever-increasing and increasingly complex workload, is therefore arguably the outstanding anomaly. At present, trade unions and citizens advice bureaux cope with quite a number of cases in tribunals, but the evidence to the Royal Commission on Legal Services was overwhelmingly in favour of providing legal aid in them, at least for more complex matters, and the Commission has made recommendations to this effect.

Concern has also been voiced about various aspects of the

Table 1
The gross income of persons entitled to legal aid, either free or on payment of contributions, based on the increases in the financial limits brought into effect on 6 April 1979

Type of applicant	Income from all sources before deduction of Income Tax, National Insurance Contributions, and Rent	
	Maximum permitting free Legal Aid	Minimum which makes applicant ineligible for Legal Aid
single person	£2,530 (£48.65 pw)	£6,003 (£115.44 pw)
married couple	£3,733 (£71.79 pw)	£7,112 (£136.77 pw)
married couple 1 child aged 4	£4,145 (£79.71pw)	£7,500 (£144.23 pw)
married couple 2 children aged 4 and 8	£4,673 (£89.87 pw)	£7,992 (£153.69 pw)
married couple 3 children aged 4, 8 and 13	£5,523 (£106.21 pw)	£8,774 (£168.73 pw)
married couple 4 children aged 4, 8, 13, and 15	£6,420 (£123.46 pw)	£9,556 (£183.77 pw)
married man apart from wife, paying £650 per annum court order	£3,250 (£62.50 pw)	£6,677 (£128.40 pw)
single parent with 2 children aged 4 and 8	£3,034 (£58.35 pw)	£6,575 (£126.44 pw)
single parent with 3 children aged 4, 8, and 13	£3,816 (£73.38 pw)	£7,366 (£141.65 pw)

Note: The examples in the above table are intended to be illustrative only and are based on the assumption of the Supplementary Benefits Commission making appropriate allowances for income tax, national insurance contributions, and an allowance of £416 (£8 weekly) for all sums paid by the applicant in respect of rent or its equivalent.

operation of legal aid in practice. On the civil side, the mode of assessment of financial eligibility has been criticized as unduly technical and time-consuming. The fact that applications have had to be submitted to the Supplementary Benefits Commission as well as the legal aid committee has added to the bureaucratic nature of the exercise. While the broad discretion of magistrates or their clerks in granting or withholding legal aid in criminal cases has evoked criticism in view of disparities in the policies of different courts (see Levenson 1979), even, in early 1979, prompting a public demonstration by lawyers outside Highbury Corner Magistrates' court.

But the limitations of legal aid are not confined to the problems of applicants in obtaining it. A major drawback is the financial difficulty experienced by those firms of solicitors for whom it represents a substantial proportion of their practice. The relatively low fees for much legal aid work and the bureaucratic complications, which in turn delay payment, make many solicitors loath to undertake it (see the findings of an experimental practice established in 1977 by the local law society in Manchester to assess the viability of new inner city practices and demand for legal services, Manchester Law Society 1979; and Hodge 1979). According to the legal aid statistics, fewer than one in five solicitors' offices contain the equivalent of one full-time worker on civil legal aid.

It is easy enough in the circumstances to understand the scepticism of those who doubt the capacity of the private sector to satisfy the public need for legal services. Indeed, the workload which many individual solicitors voluntarily undertake on citizens advice bureaux rota schemes, duty solicitor schemes, and at other advice centres, out of office hours, merely emphasizes the extent of the demand. Moreover, we have made only passing reference to the large number of people of moderate means who fall outside the eligibility limits for legal aid. Most litigation is too expensive for them to finance from their own resources. Are there any ways of remedying this defect?

One possibility would be to permit lawyers to operate on a contingent fee basis, a practice prohibited in England, but a common method of financing claims for damages in the United States. The lawyer agrees not to charge a fee if he loses, but to take a percentage of the court's award if he wins. This speculative approach to litigation has traditionally been strongly opposed by the English legal profession as rank commercialism. For the lawyer to have such a vested interest in the outcome of the case is considered contrary to public policy. It is argued that such a system would encourage lawyers to charge exorbitant fees and to undertake only cases they seemed likely to win. Also, under the English system, a losing plaintiff pays the defendant's costs and it would be unreasonable for the defendant's entitlement to costs to be affected by the plaintiff's financial relationship with his lawyer.

Some of these dangers are far from insuperable. Fees can be regulated. Doubtful cases could be financed as at present, the contingent fee system existing as an alternative only. But there would still be the problem posed by the lawyer's financial interest in the outcome, and the successful defendant's costs. A possible solution has been mooted by *Justice* (1977), namely a Contingency Legal Aid fund. Lawyers would be paid by the fund for acting in a claim for damages, whether they won or lost. The fund would have a power to reject hopeless applications and would be financed by winning litigants paying a proportion of their awards into it. Such a scheme would avoid the worst excesses of the United States system.

In effect, this proposal is aimed at supplementing the legal aid scheme by employing insurance techniques to help potential plaintiffs of average means, seeking monetary awards. A contingent fee approach is of no avail to defendants and is inappropriate for other kinds of legal dispute. There is, in principle, no reason why more extensive use should not be made of insurance in financing litigation. One or two insurance companies already offer cover for legal costs and expenses incurred in pursuing or defending a variety of civil claims. However, for most individuals, the possibility of having to pay legal costs as a result of litigation is too remote a prospect to make this a likely solution on a large scale.

As indicated at the beginning of the chapter, there are a number of reasons why many people never reach or even contemplate going to a solicitor's office. The provisions for legal aid and advice which we have outlined are of value only insofar as they are used. We must now consider what efforts have been made to further this end.

Law Centres

In America in the 1960s the idea of using legal services as a means of effecting social change was given concrete form. The Legal Services Programme, under the aegis of the Office of Economic Opportunity, played a strategic role in the Government's 'war on poverty'. It established neighbourhood law firms in deprived urban areas, in an effort to reach those people least likely to seek legal assistance. These firms gave a high priority to fighting test cases, with the express aims of exposing institutional abuses and improving the conditions of the socially disadvantaged.

This programme proved to be a catalyst for the development of law centres in this country. In 1968 the Society of Conservative Lawyers were in favour of subsidizing private firms willing to practise in deprived urban areas, failing which they tentatively suggested small-scale experiments with American-style neighbourhood law firms. At the same time, the Society of Labour Lawyers (1968) was advocating the establishment of state-funded centres with salaried lawyers. The Law Society initially expressed opposition to this approach, which it argued would, at great expense, introduce a second-rate and socially divisive service. Instead, it proposed improving the facilities for legal advice – by what was to become the Green Form scheme – and setting up an Advisory Liaison Service with solicitors, employed by the Law Society, acting as a link between agencies such as the citizens advice bureaux and private firms of solicitors.

However, in the following year the Law Society shifted its ground. It suggested that its proposed Advisory Liaison Service should be permitted to set up their own local legal centres, but, as we have seen, though this request was granted in 1972, none have as yet materialized. In the meantime, the first law centre had been established in North Kensington in 1970. By the end of 1978, there were some thirty established law centres, staffed by salaried lawyers and community workers, and a further twenty were in the process of being set up. But central government and local authority spending cuts have since resulted in some closures and a cutback in plans for expansion.

Law centres differ from private firms of solicitors in several major respects. They provide free services and are permitted to advertise. To allay fears of unfair competition, they are required to obtain waivers from the Law Society for these departures from the profession's rules of practice. In 1977 an understanding was reached whereby law centres undertook that they would not in normal circumstances handle much of the staple work of private practitioners, such as conveyancing, probate, divorce, and adult crime. Instead, they concentrate on fields like housing, landlord and tenant disputes, social security, immigration, and the law as it affects children. A number of law centres consciously adopt the policy pioneered by the American neighbourhood law firms, taking an active part in community issues and launching educational programmes and proposals for law reform.

The hostility with which the centres were initially regarded by private practitioners has substantially abated. Aside from the fact that, in the main, they deal with different kinds of work, law centres, far from posing a threat to the private profession, have in various ways generated work for it. Many of the grievances of their clientèle will create a need for legal advice and representation on behalf of the opposing side. They also pass on work to private firms, either because it is not within their their scope, or because they do not undertake individual casework as a matter of policy, or simply to enable them to cope with an often heavy workload (in 1975–76 the Paddington Centre made 492 such referrals and Camden 684). Nonetheless, a measure of suspicion remains and surfaces from time to time, as when, in 1976, local solicitors persuaded the Hillingdon Law Society to try – in the event without success – to prevent the establishment of a law centre in the area.

More intractable, perhaps, are the problems arising from the relationship of law centres with local authorities – and the Hillingdon Law Centre was in fact closed down in 1979, partly as a result of its conflict with the council over the question of independence. Occasional clashes are only to be expected. Much law centre work involves disputes with the local authority – whether on behalf of individual claimants or in regard to some local issue – while the centres are largely financed by a combination of local and central government funds.

Law centres may lay claim to two main achievements. First they have helped to counteract the reluctance of poorer members of the community to pursue their legal rights. This has been achieved by, as it were, demystifying the provision of legal services – setting up shop in busy high streets, encouraging informality, remaining open in the evenings and on Saturdays, operating round the clock emergency telephone services. In short, they project an image of accessibility. Second, they have participated effectively in the local community, helping groups such as tenants' associations and organizing campaigns to improve housing standards and other local facilities (see Adamsdown Community Trust 1978). In fact, community work and aiding disadvantaged groups seem to have been displacing individual casework as their main priority.

Byles and Morris (1977), in their study of the North Kensington Law Centre, concluded that law centres 'have established themselves as part of the fabric of legal services in this country'. Certainly they have made considerable progress in the space of a decade. But for some time yet they are likely to face problems in obtaining adequate resources and in clarifying their aims. More centres are required outside the London area. Insufficient funds and the lack of a satisfactory funding policy have left many centres in a precarious financial state. Administrative efficiency tends to suffer and, given the pressure of work and the very nature of the enterprise, a high turnover of predominantly young staff is commonplace.

The question of the appropriate role of the centres remains unresolved. Some have reduced individual casework to a minimum. A few refuse on principle to represent landlords or employers in any circumstances, laying themselves open to the charge of being doctrinaire and partisan to a degree incompatible with the lawyer's ethical obligation. On the other hand, conscious alignment with disadvantaged groups within the community has been defended as a desirable corrective to the *status quo*, rather as American lawyers in the 'war against poverty' saw themselves as counteracting the traditional role of attorneys in representing the legislative interests of big business. The focus on community action and group orientation further underlines the ambiguity of the concept of 'unmet need' and the artificiality of assessing it purely in an individualized and narrowly legalistic sense.

It may well be that law centres have most to contribute in tackling general problems of urban deprivation, yet a trend away from individual casework seems regrettable unless adequate alternatives exist which people are prepared to use. Is this in fact the case? Certainly there are a variety of organizations which provide advice and/or representation. A number of Citizens' Advice Bureaux have salaried lawyers. Some now offer assistance, including representation, for tribunal hearings, as of course do a number of trade unions in disputes arising from employment. Duty solicitor schemes have been established in a number of magistrates' courts. There are community housing aid, welfare rights and development projects, consumer advice centres, some with salaried lawyers and others which make arrangements for voluntary legal advice on a rota basis. National pressure groups like Shelter and the Child Poverty Action Group have legal departments, primarily devoted to test-case litigation. But this plethora of facilities is insufficiently coordinated, unevenly distributed, and varies enormously in the quality of services offered and in financial resources.

Justice (1977), in its evidence to the Royal Commission on Legal Services, stressed the importance of greater coordination and geographical proximity. It called for:

' ... advisory and referral centres to which every citizen can have ready access, and which will help him with the ready identification and preliminary analysis of his problem (or, more likely, cluster of problems) and tell him where to go for their solutions, and what to do and say when he gets there. That service is one which should not be placarded as a "Law Centre", "Housing Action Centre", "Claimant's Union Office", "Consumer Bureau" or "Marriage Guidance Council", since such titles presuppose that the client has already correctly classified his problems' (p.5).

Justice suggested that this service should be centred on the Citizens' Advice Bureaux (CABX), because of their established reputation in the field. The key role of CABX was a frequent theme of evidence to the Royal Commission, and one which the Commission was itself to endorse.

Such an approach would help solve many problems. There are over 700 CABX, providing a valuable and much used source of free advice. In 1976–77 they dealt with some 2.9 million enquiries, roughly a third of which, it has been estimated, contained a legal element. The National CAB Council provides local bureaux with a detailed information service and staff must undergo some training. However, many bureaux are very short of funds; over 95 per cent of staff are voluntary workers; and local autonomy has resulted in wide variations in the services provided. Also the stock image of middle-class benevolence dispensed by middle-aged ladies dies hard.

The traditional ethic of imparting neutral information rather than pursuing grievances has been both the strength and weakness of the bureaux. The current controversy over whether CABX should provide a para-legal advocacy service in tribunals highlights the dilemma. Protagonists see this as a means of providing claimants with a more sympathetic form of representation than they might obtain from lawyers and as a way of ensuring formality without excessive legalism. But many CAB workers fear that it will inevitably endanger good relationships with the Department of Health and Social Security and the Department of Employment and that it is inconsistent with their stance of neutrality. One must not lose sight of the extent to which the orientation of the advisory organization and the sympathies of its workers will determine its characterization of a problem and its approach to resolving it. Furthermore, the voluntary worker may have as much difficulty as the client in correctly classifying his problems, simply because in some cases it is difficult to lay down criteria about the appropriate advice or the desirability of referral.

If so many people are unwilling to seek the services of a solicitor independently, we need to examine the criteria for referral employed by advisory agencies: 'The referrers, as much as the lawyers, play a part in delivering legal services' (Phillips 1979:31).

This theme was the subject of some recent research into the

attitudes and practices of social workers, based on the premise that 'Social Services Departments are often the first port of call for highly inarticulate and disadvantaged people facing some problem or crisis' (Phillips:31). The broad conclusion reached by Phillips, on the basis of direct observation of two social services departments, was that a mixture of ignorance and hostility made social workers reluctant to consider legal solutions to problems or to refer clients to lawyers, whom they saw as 'hindering the achievement of social work solutions to social work problems' (p.34). At root the issue is one of values. As we saw earlier, social workers naturally interpret their clients' needs primarily in terms of welfare values, which may conflict with their strict legal rights. But even if the social worker's judgement of his client's needs is often sound, it is plainly undesirable for such decisions to be taken without an adequate appreciation of the possible options.

In another recent study of the relationship between social work practice and the provision of legal services, Grace and Wilkinson (1978b) also stress the fundamental incompatibility between the nature of social work and of legal work. The former they see as essentially based on a principle of 'guidance'. That is, the social worker is concerned with 'what is right for' the client (though they emphasize that this is *negotiated* with the client and does not reflect a simple one-way power relationship). The legal relationship, on the other hand, is essentially 'instructional'. It is concerned with the client's 'rights', and is based, in principle, at least, on instruction of the adviser by the client, though the authors concede that in practice the roles may be reversed. Thus a social worker might be committed to the idea of clients being advised of their rights, yet sometimes believe it necessary to conceal them from parents when a care order had been decided upon for their child. Even 'radical' social workers, it is argued, who *do* see themselves as 'rights' orientated, tend *in practice* to give primacy to the guidance principle.

Grace and Wilkinson conclude:

> 'that the social work role in legal services needs to be severely and strictly limited. Any attempt to foster extensions of social work in satisfying 'unmet legal need' or to enlist social workers in the contemporary drive to improve the provision of legal services would, in our view, be to the detriment of social workers, legal services, and the clients of both' (p.6).

However, it is arguable that this view distorts the reality of the instructional principle in both the legal and social work profession, the client frequently being on the *receiving* end.

In conclusion, the various suggestions for improving legal services by extending facilities for advice and representation and pouring more money into the legal aid system should help to ensure that more people will in fact, as well as theory, have access to the law as a means of establishing their rights. But such facilities will, by and large, be restricted to serving the needs of individuals. They are not a response to the challenge increasingly to be heard, for example within the law centre movement, that the notion of 'delivering legality' is inextricably bound up with the broader issues of social inequality and the differential competence of institutional and individual litigants (see Galanter 1974).

The Report of the Royal Commission on Legal Services: a Résumé

In October 1979, after three years of deliberation, the Royal Commission on Legal Services published its findings. The Report, which runs to 864 pages and contains 369 recommendations, has been widely interpreted as a resounding defeat for the legal profession's critics. As regards the profession's general organization and structure, it proposes no reforms of a fundamental nature. The Commission concluded that 'the two branches of barristers and solicitors should continue to perform their separate and complementary functions.' It advocates not merely retention of the solicitors' conveyancing monopoly, but its extension to cover preparation of the contract as well as the instrument of transfer. The barristers' monopoly of advocacy in the higher courts is also endorsed, though by a bare majority only.

The bulk of the Commission's recommendations for change seem to be designed to improve the public image of lawyers rather than to lay the foundations for any future strategy. Thus there are a number of provisions which reflect the perceived need for greater 'consumer consciousness' on the part of the profession – clarifying the calculation of solicitors' fees; permitting them to advertise individually and publicize details of any fixed charges or specialized services; the call for a code of written standards to cover many aspects of legal work and a tightening up of disciplinary procedures.

Having concluded that the solicitors' conveyancing monopoly should be retained, which would effectively perpetuate their limited availability for other kinds of work, the Commission had little option but to advocate substantially increased state funding for legal aid and for the provision of legal services in the area of social welfare law. It proposes that there should be no upper limit on personal eligibility for legal aid and higher income and capital thresholds for contributions; a statutory right to legal aid in the criminal courts, and an extension of the scheme to include tribunals. Law Centres, to be renamed Citizens Law Centres, would be wholly financed out of central government funds. They should not undertake community work and campaigns, but concentrate on providing legal services to individuals in their locality, especially in the field of welfare law. The CAB system should be expanded and regarded as the basic generalist advice service.

However, at the time of writing, neither the general economic climate nor broad governmental policy augur well for any proposals which necessitate substantial state expenditure. It is difficult to avoid the conclusion that an opportunity has been lost and that the Commission has largely settled for mild exhortation and some minor tinkering with the system, choosing not to confront the fundamental issues relating to the social role of the legal profession and the future pattern of the provision of legal services.

Suggested Reading

Abel-Smith, B., Zander, M., and Brooke, R. (1973) *Legal Problems and the Citizen*. London: Heinemann.

Byles, A. and Morris, P. (1977) *Unmet Need: the Case of the Neighbourhood Law Centre*. London: Routledge and Kegan Paul.

Galanter, M. (1976) Delivering Legality: Some Proposals for the Direction of Research. *Law and Society Review* **11**:225.

Hazell, R. (ed.) (1978) *The Bar on Trial*. Quartet Books.

Justice (1977) *Lawyers and the Legal System*. London: Justice.

Morris, P., White, R., and Lewis, P. (1973) *Social Needs and Legal Action*. London: Martin Robertson.

Royal Commission on Legal Services (1979), Cmnd. 7648. London: HMSO

Zander, M. (1978) *Legal Services for the Community*. London: Temple Smith.

6

Some Limits and Social Consequences of Law

Introduction

At the beginning of this book we defined our subject matter, in its most general sense, as being the interaction between the legal and the social. So far, however, the emphasis has been almost exclusively on one side of that relationship: the way the social influences the legal (that is, the way both the formulation and application of legal norms reflect wider social processes). Yet clearly, legal rules are designed to achieve ends of some kind and hence are based on an assumption that the relationship works both ways, that the legal can bring about social changes (usually in the sense of influencing the way people behave towards each other). However, the imbalance in the literature on the sociology of law (reflected also in this book) almost certainly results from the fact that the relationship *is* very one-sided: the formulation and operation of law is much more a *result* of social, economic, and political conditions than it is a *cause* of them. Nonetheless in this chapter we will try to redress the balance somewhat by considering the other side of the relationship.

Perhaps because of the limited role attributable to the law as an agent of change, the emphasis in this area has tended to be on the 'limits' of law: defining the boundaries of what may be expected of law and the spheres in which it may or may not be expected to have an impact. Such an approach is clearly restricted to the potentialities of law for achieving change *within* existing political and economic structures. The potential of major changes in the law to alter fundamentally the very basis of society is excluded from the analysis, not because it is ruled out as a possibility (though it would be, of course, by some), but rather because it belongs to a different level of analysis – the level at which the sociology of law shades into political sociology. The focus of attention in this chapter will consequently be on the limits and social consequences of law within the existing social, political, and economic structures of western democratic society, although, as we will see, this does not exclude the possibility that such structures may be regarded as imposing restrictions on the potentialities of law.

Discussions of the limits of law have a tendency to confuse two rather different meanings of the term 'limits'. On the one hand there is the idea of 'moral' limits; that is, arguments about the extent to which legal control is morally acceptable. This topic includes all discussion of what ought or ought not, as a matter of principle, to be brought within the ambit of law. On the other hand, there is the notion of 'practical' limits. This refers to arguments about what law *can* achieve, about areas where, for practical reasons, it inevitably fails to achieve its aims, regardless of moral considerations concerning its use.

It is the practical limits of law with which we will be concerned in this chapter. This does not, however, mean that we are assuming some simplistic fact-value distinction. Discussion of the practical limits of law is inextricably bound up with moral considerations, such as the point at which failure of enforcement or usage of laws constitutes their failure *as* laws, or when the unintended consequences of legal intervention make it unacceptable, regardless of success or failure in other terms. Also, there is an obvious tendency for people to be much more ready to accept arguments about the practical failure of law in areas where they are opposed to legal control (a good example being the universal acceptance of the view that the attempt at prohibition in the United States established the impossibility of legally controlling the production and consumption of alcohol). What we are assuming, however, is that we can separate and exclude the more fundamental moral and philosophical arguments about the limits of law. The issue of abortion provides a useful illustration. There are arguments of a fundamental *a priori* nature, based on religious or moral grounds, to the effect that abortion should be a crime because it is 'wrong'. There is equally the view that abortion, whether on demand or under certain specified circumstances, should be legal and regulated by law, because of the harmful practical consequences which otherwise ensue – the medical dangers of back-street abortion and financial exploitation. It is only the second kind of argument which concerns us here, but it is important to appreciate that it too is *ultimately* a moral argument. In other words, the weight to be attached to the unintended practical consequences of prohibiting abortion inevitably involves a degree of moral evaluation.

Perhaps we should begin by making a broad distinction between two different ways in which law can fail, derived from two rather different kinds of goals that it sets out to achieve:

(1) *Failure of usage.* One goal of law is to provide an orderly framework in which people can establish rights and obligations and have disputes settled. To the extent that they avoid using the law for these purposes and turn to alternative means, it may be deemed to have failed. If this non-use can be related to inherently inappropriate features of law, such failure can in turn be deemed one of the limits of law. This kind of limit relates mainly to the area of civil law.

(2) *Failure of control.* The other broad aim of law is that of controlling various forms of behaviour. Sometimes it incorporates a more ambitious 'social engineering' function in that the control of behaviour is intended to achieve more fundamental social goals (such as, for example, racial harmony, or sexual and racial equality). Law as control is mainly, though as we saw in Chapter 4, not entirely, associated with the criminal law. Its limits in this context are defined in terms of behaviour which cannot be effectively controlled by law – that is, where the violation rate would be so high as to mean that the law was having little or no effect (or, alternatively, where the harmful side-effects of legal control outweigh what little controlling effect it does have).

Failure of Usage

We have already dealt in Chapter 4 with circumstances under which civil law tends to be avoided as a means of establishing rights and obligations or settling disputes, since they accounted for much of the 'gap' between what is intended to take place and what actually happens. We will briefly recapitulate some of the main reasons here.

Generally speaking, it was suggested that where agreements were made, or disputes arose, between people in some kind of continuing relationship, the use of law as a means of regulation and control tended to be avoided. 'Contracts' between businessmen were frequently drawn up in an informal, non-legal manner and resort to law generally avoided. Similarly, it was suggested that one reason for the avoidance of court resolution in some categories of accident claims (most notably industrial accidents) was also its incompatibility with the nature of the relationships involved (although the high incidence of out-of-court settlement was more influenced by practical and financial considerations). Finally, in marital disputes, although total avoidance of legal processes is not usually possible, formal legal intervention is often regarded as unsuitable, when continuing relationships are necessary and fraught with emotion.

In such circumstances, adversarial procedures in particular clearly do not provide the best kind of solution. Even if the winner does have justice on his or her side, a process which produces a disgruntled loser jeopardizes and strains future relationships. In these cases negotiated compromises enabling both sides to retain their self respect and regard for each other are more important. Admittedly, it could be argued that it is specifically *adversary* procedure rather than law in general that is inappropriate in such cases. Although this may be partly true, there is nevertheless evidence to suggest that something more fundamental is wrong – perhaps stemming from the ultimate defining feature of law being its threat of external coercion, which simply creates the wrong atmosphere for such relationships.

This conclusion – that there are clear limits to the range of interpersonal relationships where legal control is appropriate – has some interesting links with the argument put forward by Chambliss and Seidman (1971), which was noted in Chapter 1. Reversing Durkheim's theory of the relationship between types of societies and types of law, Chambliss and Seidman argue that simple societies tend to be characterized by restitutive law (based on a 'give a little, take a little' approach) while complex industrial societies are characterized by repressive law (based on a 'winner takes all' approach, which applies, generally, to civil as well as criminal law). This distinction is rooted in precisely the differences in the kinds of relationship which we have been looking at. Because in simple societies they are primarily intimate and continuing it is necessary for law to be either restitutive in nature or, more importantly for the present argument, for 'law' not to exist at all. We can also apply this argument to modern western society. Although it entails much more extensive networks of impersonal relationship, where law has consequently taken over the regulatory function (and tends to be 'repressive' in Chambliss and Seidman's sense), this does not mean that *personal* relationships have become any less important (unless we strongly subscribe to the arcadian myth). And it is in these more intimate and continuing relationships, as we have seen, that law even when it is available, tends also to be avoided.

Finally, there is perhaps an area of 'failure of usage' in the criminal law too, and for roughly equivalent reasons. In Chapter 3 we saw that one of the main police justifications for discretionary non-enforcement of the law (and that, of course, means their 'failure' to use it) is that it often seems 'inappropriate'. Admittedly, the similarity ends there, as the major reason for the inappropriateness is rather different. It is not usually the case that there is any need for compromise to preserve continuing relationships. Rather, because laws are specified in general terms, there always tend to be particular instances where, although the letter of the law has been violated, the circumstances make it seem morally inappropriate to enforce it. Yet, despite this difference, there is a common underlying theme to such arguments about the limits of both civil and criminal law: in both cases law is rendered inappropriate by wider social and moral considerations which make it appear a blunt, insensitive, and therefore unsuitable instrument, especially when compared with other, informal ways of regulating and controlling human relationships and behaviour.

Failure of Control

The second major respect in which the law can be deemed to have failed is in its attempts at controlling (or reducing the incidence of) certain forms of behaviour. As we have noted, this aim is usually associated with the criminal law. We may consider the matter in terms of two related questions:

(i) what are the necessary preconditions for law to succeed in altering or modifying behaviour and, in some instances, attitudes?
(ii) are there some forms of behaviour which present particular difficulties such that legal intervention is especially likely to fail, or to have undesirable consequences which outweigh any controlling effect?

Preconditions for Success

Arguments under this heading tend to mirror the consensus/conflict dispute that we have already encountered. One commonly held view is that law will only succeed where it is supported by a general consensus of the population (see, for example, Friedmann 1972, ch.1), though the argument is usually seen as only applying to 'democracies'. Such an assertion finds popular support from the almost invariably quoted example of the 'failure' of prohibition in the United States of America.

On the face of it, such a requirement for the *success* of law almost seems to rule out any need for it in the first place. Sutherland and Cressey (1966) put it this way: 'When the mores are adequate, laws are unnecessary; when the mores are inadequate, the laws are ineffective' (p.11).

Yet there *are* laws which most people would agree are both necessary and effective. Further, *criminal* law in particular is ultimately definable by reference to the legitimate use of coercive force against offenders – its very rationale is the necessity of *discouraging* people who *want* to commit the acts concerned. This does not seem to fit in very well with the consensual argument. So is it simply false, or is Sutherland's point misleading? Clearly the latter is the case, though Sutherland does highlight a dilemma in the consensual view which we have encountered before: if 'consensus' does not denote *total* consensus (and it obviously cannot) but something less, such as 'majority', then it actually leaves open the possibility of considerable conflict, especially if we allow for differences in power between different sections of the community. Thus, contrary to Sutherland's argument, consensual (in the sense of 'majority') support for a law is quite compatible with a necessity for that law, on the grounds that it controls the recalcitrant minority and ensures that the will of the majority prevails.

But the position is more complicated still. For it is a feature of human behaviour that we will sometimes break rules that we generally support, if we think we can get away with it, as few motorists, for example, would deny. This is because our moral beliefs are always contingent on many other considerations (our own personal interests, social pressures from others and so on). This human tendency is sometimes acknowledged to be one of the grounds justifying legislation. Thus the first report of the Race Relations Board (1967) gave as one of its reasons for the necessity of legislation that: 'A law gives support to those who do not wish to discriminate, but who feel compelled to do so by social pressure' (para.65).

However, even if all these qualifications are made, a version of the consensualist argument still remains to be considered: that laws will fail unless a majority supports or at least does not actively oppose them. Since prohibition is the example most commonly cited in favour of this view, we will examine it first. It is, in any event, quite a good example, if only because it raises many of the questions involved in claims about the failure of laws.

The prohibition laws are assumed to have failed because of the very considerable evidence that they were widely violated. This, however, seems a rather inadequate criterion for writing them off as a viable form of legal control. After all, there is also considerable evidence that the laws against shoplifting are widely violated, yet this is never used as an argument against them. Why was it, then, in the case of prohibition? The answer seems to be because in this case, unlike that of shoplifting, there was an organized moral opposition, using arguments based on freedom of choice, able to keep alive the plausibility of the option of abolishing the law. It was able to use the evidence of 'failure' against the laws and also to point to the unacceptably high level of interference with individual freedom that would be necessary if they *were* to be effectively enforced. Thus, in his analysis of the Prohibition Era, Sinclair (1962) concludes:

'The drys insisted on a prohibition law which could not be enforced by their policemen and prosecutors and judges. The failure of this enforcement was, to the wets, a proof of the failure of the law. In fact, such a revolutionary theory as national prohibition could never have been enforced without a revolution in criminal procedure. Yet this second revolution was not supported by the drys, for they saw themselves as the defenders of the ancient customs and liberties of America' (p.214).

The example of prohibition does appear to bear out the consensualist argument. As Sinclair shows, in the areas where there was fairly widespread support for the law (for example, the rural south and west) there was effective enforcement and effective prohibition. It was in the urban areas, where this support was lacking, that the laws most patently failed. However, this does *not* show that the laws were *inherently* incapable of succeeding in these settings. Rather, as the quotation from Sinclair suggests, it was because the level of enforcement activity necessary for success would have been unacceptable even (or perhaps especially) to those who favoured the laws. Thus, when President Hoover increased the efficiency of the Prohibition Bureau, more effective enforcement did occur – although all this achieved, in the end, was the hastening of repeal. The consensualist view does, consequently, appear to be restricted in applicability to 'democratic' societies, where public resistance to control has ways and means of asserting itself.

There are, nevertheless, some paradoxical elements in this argument – not least that it seems to rule out the possibility of non-consensual statutes such as prohibition ever becoming law in the first place. Also, it defines the limits of law in an extremely passive way: law can only recognize and endorse changes which have occurred, or, at most, reinforce and strengthen them. Yet, at the same time, there are clearly some forms of law which are seen as deliberately setting out to take a lead and actually produce change of some kind. Obvious examples are legislation against racial and, more recently, sexual discrimination. Although it is difficult to ascertain whether such legislation is opposed by majority popular feeling, there is certainly sufficient evidence of direct discrimination and its manifestation in the inferior position of both blacks and women (see the Home Office White Paper *Racial Discrimination* 1975; and Coussins 1976) to support the contention that such legislation is belied by existing *practice*. As we saw however in the quotation from the first Race Relations Board Report, it is often assumed that the opposition is of the passive 'conforming-to-tradition' variety, rather than that of a confirmed moral stance. This, however, hardly makes such legislation any less ambitious, especially since it seems that it is aimed not just at altering the behaviour, but the very minds of men and women. The same Race Relations Board Report, for example, claims that: 'A law reduces prejudice by discouraging the behaviour in which prejudice finds expression' (para.65).

Since the inferior position of racial minorities and women appears to be tied up with the fundamental social, political, and economic processes of our society, the prospects of anti-discrimination legislation succeeding while it operates *within* these constraints is regarded by many as slight. What then have been the achievements of such legislation? In this country (particularly in relation to sex), it has not been in force long enough for us to be able to draw any firm conclusions. We have seen that legislation on race commenced with the 1965 Act, but that only since 1968 were the key areas of housing and employment included. Such evidence as there is, however, is not very encouraging. The Home Office White Paper *Racial Discrimination*, published in 1975 as a prelude to the 1976 Act, concluded that there had been virtually no change in relation to employment and housing. The only undoubtedly real change produced by the legislation has been the virtual elimination of the expression of racial discrimination in signs and advertisements. But since this bears no necessary relation to discriminatory *behaviour*, it is a classically 'cosmetic' achievement. Whether the overall failure is inherent, or a result of the unquestionably pallid form and restrictive interpretation of the 1965 and 1968 Acts (see Chapter 2, pp.59–61 and Chapter 4, pp.170–72) remains to be seen once the 1976 Act has been fully operational for some time.

Since the Sex Discrimination and Equal Pay Acts came into force only at the end of 1975, it would be premature to speculate about their effects too. There is, however, already some evidence of judicial interpretation at variance with the spirit of the legislation. Although the Equal Pay Act was passed in 1970, a five-year period was allowed for its full implementation. There has in fact been some change in women's relative earnings: between 1970 and 1975 women's average gross hourly wages as a percentage of men's rose from 63.1 per cent to 72.1 per cent though the rate of relative increase seems to have flattened out since 1975. These figures have been interpreted both as a sign of failure (Coussins 1976) and as a glimmer of hope (Byrne and Lovenduski 1978). The picture is complicated by the fact that there had been a steady decline in women's relative earnings in the two decades before the Act was passed, so that by 1975 the position was little different from what it had been in 1950. However, this could equally be interpreted as an even greater success for the Act, in that it could be credited with reversing the trend. But it is obviously dangerous to read very much into this change, especially since it has shown signs of levelling off since 1975. Overall, the position is perhaps a little discouraging. Most cases dealt with under both Acts are employment-related and comparative earnings are probably among the best indices of improvement in the position of women (better, for example, than simply whether more women are being admitted to formerly male-dominated occupations). The facility with which the spirit of the employment provisions has been evaded suggests that organized trade union activity is a much more hopeful avenue for success than utilization of the Acts (see Coussins 1976). However, it must again be emphasized that it is much too soon to try and draw hard-and-fast conclusions on sex discrimination legislation.

It is perhaps of interest to look at comparative evidence from the United States where, at least in the case of racial discrimination, changes brought about by a combination of legislation and creative judicial interpretation took place somewhat earlier. Again, the evidence is ambiguous, being encouraging or discouraging according to whichever index is taken to be the most indicative of advance (see Rodgers and Bullock 1972; Claiborne 1979). In the sphere of political participation, for example, there has been considerable advance resulting from the 1965 Voting Rights Act: black registration in southern states increased from 43 per cent in 1964 to 66 per cent in 1970. Another achievement has been the marked decline in the practice of racial segregation. Attitudes also seem to have changed, especially since the historic Supreme Court decision in 1954 (*Brown* v. *Board of Education*): between 1942 and 1964 those expressing approval of racial integration in schools rose from 40 per cent in the north and 2 per cent in the south, to 75 per cent and 30 per cent respectively (see Hyman and Sheatsley 1970). However, it has been persuasively argued that the areas where prejudice and discrimination really matter are education, housing, and jobs. And, as is also revealed in the British evidence, it is here that significant improvement in the position of blacks is conspicuously lacking. It may well be that it could be substantially improved only by the more radical approach of 'reverse discrimination', as heralded in 1978 in the United States by the *Bakke* decision, which recognized in principle the legitimacy of affirmative action in college quotas for blacks. In the same year in this country, Camden Borough Council was reported to have proposed a measure of 'positive racial discrimination' in job applications. But the hostility provoked by both of these pronouncements serves as a reminder that limits of law are apparent in radical measures just as they are in gradualist ones.

The conclusion on anti-discrimination legislation appears to be that it has as yet made little headway. This, however, is not so much because it is, or has been, out of line with general public opinion (although that may have played its part). More importantly, it appears usually to run counter to the practices of those people who control the provision of opportunities for achievement in such crucial areas as education and employment. Whether or not they are part of a wider societal consensus is not, in the end, necessarily decisive. It is the conduct of those with power to influence the outcome which determines the success or failure of such laws. For while it is easy to demonstrate the existence of discrimination in *general* terms (from data on the objective position of women and blacks), it is notoriously difficult, if not impossible, to prove conclusively in particular instances.

The conclusion that the power to determine the outcome of events is not vested in a generalized 'public opinion' is by now a familiar one. Two further examples of the limits of law are worth mentioning in this connection. First, 'white collar crime' (see Sutherland (1945) for the original formulation of this concept) has always been regarded as an area in which law tends to fail through under-enforcement. White collar crime denotes behaviour of the business community which violates laws governing business activities. Sutherland's original examples were violations of the American Anti-Trust Laws, but the category includes the violations of factory legislation, anti-adulteration, and anti-pollution legislation which we discussed in Chapter 2. A distinctive feature of the general pattern of under-enforcement is the particularly marked reluctance to use criminal processes, even where they are available. This is not because of any lack of general public support for such laws, but because the high social and economic status of those they are aimed at controlling facilitates their effective evasion (although, as we also saw in Chapter 2, this is not *inevitably* the case).

A more recent example relates to a different source of power. The

Industrial Relations Act 1971 was an undoubted failure, not only in the sense that it was ultimately repealed, but that concerted opposition prevented it from ever really getting off the ground. Again, this failure was certainly not due to general public opinion. It resulted from the organized opposition of the Trade Union movement, aided by relative indifference on the part of important sections of the business community.

It seems that just as laws emerge and change through powerful groups managing to impose their will, they fail through powerful groups managing to oppose or evade them. Although, in both cases, the support of public opinion is one source of such power it is by no means the only one, nor necessarily the most decisive. In the case of laws failing, this is probably because many laws do not have a sufficiently direct impact on the general population to arouse the possibility of concerted opposition. When they do, as in the case of prohibition, such opposition *does* become a decisive factor, though not in the sense that it makes enforcement impossible, but rather that the level of enforcement activity necessary to overcome it is likely to be unacceptable, even to those in favour of the law.

All this suggests that if laws do fail, in the sense of being widely violated, the cause is likely to be a failure of *enforcement*, which is itself explained by lack of consensual support or by inefficient, inadequate, or corrupt enforcement machinery. Underlying such arguments is the apparently commonsense view that the criminal law, when it *is* enforced against a sufficiently large proportion of offenders, *is* effective – that is, that deterrence (or, for that matter, rehabilitation) works. Since the whole of the penal system rests on such an assumption, it is worth considering in a little more detail.

We have already seen, in earlier chapters, that the deterrent, crime-controlling view of the effects of criminal sanctions has not gone unchallenged. The 'labelling' perspective of writers such as Lemert (1967) and J. Young (1971) suggested virtually the opposite: the stigma of being labelled 'criminal' isolates offenders from the conventional community, leading to the formation of crime-supporting subcultures and, ultimately, a 'criminal identity' which precipitates more criminal activity than would otherwise have occurred. Indeed, one of the leading writers of this school (Erikson 1966) has suggested that societies actually 'need' crime and criminals (to define the 'moral boundaries' of permissible behaviour) and that these crime-promoting consequences of the penal process are both functional and (though presumably only at some 'subconscious' level) deliberate.

However, such empirical evidence as there is lends little support to this rather more extreme version of labelling theory. Reconviction statistics have always shown that the majority of first offenders are not subsequently reconvicted (Hammond 1964), suggesting that the usual impact of being 'labelled' is the opposite of that proposed by labelling theorists. This does not rule out the possibility that in some cases, or under certain circumstances, the labelling effect occurs, but the main weakness of the theory is that it has never specified *which* cases and *what* circumstances.

Attempts to test the efficiency of criminal sanctions in controlling crime have tended to be equally inconclusive. Before examining them, however, it is necessary to distinguish two separate components of the argument. On the one hand there is controversy about the effects of increasing the punitiveness of the sanctions for particular offences (the 'severity' effect). On the other hand there is the question of whether it is offenders' (or potential offenders') perceptions of the probability of being caught (the 'certainty' effect) which is more decisive. The two strands are not entirely separate, of course, since the 'certainty' effect normally presupposes *some* degree of perceived punitiveness (or unpleasantness) in the sanction. In practice, however, research findings have tended to be rather different for these two effects (see National Swedish Council or Crime Prevention 1975, and Gibbs 1975). There is no consistent evidence to support the contention that increasing the severity of punishments (for example, by using capital or corporal punishment, or by longer prison sentences) has any especially deterrent effect. Indeed, the findings tend to mirror those we encountered in Chapter 3 when we were looking at the effectiveness of rehabilitative programmes: neither the type of treatment nor the amount of punishment seems to make much difference to either general crime rates or individual reconviction rates.

Evidence on the 'certainty' effect, however, is rather more positive. Many studies have demonstrated that increasing the perceived probability of detection has a marked effect in reducing crime rates (see the National Swedish Council for Crime Prevention (1975), especially Buikhuisen, p.77). A good example has been the history of 'drinking-and-driving' legislation in this country (see Ross 1973). When the Road Safety Act 1967 introduced new penalties and new provisions for the enforcement of the law against driving while under the influence of drink, the immediate effect was a dramatic reduction in such behaviour. Ross uses two indices to demonstrate this: the reduction in road deaths, especially at night, exactly coinciding with the introduction of the law, and the reduction in road accident deaths where those involved had high levels of alcohol in their blood. Subsequent developments were equally interesting demonstrating that although it is the *perceived* risk of detection that is important in controlling behaviour, such perceptions are quickly influenced by reality. Ross shows that by 1970 all the immediate impact of the 1967 Act had disappeared. The reason, he says, was that people's initial perceptions of the increased risks of detection were grossly exaggerated. Partly due to the difficulties of enforcing such laws and partly because of the low priority given to them by the police, the reality failed to live up to expectations, with the result that the perceived level of impunity rose.

The conclusion appears to be that effective enforcement of the criminal law *does* control behaviour, while increasing the severity of the punishment (at least within the broad range of opinion as to what is retributively acceptable for particular types of offence) does not. This is important because it is obviously easier, cheaper, and more popular to increase penalties than it is (as Ross's example illustrates) to increase the efficiency of enforcement. Also, when laws appear to be 'failing' there are invariably popular demands for increased penalties. The evidence suggests that this is likely to be the least successful method of increasing the effectiveness of laws. While the combination of a high level of impunity with severe punishment of those who *are* caught is also likely to engender a considerable sense of injustice.

PROBLEMATIC AREAS OF LEGAL CONTROL

So far we have looked generally at the ways in which law may 'fail to control'. We now turn to our second question: are there particular forms of human behaviour which are particularly problematic so far as legal control is concerned? As we indicated at the beginning, the question here is not just one of the *failure* of enforcement, but also of the *consequences* of enforcement. In other words, sometimes legal control may have unintended and undesirable consequences that outweigh any benefits it may have in terms of controlling the behaviour concerned.

The Legislation of Morality

One area of behaviour which has been the subject of much attention and research is what is often referred to as 'victimless' crime (where the law is said to be attempting the 'legislation of morality'). These two expressions, though emphasizing different points, overlap considerably in the kind of behaviour to which they refer: 'private'

viduals or groups of individuals, which attracts
as primarily on the ground that it is 'morally' offen-
hough the offender is sometimes also said to be
self). The category thus includes legislation aimed
nbling, homosexuality, prostitution, pornography,
drugs (including alcohol, as in the case of
prohibition). The legitimacy of legal intervention in private morality
has generated a considerable amount of debate. As we emphasized at
the beginning of this chapter, however, we are not here directly
concerned with the question of whether such behaviour ought or
ought not to be subject to legal control, but with its practical
limitations and the consequences of attempting it.

Perhaps one of the most important writers to have drawn
attention to the problems associated with legislating against 'victimless' crime is Schur (1962 and 1965). Much of his concern has been
with drug control, but his conclusions are intended, in varying
degrees, to cover many of the other forms which 'victimless' crime
may take.

There are two features of these crimes which make enforcement
particularly problematic. First, the very fact that they lack a victim
robs them of the one person who is most likely to report them to the
police and (as we saw in Chapter 3) reveal either the offender in
person or the vital evidence necessary for his detection. Second, the
usually ambiguous moral status of such offences means that they
tend to generate protective minorities and sub-cultures opposed to
the laws themselves, thereby adding to the difficulties of
enforcement. However, these problems are not such as to make
effective enforcement *necessarily* impossible. They merely indicate
that enforcers need to make strenuous efforts and take special
initiatives. But it is here – particularly in the sphere of 'special
initiatives' – that the undesirable consequences of legislating against
such crimes allegedly make their appearance.

The first harmful consequence, according to Schur, stems once
again from the absence of the person (the victim) who usually makes
the crime and offender known to the police. This means that they
normally have great difficulty in obtaining evidence. When there are
also strong pressures from superiors or from outside sources such as
the mass media to 'clean up' particular types of crime, the police
have a strong incentive to use unsavoury or even illegal methods
(such as planting evidence in the case of drugs, or using decoys
against homosexuals). The same factors – strong demands for
control combined with relative ineffectiveness – also have a
tendency to produce disproportionately harsh legal measures. With

the emergence of 'the drug problem' in this country in the 1960s, the police were given special powers of search, the courts were unusually restrictive in their interpretation of statutory provisions, the relative strictness of which persists, for example, in the current Misuse of Drugs Act 1971 which places the onus of proof on the defence for certain offences.

Such crimes are also often associated with the provision of goods and services which are in considerable demand by at least some sections of the community. One consequence of this demand is that it fosters an entrenched, illicit trade by erecting what Packer (1968) has called a 'crime tariff'. 'The effect is to secure a kind of monopoly profit to the entrepreneur who is willing to break the law . . . sheltered from the competition of those who are unwilling to do so' (p.278). Prohibition provided the classic example: it gave a boost to large-scale organized crime which has remained with America ever since (branching out into other 'crime tariff' areas such as narcotics, gambling, pornography, and vice).

The high level of demand combined with the tariff effect also facilitates police corruption. The large sums of money involved and the high profits provide funds for bribery on an extensive scale. The lack of obvious victims, together with the demand, tends to lead to a relative absence of moral commitment to enforcement on the part of the police, making the offer of bribes more difficult to resist.

A third alleged consequence of legislating against victimless crimes was one that particularly concerned Schur. It involves a version of the labelling theory: criminalizing private behaviour creates alienated stigmatized subcultures that are driven into other criminal activity as a result. Schur made this point with particular reference to drug control in the United States in contrast to Britain. In the United States, he claimed, drug abuse is treated almost exclusively as a 'crime' problem, while in Britain it is regarded primarily as a medical one. The crucial difference is that the British system allows for the legal provision of drugs to support addicts, provided it constitutes part of a treatment programme, while the United States system does not. Schur outlined various adverse consequences of the United States' approach, including the 'labelling' effect. Two others stand out as being particularly important from the point of view of the 'limits of law' argument. First, the fact that supplies of addictive drugs are *only* available from criminal sources produces a powerful tariff effect which in turn produces a strong financial incentive to encourage addiction. A second consequence is that addicts must continually find large sums of money to support their addiction, thus precipitating further crime. Schur concluded that these factors at least partly accounted for both the much greater prevalence of narcotic addiction in the United States and its much greater association with other forms of criminal activity. However, he put forward this thesis in the early and mid 1960s. Subsequent events in relation to drug control in this country were to suggest that the distinctions he had drawn between the two countries' systems were perhaps a little exaggerated. Yet at the same time, such events, together with parallel developments and revelations in relation to pornography, were to lend considerable support to Schur's *general* arguments about the legislation of morality.

Almost at the same time as Schur was writing, a 'drug scene' was beginning to emerge in this country together with demands for and the provision of stricter controls. Despite the fact that the legal supply of drugs to support addicts remained part of the 'British system' (probably avoiding some of the more extreme consequences of narcotic control in the United States), the reality of the drug scene, which was mainly centred on the use of cannabis, LSD, and amphetamines, was that it was defined as crime in much the same way as in the United States, with many similar consequences. We have already seen, in Chapter 3, how this led some writers (for example J. Young 1971) to suggest that increased attention to the legal control of cannabis produced precisely the kind of drug-subculture formation and 'deviance amplification' described by Schur. But more significant were later revelations of the activities of the London CID Drug Squad during this period (see Cox, Shirley, and Short 1977). A *Sunday Times* inquiry, and the subsequent trial and conviction for perjury of three senior members of the Drug Squad in 1973, showed that the methods used by the squad to overcome the undoubted difficulties of convicting drug dealers had reached remarkable extremes. The system of using informers had been extended to one of 'licensed dealers' who were granted immunity and used to 'set-up' other dealers in order to provide convictions. Not only were the licensed dealers usually more serious law-breakers than those who were convicted, but there was also a practice of paying them off with a proportion of the drugs that had been confiscated (this was referred to as 'recycling'). It was police perjury in relation to one of these 'set ups' which finally provided the basis for their conviction. Cox's conclusions echo those of Schur and Packer:

'As a species of crime, drug trafficking and possession have ... distinctive features. As in other areas of the law that attempt to prescribe moral regulations – for instance, those affecting gambling, drinking, prostitution and pornography – a significant minority of the population disagree with the law's basic principles. The existence of such a minority has always increased the likelihood of police malpractice, if only because the police inevitably become more cynical about enforcing a law that is held in such disrepute' (p.87).

The consequences of the generation of such cynicism, combined with the profits to be made out of the proscribed behaviour, were even more dramatically illustrated in the subsequent trial and conviction, on corruption charges, of five senior members of the Obscene Publications Squad (the 'dirty squad') in 1976. The accused were, in effect, running 'protection rackets': selected pornography dealers were allowed to trade freely in return for rake-offs from their profits paid directly to the police. Among the bizarre stories recounted were the incident in which a major pornography dealer, wearing a borrowed CID tie, was taken to recover his own hard-core material from the vaults of Holborn police station for resale, and the fact that one of the accused received fees for acting as sub-editor on some of the magazines.

Despite the fact that such sensational revelations made a mockery of the legislation, do they really prove that attempts to legislate morality in areas such as drugs and pornography are inevitably doomed to failure? A relevant consideration in answering this question is that serious as such evidence of corruption is, it is by no means restricted to the legislation of morality. Once again the London CID provided an instructive example. The drugs and pornography trials were, in fact, preceded by trials of other members of the CID in 1972 on charges of bribery and blackmail in relation to their handling of quite different areas of organized crime, such as robbery, where there is no 'significant minority of the population' who are morally opposed to the law. In other words, the corruption in the Drugs and 'Dirty' squads was only part of much deeper and more widespread corruption in the CID at that time. The obstacles to obtaining the conviction of influential, wealthy, and organized criminals in London seem to have led to an insidious process building up from the use of dubious methods of securing and utilizing informants, to open bribery and corruption, which went back over a long period of time (see Cox, Shirley, and Short 1977).

Nevertheless, as we have seen, the special factors associated with the legislation of morality such as lack of an obvious victim, indifference, or active opposition to the law among sections of the public, together with the cynicism they generate among law enforcers, undoubtedly add to the risks of such conduct. They also raise (in a way that similar problems of enforcement in other areas of crime, such as robbery, do not) the blunt question of whether it is worth having the law at all. But in the end the problem is the same as the one we touched on earlier in relation to abortion. The issue is not so much one of objectively determinable 'practical limits' of the law, but rather one of morality – is the level of control which is achievable worth the risk of such adverse side-effects? The answer will inevitably depend on the reprehensibility with which the behaviour concerned is regarded.

Industrial Relations

We have already mentioned the significance of industrial relations as an area illustrating the limits of law. The failure of the Industrial Relations Act 1971 was a failure to impose what has been described as 'the most ambitious and interventionist legislative structure in the western world' (Thomson and Engleman 1975) upon industrial relations in this country. Subsequent developments, such as the chaos and bitterness engendered over the nature of the law on picketing and its enforcement in the protracted Grunwick dispute of 1977 and during the industrial action taken in the winter of 1978–9, have certainly done little to improve the image of law as an effective instrument of control.

The failure of the Industrial Relations Act was seen as an example of the influence of organized, powerful pressure groups as against unorganized, 'public opinion', in determining the outcome of particular pieces of legislation. But the arguments about the role of law in industrial relations go much further than this. The failure of the Act and the difficulties encountered in operating the law on picketing can be seen simply as specific examples of a more general problem: the very nature of industrial relations makes them peculiarly unsuited to legal regulation. In varying degrees, such a conclusion has been reached by many experienced observers (as well as by the most exhaustive official inquiry into industrial relations in this country – the Donovan Commission, 1968). Perhaps the most distinguished exponent of this view was the comparative labour law-yer Otto Kahn-Freund. Consequently, we will look at his arguments in a little more detail (see Kahn-Freund 1977).

The essential starting point, and crucial feature of the relationship between labour and management, is that the two sides have divergent, ultimately irreconcilable interests ('There must always be someone who seeks to increase the rate of consumption and some who seek to increase the rate of investment'). This is as true of communist as it is of capitalist societies, and failure to recognize it is inevitably disastrous. Consequently, mature systems of industrial relations in democratic societies (and Kahn-Freund insists, despite the present difficulties, that such a description applies to this country) must rest 'on a balance of the collective forces of management and organized labour'. However, the balance of power in the employment relationship between employer and *individual* employee is inherently unequal. Hence, the main object of labour law is to be a 'countervailing force to counteract the inequality of bargaining power'. It restricts the scope of the workers' duty of obedience and extends their freedom of action.

But, as Kahn-Freund illustrates with various historical examples (pp.7–8), the law cannot, *on its own*, achieve this enhancement of the power of labour. If labour is weak and unorganized, such laws will be circumvented and neutralized. Labour's power comes, ultimately, from its organization:

> ' As a power countervailing management the trade unions are much more effective than the law has ever been or can ever be. This is not only true in this country, it also applies where the law has played a larger part in the development of labour relations than in Britain; in Continental countries such as France or Germany, in Australia and New Zealand, and in the United States and Canada. Everywhere the effectiveness of the law depends on the unions far more than the unions depend on the effectiveness of the law' (p.10).

It should be clear, however, that this does not mean that law has *no* role in industrial relations. Indeed, Kahn-Freund allows that on some matters it is crucial – such as safety at work. And in others, such as minimum wage legislation, it 'should not be decried'. But once again, the success of such legislation will depend on the strength with which it is supported by union power. Also, it is in the most important area – the determination of wage levels – where law is of least effect. Nevertheless, in all areas, including wage negotiation, management and labour do have one interest in common: that there should be 'reasonably predictable procedures' for regulating the inevitable conflicts that arise. Here, also, law may play a part, though only in 'regulating' conflicts. It cannot expect to eliminate them, nor can it replace the use of the sanctions which both sides have at their disposal for asserting their interests. In this respect, he concludes 'there is a certain parallel between labour relations and international relations'.

In Kahn-Freund's analysis, it is because 'mature' industrial relations require the balance of powerful, organized forces that *external* sanctions cannot be effectively imposed. Yet the distinctive feature of law as a controlling mechanism (as opposed to other, informal, kinds) is precisely its ultimate reliance on such an external sanction. Indeed, this is what is meant in the familiar demand for law to 'curb union power'. Thomson and Engleman (1975) in their conclusions on the failure of the Industrial Relations Act, make a more general point about this dilemma:

' . . . law requires reserve powers of enforcement, and as pressure groups within society have become more powerful vis-a-vis the state in modern industrial societies, law has become an increasingly difficult instrument for the state to utilise. Even when a broad consensus is achieved, some groups may be able to challenge successfully the specific implementation of law. This is, of course, the central problem not only of a capitalist, but of any pluralist society, and the dilemma it presents has rarely been satisfactorily resolved' (p.154).

In the sphere of industrial relations, particularly as portrayed by Kahn-Freund, these conclusions about the limits of law are not optimistic ones. However, the inevitability of conflict between labour and management (he was dismissive of the currently fashionable idea that 'worker participation' can overcome it) must be seen in a wider context. Although, at the level of industrial relations, 'consumption' and 'investment' are divergent interests, at the *societal* level they are both everyone's interest. Further, the 'balance of forces' which precludes legal control implies a degree of equivalence which in fact rarely obtains. There is always the possibility that one side will achieve more power than the other, to the detriment of the interests of society as a whole. Yet law cannot in itself, it seems, redress the balance (see Kahn-Freund's conclusion that it was only through organization that labour managed to make their legal powers a reality). Unfortunately, if law cannot solve such problems, there is always the danger that more authoritarian solutions will begin to present themselves in a more favourable light.

Suggested Reading

Byrne, P. and Lovenduski, J. (1978) Sex Equality and the Law in Britain. *British Journal of Law and Society* 5: 148.

Claiborne, L. (1979) *Race and Law in Britain and the United States* (2nd ed.) London: Minority Rights Group.

Cox, B., Shirley, J., and Short, M. (1977) *The Fall of Scotland Yard*. Harmondsworth: Penguin.

Kahn-Freund, O. (1977) *Labour and the Law*, (2nd ed.). London: Stevens.

Gibbs, J. (1975) *Crime, Punishment and Deterrence*. Oxford: Elsevier.

Packer, H. (1968) *The Limits of the Criminal Sanction*. Stanford: Stanford University Press.

Racial Discrimination (1975) White Paper. Cmnd. 6234. London: HMSO.

Ross, H. (1973) Law, Science and Accidents: The British Road Safety Act 1967. *Journal of Legal Studies 2:* 1

Schur, E. (1965) *Crimes Without Victims*. Englewood Cliffs, NJ: Prentice Hall.

Sinclair, A. (1962) *Prohibition: the Era of Excess*. Boston: Little Brown and Co.

Thomson, A. and Engleman, S. (1975) *The Industrial Relations Act: a Review and Analysis*. London: Martin Robertson.

7
Conclusion

In the preceding chapters we have looked at some aspects of the interaction between the legal and the social, mainly in the context of contemporary England. Our approach has been essentially descriptive rather than theoretical, for reasons which we gave in Chapter 1: much of the reality of the law in action is not readily encompassed by the theoretical concerns of current sociology.

To say that we have been mainly descriptive is not in any way to suggest that we have been, or indeed that it is possible to be, 'value-free'. We have been guided, where appropriate, by 'gaps' between apparent intention and actual practice as well as by an ideological concern with the kind of conception of 'justice' which is implicit in concepts such as due process. That is, we have been guided by the kinds of problem which currently preoccupy those working in the field of 'socio-legal problems'. This means that we have omitted other ways of looking at the law in action. With the exception of our discussion of the emergence and change of legal norms (see the conclusions to Chapter 2), we have also omitted speculation of a fundamental nature about the relationship between law and the wider social, political, and economic structure. Such selectivity seems too inevitable to require justification, and we readily acknowledge that other people may consider quite different issues to be more important.

It is because we have chosen this perspective that the problem of the 'gap' has loomed so large in previous chapters. We fully accept that 'It is not news that the law in the books does not correspond to the law in action' (Friedman and Macaulay 1977:20–1), and that there is no *a priori* reason to expect harmony between law and behaviour, rather than, for example, dissonance or 'a purely accidental conjunction' (see Abel 1973:184–89). But this does not make it superfluous to examine the relationship between formal law and legal reality. As we saw when looking at the role of bargaining in both civil and criminal matters, formal provisions, by their very existence influence the reality, even when the gap is a wide one. The unspoken threat of full-scale proceedings helps to explain both the high incidence and particular character of negotiated justice. To this extent, at least, the form is a part of the reality.

The conception of law as a self-contained body of rules has had a powerful hold on people's minds, conspicuously so in the English juristic tradition. Accordingly, the notion that there *should* be a one-to-one correspondence between formal law and legal reality has persisted, and partly accounts for the emphasis in contemporary social-legal research on the 'gaps'. But it has not been our purpose to assert that the lack of such correspondence is invariably undesirable. The legal reality may be objectionable for wholly different reasons, or indeed it may have more to commend it, as when it serves to sustain the long-term relationships of parties in dispute.

Concentration on the gaps can prove sterile if analysis is *confined* to pointing out how legal reality deviates from formal provisions. We have tried to show that the relationship between legal form and legal reality is a complex one, not only because of the influence which they have on one another, but also because of the often ambiguous nature of the form as well as the reality. It is precisely because law is socially constructed that such ambiguities and disjunctures arise and it is therefore important to retain a sense of the fluidity of law in respect of its formulation and operation alike.

As regards what we have described as the static aspect of the interaction between the legal and the social, we can summarize the main recurrent features on which we have focussed as follows:

> the tension between rules and discretion in the attempt to reconcile the competing demands of due process and substantive justice;
>
> the pervasiveness of bargaining in the administration of justice;
>
> the potential conflict between law conceived as a mechanism for resolving disputes between individuals and as an instrument of social change;
>
> the propensity of bureaucratic imperatives to undermine formal legal provisions, and the legal system's relative inaccessibility and lack of responsiveness to people's needs.

One of the main points which emerges is that the law is required to perform a variety of functions, not all of which are mutually compatible, or at least easily reconcilable. Nor are they capable of being listed in some non-controversial order of priority. It follows that there is a strong element of wishful thinking in the belief that the legal system would be substantially improved *if only* we had a Bill of Rights (see Duncanson 1978), or a statutory code of criminal procedure, or abandoned the adversary system, or whatever the fashionable panacea happens to be.

Thus the current popular call for a Bill of Rights in this country seems to us to involve precisely the kind of misconceptions about legal form and legal reality with which this book has been concerned. This is because a document proclaiming fundamental human rights, even if it were to amount to something more than vacuous rhetoric, would be likely to be either ambiguous, controversial, or both, in its formal provisions and consequently vulnerable to the vagaries of judicial interpretation. As Lloyd (1976) has persuasively argued, the judges are not well-equipped by background and training to undertake such a role: '...decisions resolving the scope and limits of human values are not so much matters which call for impartial scrutiny as for moral and political convictions' (p.126).

Similarly, though we would in fact favour replacing the much-criticized Judges' Rules by a statutory code aimed at clarifying police powers and the rights of suspects, it would be unrealistic to expect too much of an essentially formal change of this kind on its own. It could hardly avoid becoming a substitute source of controversy, would be heavily influenced by bureaucratic demands, and undermined by the various constraints of day-to-day policing.

Equally, it is difficult to envisage any diminution in the various pressures and tensions which we have enumerated, or in the level of negotiated justice, whatever formal model of procedure obtains. For these reasons, it is understandable that attention is increasingly being paid to those early stages in both criminal and civil proceedings which frequently determine the outcome of disputes and often indeed are the only stages prior to some negotiated settlement. We do need close scrutiny of the circumstances under which the bargain is struck. The focus on low-level interaction – between policeman and suspect, insurance assessor and accident victim, clerical officer and welfare claimant – is justified precisely because such encounters are typically decisive. Hence also the value of close control over pre-trial procedures and the early availability of legal services.

As far as the criminal process is concerned, *formal* steps to minimize police discretion and clarify police powers can only be effective if there is more stringent regulation of interrogation. There is undoubtedly room for improving the situation by measures such as taperecording, extending the duty solicitor scheme, and giving real substance to the suspect's right of access to a lawyer. At the same time the rights of the police to search and detain for questioning need to be more clearly defined. For reasons noted earlier, we would also advocate the setting up of an independent prosecution process on the lines of the one which exists in Scotland.

Assuming, as is only realistic, continued inequalities in the distribution of resources, there is also a need in the sphere of civil litigation to reduce imbalance between parties. Improving legal aid, law centre and CAB funding can obviously help, but as Galanter (1976) has argued in the American context, 'delivering legality' often requires much more.

Galanter has drawn particular attention to the advantages that the 'repeat player' – such as the large corporation – enjoys over the 'one shotter' in the conduct of litigation, through greater ability to structure the transaction. Litigation is often a routine occurrence for the institution, which has access to legal expertise, can make economies of scale, and can afford to take a long term view. In short, it has a degree of bargaining credibility denied to the individual, even when he is a person of substance: 'The most significant disparities in the use of law and in the provision of legal services, I submit, are not between rich and poor individuals but between individuals and organizations' (p.231).

One can seek to redress the balance by effecting change at the level of rules and institutions and by improving legal services. But in many situations, Galanter argues, none of these strategies is as likely to make as much impact on the problem of access to legality as enhancing the capability or 'competence' of parties, especially by means of organization. In this country one might point to the organizational backing which litigants receive from trade unions and various pressure groups, as well as the benefits to be derived from enlisting the support of the media, as was demonstrated in the case of the thalidomide children. Nor should the potential role for paralegals be underestimated, given that 'Most recourse to law . . . is aimed not at systematic change but at securing routine gains and protections in recurrent situations' (p.240).

Bibliography

Abel, R. (1973) Law Books and Books about Law. *Stanford Law Review* **26:** 175.

Abel-Smith, B. and Stevens, R. (1967) *Lawyers and the Courts.* London: Heinemann.

_____ (1968) *In Search of Justice.* London: Allen Lane.

Abel-Smith, B., Zander, M., and Brooke, R. (1973) *Legal Problems and the Citizen.* London: Heinemann.

Adamsdown Community Trust (1978) *Community Need and Law Centre Practice.* Adamsdown Community Trust.

Aldisert, R. (1977) An American View of the Judicial Function. In H. Jones (ed.), *Legal Institutions Today: English and American Approaches Compared.* American Bar Association.

Allen, Sir D. (1977) Letter of Guidance to Government Departments. 6 July.

Allott, P. (1977) The Courts and the Executive: Four House of Lords Decisions. *Cambridge Law Journal* **36:** 255.

American Friends Service Committee (1971) *Struggle for Justice.* New York: Hill and Wang.

Applebey, G. (1978) *Small Claims in England and Wales.* Birmingham: Institute of Judicial Administration.

Armstrong, G. and Wilson, M. (1973) City Politics and Deviancy Amplification. In I. Taylor and L. Taylor (eds.), *Politics and Deviance.* Harmondsworth: Penguin.

Atiyah, P. (1975) *Accidents, Compensation and the Law* (2nd ed.). London: Weidenfeld and Nicolson.

Atkinson, J. (1979) *Order in Court: the Organisation of Verbal Interaction in Judicial Settings.* London: Macmillan.

Baldwin, J. (1974) Problem Housing Estates – Perceptions of Tenants, City Officials and Criminologists. *Social and Economic Administration* **8**: 116.

Baldwin, J. and Bottoms, A. (1976) *The Urban Criminal*. London: Tavistock.

Baldwin, J. and McConville, S. (1977) *Negotiated Justice*. London: Martin Robertson.

____ (1978a) The Influence of the Sentencing Discount in Inducing Guilty Pleas. In J. Baldwin and K. Bottomley, *Criminal Justice*. London: Martin Robertson.

____ (1978b) The Appearance of Justice, *New Society*, 31 August.

____ (1978c) Preserving the Good Face of Justice: Some Recent Plea Bargaining Cases. *New Law Journal* **128**: 872.

____ (1979a) Police Interrogation and the Right to See a Solicitor. *Criminal Law Review* 145.

____ (1979b) The Representativeness of Juries, *New Law Journal* **129**: 284.

____ (1979c) *Jury Trials*. London: Oxford University Press.

Bankowski, Z. and Mungham, G. (1976a) *Images of Law*. London: Routledge and Kegan Paul.

____ (1976b) The Jury in the Legal System. In P. Carlen (ed.), *The Sociology of Law*. Sociological Review Monograph No. 23.

Banton, M. (1964) *The Policeman in the Community*. London: Tavistock.

Bartlett, D. and Walker, J. (1978) Inner Circle. In J. Baldwin and A. Bottomley (eds.), *Criminal Justice: Selected Readings*. London: Martin Robertson.

Beale, H. and Dugdale, T. (1975) Contracts between Businessmen: Planning and the Use of Contractual Remedies. *British Journal of Law and Society* **2**: 45.

Bean, P. (1976) *Rehabilitation and Deviance*. London: Routledge and Kegan Paul.

Becker, H. (1963) The Marijuana Tax Act. In H. Becker, *Outsiders: Studies in the Sociology of Deviance*. New York: Free Press.

____ (1964) *The Other Side: Perspectives on Deviance*. New York: Free Press.

Bell, K. (1969) *Tribunals in the Social Services*. London: Routledge and Kegan Paul.

Bendix, R. (1960) *Max Weber: an Intellectual Portrait*. London: Heinemann.

Berman, H. (1972) The Educational Role of the Soviet Court. *International and Comparative Law Quarterly* **21**: 81.

Bittner, E. (1967) The Police on Skid Row. *American Sociological*

Review **32:** 699.

Black, D. and Reiss, A. (1970) Police Control of Juveniles. *American Sociological Review* **35:** 63.

Blom-Cooper, L. and Drewry, G. (1972) *Final Appeal.* London: Oxford University Press.

Boateng, P. (1979) 'Sus' Law. *Rights!* **3:** 10. London: National Council for Civil Liberties.

Bordua, D. (ed.) (1967) *The Police: Six Sociological Essays.* New York: John Wiley.

Bottomley, K. (1970) *Prison Before Trial.* Occasional Papers on Social Administration, No.39. London: Bell.

_____ (1973) *Decisions in the Penal Process.* London: Martin Robertson.

Bottoms, A. and McClean, J. (1976) *Defendants in the Criminal Process.* London: Routledge and Kegan Paul.

Bowles, R., and Phillips, J. (1977) Solicitors' Remuneration: A Critique of Recent Developments in Conveyancing. *Modern Law Review* **40:** 639.

Box, S. (1971) *Deviance, Reality and Society.* New York: Holt, Rinehart and Winston.

Bull, R. (1979) The Influence of Stereotypes on Person Identification. In D. Farrington, K. Hawkins, and S. Lloyd-Bostock (eds.). *Psychology, Law and Legal Processes.* London: Macmillan.

Burman, S. (1976) Symbolic Dimensions of Law Enforcement. *British Journal of Law and Society* **3:** 204.

Burnham, J. (1945) *The Managerial Revolution.* Harmondsworth: Penguin.

Byles, A. and Morris, P. (1977) *Unmet Need: The Case of the Neighbourhood Law Centre.* London: Routledge and Kegan Paul.

Byrne, P. and Lovenduski, J. (1978) Sex Equality and the Law in Britain. *British Journal of Law and Society* **5:** 148.

Cain, M. (1973a) The Main Themes of Marx and Engels' Sociology of Law. *British Journal of Law and Society* **1:** 136.

_____(1973b) *Society and the Policeman's Role.* London: Routledge and Kegan Paul.

_____ (1974) The Problem of the Teaching of the Sociology of Law in the U.K. International Sociological Association VIII World Congress of Sociology and Law, Toronto.

Cain, M. and Hunt, A. (1979) *Marx and Engels on Law.* London: Academic Press.

Calligan, S. (1975) Dealing with Domestics. *Police Review* **4319:** 1345, 24 November 1975.

Campbell, C. (1974) Legal Thought and Juristic Values. *British Journal of Law and Society* **1**: 13.

Campbell, C. and Wiles, P. (1976) The Study of Law in Society in Britain. *Law and Society Review* **10**: 547.

Carlen, P. (1976) *Magistrates' Justice*. London: Martin Robertson.

Carson, W. (1970) White Collar Crime and the Enforcement of Factory Legislation. In W. Carson and P. Wiles (eds.), *Crime and Delinquency in Britain*. London: Martin Robertson.

_____ (1974a) The Sociology of Crime and the Emergence of Criminal Laws. In P. Rock and M. McIntosh (eds.), *Deviance and Social Control*. London: Tavistock.

_____ (1974b) Symbolic and Instrumental Dimensions of Early Factory Legislation. In R. Hood (ed.), *Crime, Criminology and Public Policy*. London: Heinemann.

Chambliss, W. (1970) A Sociological Analysis of the Law of Vagrancy. In W. Carson and P. Wiles (eds.), *Crime and Delinquency in Britain*. London: Martin Robertson.

_____ (1974) The State, the Law and the Definition of Behaviour as Criminal or Delinquent. In D. Glaser (ed.), *Handbook of Criminology*. Chicago: Rand McNally.

_____ (1975) The Political Economy of Crime. In I. Taylor, P. Walton and J. Young (eds.), *Critical Criminology*. London: Routledge and Kegan Paul.

Chambliss, W. and Seidman, R. (1971) *Law, Order and Power*. London: Addison-Wesley.

Chatterton, M. (1978) Police in Social Control. In J. Baldwin and A. Bottomley (eds.), *Criminal Justice: Selected Readings*. London: Martin Robertson.

Children in Trouble (1968) Cmnd.3601. London: HMSO.

Christie, N. (1974) Utility and Social Values in Court Decisions on Punishment. In R. Hood (ed.), *Crime, Criminology and Public Policy*. London: Heinemann.

Christoph, J. (1962) *Capital Punishment and British Politics*. London: Allen and Unwin.

Cicourel, A. (1976) *The Social Organisation of Juvenile Justice*. New York: John Wiley.

Claiborne, L. (1979) *Race and Law in Britain and the United States* (2nd ed.). London: Minority Rights Group.

Clarke, M. (1976) Durkheim's Sociology of Law. *British Journal of Law and Society* **3**: 246.

Clifford, B. (1979a) The Relevance of Psychological Investigation to Legal Issues in Testimony and Identification. *Criminal Law Review* 153.

_____ (1979b) Eyewitness Testimony: the Bridging of a Credibility Gap. In D. Farrington, K. Hawkins, and S. Lloyd-Bostock (eds.) *Psychology, Law and Legal Processes*. London: Macmillan.

Cohen, S. (ed.) (1971) *Images of Deviance*. Harmondsworth: Penguin.

_____(1979) Guilt, Justice and Tolerance: Some Old Concepts for a New Criminology. In D. Downes and P. Rock (eds.) *Deviant Interpretations*. London: Martin Robertson.

Consumer Council (1970) *Justice Out of Reach*. London: HMSO.

Cotterrell, R. (1977) Durkheim on Legal Development and Social Solidarity. *British Journal of Law and Society* **4:** 241

Coussins, J. (1976) *The Equality Report*. London: National Council for Civil Liberties.

Cox, B., Shirley, J., and Short, M., (1977) *The Fall of Scotland Yard*. Harmondsworth: Penguin.

Criminal Law Revision Committee (1972) Evidence (General), 11th Report, Cmnd.4991. London: HMSO.

Cross, R. (1976) *Statutory Interpretation*. London: Butterworth.

_____ (1977) *Precedent in English Law* (3rd ed.). Oxford: Clarendon.

Damaska, M. (1975) Structures of Authority and Comparative Criminal Procedure. *Yale Law Journal* **83:** 480.

Damer, S. (1976) Wine Alley, the Sociology of a Dreadful Enclosure. In P.Wiles (ed.) *The Sociology of Crime and Delinquency in Britain*, Vol. 2. London: Martin Robertson.

Davies, C. (1969) Imprisonment Without Sentence. *New Society*, 27 March.

_____ (1971a) Pre-Trial Imprisonment: A Liverpool Study. *British Journal of Criminology 11:* 32.

_____ (1971b) Sentences for Sale: A New Look at Plea Bargaining in England and America. *Criminal Law Review* 150, 218.

Davis, K.C. (1975) *Police Discretion*. Minnesota: West Publishing Co.

Deedes, W. (1970) Committee on Powers of Arrest and Search in Relation to Drug Offences. London: HMSO.

Dell, S. (1971) *Silent in Court*. London: Bell.

Denning, Lord (1979) *The Discipline of Law*. London: Butterworth.

Dent, H. and Stephenson, G. (1979) Identification Evidence: Experimental Investigations of Factors Affecting the Reliability of Juvenile and Adult Witnesses. In D. Farrington, K. Hawkins, and S. Lloyd-Bostock (eds.) *Psychology, Law and Legal Processes*. London: Macmillan.

Devlin, Lord (1976a) Judges and Lawmakers. *Modern Law Review* **39**: 1.
____ (1976b) Committee on Evidence of Identification in Criminal Cases. H.C. 338. London: HMSO.
____ (1978) *The Observer*, 24 October.
Devlin, P. (1956) *Trial by Jury*. London: Stevens.
Devons, E. (1965) Serving as a Juryman in Britain. *Modern Law Review* **28**: 561.
Diamond, A. (1977) Law Reform and the Legal Profession. *Australian Law Journal* **51**: 396.
Dickson, D. (1968) Bureaucracy and Morality: An Organisational Perspective on a Moral Crusade. *Social Problems* **16**: 143.
Diplock, Lord (1965) The Courts as Legislators; Presidential Address to the Holdsworth Club. University of Birmingham.
Disclosure of Official Information (1979) Disclosure of Official Information: A Report on Overseas Practice. London HMSO.
Donovan Commission (1968) *Report of the Royal Commission on Trade Unions and Employers' Associations*. Cmnd. 3623. London: HMSO.
Duncanson, I. (1978) Balloonists, Bills of Rights and Dinosaurs. *Public Law* 391.
Dworkin, R. (1977) *Taking Rights Seriously*. London: Duckworth.
Eekelaar, J. (1978) *Family Law and Social Policy*. London: Weidenfeld and Nicolson.
Eekelaar, J. and Clive, E. (1977) *Custody After Divorce*. Centre for Socio-Legal Studies, Wolfson College, Oxford.
Elston, E., Fuller, J., and Murch, M. (1975) Judicial Hearings of Undefended Divorce Petitions, *Modern Law Review* **38**: 609.
Equal Opportunities Commission (1977) *First Annual Report, 1976*. London: HMSO.
Erikson, K. (1966) *Wayward Puritans: A Study in the Sociology of Deviance*. New York: John Wiley.
Farrar, J. (1974) *Law Reform and the Law Commission*. London: Sweet and Maxwell.
Feldstein, M. (1967) *Economic Analysis for Health Service Efficiency*. Chicago: Markham.
Finer, Mr. Justice (1974) *Report of the Committee on One-Parent Families*. Cmnd. 5629. London: HMSO.
Fisher, H. (1977) Report of an Inquiry into the circumstances leading to the trial of three persons on charges arising out of the death of Maxwell Confait and the fire at 27 Doggett Rd., London SE6. London: HMSO.

Fitzgerald, M. (1977) *Prisoners in Revolt*. Harmondsworth: Penguin.

Forde, M. (1978) Transnational Employment and Employment Protection. *Industrial Law Journal* 7: 228.

Forester, T. (1978) Tribunals of the People. *New Society*, 23 November.

Forgan, L. (1978) *The Guardian*, 4 December.

Foster, K. (1973) The Location of Solicitors. *Modern Law Review* 36: 153.

Francis, H. (1971) *Report of the Committee on the Rent Acts*. Cmnd. 4609. London: HMSO.

Frank, J. (1963) *Courts on Trial*. New York: Atheneum.

Franks, O. (1957) *Report of the Committee on Administrative Tribunals and Enquiries*. Cmnd. 218. London: HMSO.

Freeman, M. (1977) The New Race Relations Act – Will it Work? *New Law Journal* 127: 304.

Friedman, L. (1977) *Law and Society: An Introduction*. Englewood Cliffs, N.J.: Prentice-Hall.

Friedman, L. and Macaulay, S. (1977) *Law and the Behavioural Sciences* (2nd ed.). New York: Bobbs-Merrill.

Friedmann, W. (1972) *Law in a Changing Society*. Harmondsworth: Penguin.

Frost, A. and Howard, C. (1977) *Representation and Administrative Tribunals*. Routledge and Kegan Paul.

Galanter, M. (1974) Why the 'Haves' Come Out Ahead: Speculations on the Limits of Legal Change. *Law and Society Review* 9: 95.

＿＿＿ (1976) Delivering Legality: Some Proposals for the Direction of Research. *Law and Society Review* 11: 225.

Gardiner, G. and Martin, A. (1963) (eds.) *Law Reform Now*. London: Victor Gollancz.

Gibbs, J. (1975) *Crime, Punishment and Deterrence*. Oxford: Elsevier.

Gifford, T. and O'Connor, P. (1979) Habeas Corpus, *Legal Action Group Bulletin* 182.

Gill, O. (1976) Urban Stereotypes and Delinquent Incidents. *British Journal of Criminology* 16: 321.

＿＿＿ (1977) *Luke Street: Housing Policy, Conflict and the Creation of the Delinquent Area*. London: Macmillan.

Glueck, E. and Glueck, S. (1950) *Unravelling Juvenile Delinquency*. New York: Harper and Row.

Goldstein, A. and Marcus, M. (1977) The Myth of Judicial Supervision in Three "Inquisitorial" Systems: France, Italy, and

Germany. *Yale Law Journal* **87**: 240.

Goodman, Lord (1979) *The Observer*, 28 January.

Gouldner, A. (1975) *For Sociology: Renewal and Critique in Sociology Today*. Harmondsworth: Penguin.

Grace, C. and Wilkinson, P. (1978a). *Sociological Inquiry and Legal Phenomena*. New York: St Martin's Press.

_____ (1978b) *Negotiating the Law: Social Work and Legal Services*. London: Routledge and Kegan Paul.

Grant, M. (1978) Planning, Politics and the Judges. *Journal of Planning and Environment Law* 512.

Grant, W. (1977) Corporatism and Pressure Groups. In D. Kavanagh and R. Rose (eds.), *New Trends in British Politics*. London: Sage.

Gray, J. (1978) The Unsolicited Goods and Services Acts 1971 and 1975: A Case Study of the Process Leading to the Enactment of Private Members' Bills. *Public Law* 242.

Greer, D. (1971) Anything but the Truth? The Reliability of Testimony in Criminal Trials. *British Journal of Criminology* **11**: 131.

Griffith, J. (1974a) *Parliamentary Scrutiny of Government Bills*. Allen and Unwin.

_____ (1974b) Judges, Race and the Law. *New Statesman* **734**: 22 November.

_____ (1977) *The Politics of the Judiciary*. London: Fontana.

Griffiths, J. (1970) Ideology in Criminal Procedure or a Third 'Model' of the Criminal Process. *Yale Law Journal* **79**: 359.

Gunningham, N. (1974) *Pollution, Social Interest and the Law*. London: Martin Robertson.

Gusfield, J. (1963) *Symbolic Crusade: Status Politics and the American Temperance Movement*. Illinois: University of Illinois Press.

Gusfield, J. (1967) Moral Passage: The Symbolic Process in Public Designations of Deviance. *Social Problems* **15**: 175.

Hailsham, Lord (1971) Address to Annual General Meeting of Law Society of Scotland, 9 May. In *New Law Journal* **121**: 624.

Hain, P. (1976) *Mistaken Identity: The Wrong Face of the Law*. London: Quartet Books.

Hall, J. (1952) *Theft, Law and Society*. New York: Bobbs Merrill.

Hammond, W. (1964) *The Sentence of the Court. A Handbook for Courts on the Treatment of Offenders*. London: HMSO.

Harman, H. and Griffith, J. (1979) *Justice Deserted*. London: National Council for Civil Liberties.

Harris, D. (1965) Pilot Survey of Financial Consequences of

Personal Injuries Suffered in Road Accidents in the City of Oxford. Summary by S. Hartz in *New Law Journal* **119**: 492 (1969).

Hart, H. (1961) *The Concept of Law*. Oxford: Clarendon Press.

Hart, J. (1963) Some Reflections on the Report of the Royal Commission on the Police. *Public Law* 283.

Hay, D., Linebaugh, P. and Thompson, E. (eds.) (1975) *Albion's Fatal Tree*. London: Allen Lane.

Hazell, R. (ed.) (1978) *The Bar on Trial*. London: Quartet Books.

Heberling, J. (1973) Conviction without Trial. *Anglo-American Law Review* **2**: 428.

Hewitt, C. (1974) Elites and the Distribution of Power in British Society. In P. Stanworth and A. Giddens (eds), *Elites and Power in British Society*. Cambridge University Press.

Hindell, K. and Simms, M. (1971) *Abortion Law Reformed*. London: Peter Owen.

Hine, J., McWilliams, W., and Pease, K. (1978) Recommendations, Social Information and Sentencing. *Howard Journal* **17**: 91.

Hirst, P. (1972) Marx and Engels on Law, Crime and Morality. *Economy and Society* **1**: 28.

Hodge, H. (1979) Starting a Legal Aid Practice – the First Year. *Legal Action Group Bulletin* 32.

Home Office (1975) *Racial Discrimination*. Cmnd. 6234. London: HMSO.

Home Office (1978a) *Criminal Statistics: England and Wales 1977*. Cmnd. 7289. London: HMSO.

____ (1978b) Judges' Rules and Administrative Directions to the Police. HO Circular No. 89/1978. London: HMSO.

____ (1978c) Identification Parades and the Use of Photographs for Identification. HO Circular No. 109/1978. London: HMSO.

Hood, R. (1972) *Sentencing the Motoring Offender*. London: Heinemann.

____ (1974) Criminology and Penal Change: A Case Study of the Nature and Impact of Some Recent Advice to Governments. In R. Hood (ed.), *Crime, Criminology and Public Policy*. London: Heinemann.

____ (1978) Tolerance and the Tariff: Some Reflections on Fixing the Time Prisoners Serve in Custody. In J. Baldwin and A. Bottomley, *Criminal Justice: Selected Readings*. London: Martin Robertson.

Hood, R. and Sparks, R. (1970) *Key Issues in Criminology*. London: Weidenfeld and Nicolson.

Hunt, A. (1978) *The Sociological Movement in Law*. London: Macmillan.

Hyman, H. and Sheatsley, P. (1970) Attitudes Towards Segregation. In R. Schwartz and J. Skolnick (eds), *Society and the Legal Order*. New York: Basic Books.

Ison, T. (1967) *The Forensic Lottery*. London: Staples Press.

Jackson, G. (1971) *Soledad Brothers: the Prison Letters of George Jackson*. London: Jonathan Cape.

Jaffe, L. (1969) *English and American Judges as Lawmakers*. Oxford: Clarendon Press.

Jolowicz, J. (1978) Some Twentieth Century Developments in Anglo-American Civil Procedure. *Anglo-American Law Review* 7: 163.

Joseph, M. (1976) *The Conveyancing Fraud*. Published by the author.

Judicial Statistics (1979) *Annual Report for the Year 1978*. Cmnd. 7627. London: HMSO.

Judicial Studies and Information (1978) Report of a Working Party. London: HMSO.

Justice (1970) *The Prosecution Process in England and Wales*. London: Justice Educational Research Trust.

_____ (1974) *Going to Law: A Critique of English Civil Procedure*. London: Stevens.

_____ (1977) *Lawyers and the Legal System*. London: Justice.

_____ (1978) *Freedom of Information*. London: Justice.

Kadish, M. and Kadish, S. (1973) *Discretion to Disobey*. Stanford: Stanford University Press.

Kahn-Freund, O. (1966) Reflections On Legal Education. *Modern Law Review* 29: 121.

_____ (1977) *Labour and the Law* (2nd ed.) London: Stevens.

Kalven, H. and Zeisel, H. (1966) *The American Jury*. Boston: Little, Brown.

Kettle, M. (1979) Anderton's Way. *New Society*, 8 March.

King, M. (1971) *Bail or Custody*. Cobden Trust.

_____ (1976) *The Effects of a Duty Solicitor Scheme: An Assessment of the Impact upon a Magistrates' Court*. Cobden Trust.

_____ (1978) A Status Passage Analysis of the Defendant's Progress through the Magistrates' Court. *Warwick Law Working Papers* No. 3. University of Warwick.

Klare, H. (1979) Comment on M. Ryan's 'The Acceptable Pressure Group'. Howard Journal **18**: 73.

Knapp, W. (1972) *Commission Report on Police Corruption*. New York: George Braziller.

LaFave W.R. (1965) *Arrest, the Decision to Take a Suspect into Custody*. Boston: Little, Brown.

Lambert, J. (1970) *Crime, Police and Race Relations*. London: Oxford University Press.

Laurie, P. (1972) *Scotland Yard*. Harmondsworth: Penguin.

Law Commission (1966) *Reform of the Grounds of Divorce*. Cmnd. 3123. London: HMSO.

―――― (1969a) *Exemption Clauses in Contracts: First Report*. Law Com. No. 24. London: HMSO.

―――― (1969b) *Financial Provision in Matrimonial Proceedings*. Law Com. No. 25. London: HMSO.

―――― (1972) *Seventh Annual Report* 1971–2. Law Com. No.50. London: HMSO.

―――― (1975) *Exemption Clauses: Second Report* (Joint Report with Scottish Law Commission). Law Com. No.69. London. HMSO.

―――― (1976) *Eleventh Annual Report* 1975-6. Law Com. No.78. London: HMSO.

Le Dain, G. (1972) *Cannabis*. A Report of the Commission of Inquiry into the Non-Medical Use of Drugs. Information Canada.

Legal Action Group (1979) Jury Service: A Personal Observation. *Legal Action Group Bulletin* 278.

Leggatt, A. (1976) Why Fusion is a Consummation not to be Wished, *Law Society's Gazette* 978: 24 November.

Legum, M. (1977) Race Relations: Another Expensive Blueprint for Failure? *The Times*, 17 August.

Leigh, L. (1975) *Police Powers in England and Wales*. London: Butterworth.

Lemert, E. (1967) *Human Deviance, Social Problems and Social Control*. Englewood Cliffs, N.J.: Prentice Hall.

―――― (1974) Beyond Mead: The Societal Reactions to Deviance. *Social Problems* 21: 457.

Lemon, N. (1974) Training, Personality and Attitudes as Determinants of Magistrates' Sentencing. *British Journal of Criminology* 14: 34.

Lennon, P. (1978) How One Woman Routs Forces of Darkness. *Sunday Times*, 12 February.

Lerman, P. (1970) *Delinquency and Social Policy*. New York: Praeger.

Levenson, H. (1979) Criminal Legal Aid: The Consistent Discrepancies. *Legal Action Group Bulletin* 6.

Lidstone, K. (1978) A Maze in Law! *Criminal Law Review* 332.

Lipton, D., Martinson, R., and Wilks, J. (1975) *The Effectiveness of Correctional Treatment: A Survey of Treatment Evaluation*

Studies. New York: Praeger.

Lloyd, Lord (1976) Do We Need a Bill of Rights? *Modern Law Review* **39**: 121.

McBarnet, D. (1978) False Dichotomies in Criminal Justice Research. In J. Baldwin and A. Bottomley (eds), *Criminal Justice: Selected Readings*. London: Martin Robertson.

McCabe, S. and Purves, R. (1972a) *By-Passing the Jury*. Oxford: Blackwell.

——— (1972b) *The Jury at Work*. Oxford: Blackwell.

McCabe, S. and Sutcliffe, F. (1978) *Defining Crime*. Oxford: Blackwell.

McCorquodale, S. (1962) The Composition of Administrative Tribunals. *Public Law* 298.

McNee, D. (1978) Evidence to *Royal Commission on Criminal Procedure*.

Macaulay, S. (1963) Non-Contractual Relations in Business: A Preliminary Study. *American Sociological Review* **28**: 55.

Mack, J. (1976) Full-Time Major Criminals and the Courts. *Modern Law Review* **39**: 241.

Mackintosh, J. (1978) (ed.) *People and Parliament*. Papers 9 and 10. London: Saxon House.

Manchester, A. and Whetton, J. (1974) Marital Conciliation in England and Wales. *International and Comparative Law Quarterly* **23**: 339.

Manchester Law Society (1979) *First Annual Report of Firm of Cooper and Pearson*.

Mann, F. (1977) Fusion of the Legal Professions? *Law Quarterly Review* **93**: 367.

Mark, R. (1973) Minority Verdict, BBC, reprinted in R. Mark, *Policing a Perplexed Society* (1977). London: Allen and Unwin.

Martin, M. (1978) System Dynamics Evaluation of Alternative Crime Control Policies: An Alaskan Viewpoint. *Justice System Journal* **3**: 242.

Matza, D. (1969) *Becoming Deviant*. Englewood Cliffs, N.J.: Prentice Hall.

Mawby, R. (1978) A Note on Domestic Disputes Reported to the Police. *Howard Journal* **17**: 160.

Megarry, R. (1962) *Lawyer and Litigant in England*. London: Stevens.

Morris, A., McIsaac, M., and Gallacher, J. (1973) Children and Law. *New Society*, 2 August.

Morris, P., White, R., and Lewis, P. (1973) *Social Needs and Legal Action*. London: Martin Robertson.

Munro, C. (1975) Without Miranda: the Legality of Police Detention. *New Law Journal* **125:** 137.

Murch, M. (1977) The Role of Solicitors in Divorce Proceedings. *Modern Law Review* **40:** 625.

Nagel, S. (1976) Impact of Plea Bargaining on the Judicial Process. *American Bar Association Journal* **62:** 1020.

National Swedish Council for Crime Prevention (1975) *General Deterrence*. National Swedish Council for Crime Prevention, Research and Development Division.

New Law Journal (1073) Correspondence columns. *New Law Journal* **123:** 952.

Newman, D. (1956) Pleading Guilty for Considerations: A Study of Bargain Justice. *Journal of Criminal Law, Criminology, and Police Science* **46:** 780.

O'Higgins, P. and Partington, M. (1969) Industrial Conflict: Judicial Attitudes. *Modern Law Review* **32:** 53.

Open Government (1979) *Open Government*. Cmnd. 7520. London: HMSO.

Ormrod (1971) *Report of the Committee on Legal Education*. Cmnd. 4595. London: HMSO.

Outer Circle Policy Unit (1977) *An Official Information Act*. Outer Circle Policy Unit.

Packer, H. (1968) *The Limits of the Criminal Sanction*. Stanford: Stanford University Press.

Page, B. (1978) The Secret Constitution. *New Statesman*, 21 July.

Partington, M. (1978) *The Legal Aid Means-Tests: Time for a Reappraisal*. London: Child Poverty Action Group.

Paterson, A. (1974) Judges: A Political Elite? *British Journal of Law and Society* **1:** 118.

Paulus, I. (1974) *The Search for Pure Food: A Sociology of Legislation in Britain*. London: Martin Robertson.

Pearson, G. (1975) *The Deviant Imagination*. London: Macmillan.

Pearson, Lord (1978) *Royal Commission on Civil Liability and Compensation for Personal Injury*. Cmnd. 7054−1. London: HMSO.

Phillips, A. (1979) Social Work and the Delivery of Legal Services. *Modern Law Review* **42:** 29.

Piliavin, I. and Briar, S. (1964) Police Encounters with Juveniles. *American Journal of Sociology* **70:** 206.

Pinto-Duschinsky, M. (1977) Corruption in Britain: The Royal Commission on Standards of Conduct in Public Life. *Political Studies* **25:** 274.

Podgorecki, A. (1973) *Knowledge and Opinion about Law*.

London: Martin Robertson.

Pollock, S. (1975) *Legal Aid – The First 25 Years*. London: Oyez.

Powis, D. (1977) *The Signs of Crime: A Field Manual for Police*. London: McGraw Hill.

Prices and Incomes Board (1968) Remuneration of Solicitors. Cmnd. 3529. London: HMSO.

____ (1971) Standin Reference on the Remuneration of Solicitors, Second Report. Cmnd. 4624. London: HMSO.

Purves, R. (1971) That Plea Bargaining Business: Some Conclusions From Research. Criminal Law Review 470.

Quinney, R. (1970) *The Social Reality of Crime*. Boston: Little, Brown.

____ (1975) Crime Control in Capitalist Society. In I.Taylor, P. Walton, and J. Young, *Critical Criminology*. London: Routledge and Kegan Paul.

Race Relations Board (1967) *First Report*. London: HMSO.

Rapoport, A. (1975) Theories of Conflict Resolution and the Law. In M. Friedland (ed.), *Courts and Trials: A Multidisciplinary Approach*. Toronto: University of Toronto Press.

Rees, T., Stevens, P., and Willis, C. (1979) *Race, Crime and Arrests*. Research Bulletin No. 8. London: HMSO.

Reid, Lord (1972) The Judge as Law Maker. *Journal of the Society of Public Teachers of Law* **12**: 22.

Renner, K. (1976) *The Institutions of Private Law and their Social Functions*. London: Routledge and Kegan Paul.

Rodgers, H. and Bullock, C. (1972) *Law and Social Change: Civil Rights Laws and their Consequences*. London: McGraw Hill.

Roshier, B. (1976) Corrective Criminology, *Working Papers in Sociology* No. 10, University of Durham.

Ross, H. (1973) Law, Science and Accidents: The British Road Safety Act 1967, *Journal of Legal Studies* **2**: 1.

Royal Commission on Legal Services (1979) Cmnd. 7648 London: HMSO.

Ryan, M. (1978) *The Acceptable Pressure Group*. London: Saxon House.

Sachs, A. and Wilson, J. (1978) *Sexism and the Law*. London: Martin Robertson.

Salmon, Lord (1976) *Royal Commission on Standards of Conduct in Public Life*. Cmnd. 6524. London: HMSO.

Sanders, A. (1979) Guilt, Innocence and Jury Acquittals. *Howard Journal* **18**: 7.

Sawer, G. (1965) *Law in Society*. Oxford: Clarendon Press.

Scarman, Mr. Justice (1968) *Law Reform: The New Pattern.* London: Routledge and Kegan Paul.

Scarman, Lord (1974) *English Law – The New Dimension.* London: Stevens.

Schur, E. (1962) *Narcotic Addiction in Britain and America.* Indiana: Indiana University Press.

——— (1965) *Crime Without Victims.* Englewood Cliffs N.J.: Prentice Hall.

——— (1968) *Law and Society.* New York: Random House.

Schwartz, R. and Miller, J. (1964) Legal Evolution and Social Complexity. *American Journal of Sociology* **70:** 159.

Scofield, M. (1971) *The Strange Case of Pot.* Harmondsworth: Penguin.

Scrutton, Lord (1923) The Work of the Commercial Courts. *Cambridge Law Journal* **1:** 6.

Sealy, L. and Cornish, W. (1973) Jurors and their Verdicts. *Modern Law Review* **36:** 496.

Select Committee on Procedure (1978) First Report, Vol. I, H.C. Papers. Session 1977–78, 588/I. London: HMSO.

Select Committee Report (1974/5) *Violence in Marriage.* 248 H.C. 553, July 1975. London: HMSO.

Shklar, J. (1964) *Legalism.* Harvard: Harvard University Press.

Sinclair, A. (1962) *Prohibition: The Era of Excess.* Boston: Little, Brown.

Skolnick, J. (1966) *Justice Without Trial.* New York: John Wiley.

de Smith, S. (1977) *Constitutional and Administrative Law* (3rd ed.) Harmondsworth: Penguin.

Society of Conservative Lawyers (1968) *Rough Justice.* Society of Conservative Lawyers.

Society of Labour Lawyers (1968) *Justice For All.* Fabian Research Series.

Stinchcombe, A. (1963) Institutions of Privacy in the Determination of Police Administrative Practice. *American Journal of Sociology* **69:** 150.

Street, H. (1975) *Freedom, the Individual and the Law* (3rd ed.) Harmondsworth: Penguin.

Sudnow, D. (1965) Normal crimes: Sociological Features of the Penal Code in a Public Defender's Office. *Social Problems* **12:** 255.

Sutherland, E. (1945) Is White Collar Crime Crime? *American Sociological Review* **10:** 132.

Sutherland, E. and Cressey, D. (1966) *Principles of Criminology* (7th ed.). Philadelphia: Lippincott.

Szasz, T. (1974) *Law, Liberty and Psychiatry*. London: Routledge and Kegan Paul.

Tangley, Lord (1965) H.L. Deb., Vol.265, Col.452.

Tarling, R. (1979) *Sentencing Practice in Magistrates' Courts*. Home Office Research Study 56. London: HMSO.

Taylor, I. and Taylor, L. (eds) (1973) *Politics and Deviance*. Harmondsworth: Penguin.

Taylor, L., Lacey, R., and Bracken, D. (1980) *In Whose Best Interests? The Unjust Treatment of Children in Courts and Institutions*. London: Cobden Trust.

Taylor, P. (1978) Plea Bargaining. *Guardian Gazette* **75**: 534.

Telling, D. (1978) Arrest and Detention – The Conceptual Maze. *Criminal Law Review* 320.

Thomas, D. (1979) *Principles of Sentencing* (2nd ed.). London: Heinemann.

Thomas, P. and Smith, P. (1978) The Fisher Report and the Judges' Rules, *New Law Journal* **128**: 548.

Thomson, A. and Engleman, S. (1975) *The Industrial Relations Act: A Review and Analysis*. London: Martin Robertson.

The Times (1977) Correspondence, 15 July.

The Times (1978) Correspondence, 1 June.

Twining, W. (1974) Law and Social Science: The Method of Detail. *New Society*, 27 June.

Wade, H. (1977) *Administrative Law* (4th ed.). London: Oxford University Press.

Walkland, S. (1968) *The Legislative Process*. London: Allen and Unwin.

Walmsley, R. (1978) Indecency between Males and the Sexual Offences Act 1967. *Criminal Law Review* 400.

Wedderburn, K. (1965) Reflections on Law Reform. *The Listener* 6 May.

White Paper (1978) *Reform of Section 2 of the Official Secrets Act 1911*. Cmnd. 7285. London: HMSO.

White, R. (1973) Lawyers and the Enforcement of Rights. In P. Morris, *et al.*, Social Needs and Legal Action. London: Martin Robertson.

White, S. (1977) The Bail Act: Will it make any difference? *Criminal Law Review* 338.

Wilcox, A. (1972) *The Decision to Prosecute*. London: Butterworth.

Williams, C. (1954) Turning a Blind Eye, *Criminal Law Review* 271.

Williams, D. (1978) Taxing Statutes are Taxing Statutes: The Interpretation of Revenue Legislation. *Modern Law Review* **41**: 404

Williams, G. (1979) The Authentication of Statements to the

Police. *Criminal Law Review* 6.

Willock, I. (1974) Getting on with Sociologists. *British Journal of Law and Society* 1: 3.

Wilson, G. (1973) The Place of Social Sciences in Legal Education. Unpublished paper Delivered at the Workshop on Law and the Social Sciences.

Wilson, J. (1968) *Varieties of Police Behaviour*. Harvard: Harvard University Press.

Winn, Lord Justice (1968) *Report of the Committee on Personal Injuries Litigation*. Cmnd.3691. London: HMSO.

Wootton, B. (1963) *Crime and the Criminal Law*. London: Stevens.

Wootton, Baroness (1968) *Cannabis*. Report of the Advisory Committee on Drug Dependence. London: HMSO.

Wright, M. (1975) Tactics of Reform. In S. McConville (ed.), *The Use of Imprisonment*. London: Routledge and Kegan Paul.

Young, J. (1971) The Role of the Police as Amplifiers of Deviancy. In S. Cohen (ed.), *Images of Deviance*. Harmondsworth: Penguin.

Young, M. (1976) *An Examination of some Aspects of the Developing Perceptions in a Local Community of Non-Medical Drug Use as Marginal, Anti-Structural, Deviant Behaviour*. A Dissertation for the Degree of B.A. (Hons.) Anthropology, University of Durham (unpublished).

Younger Report (1974) *Young Adult Offenders (Report of the Advisory Council on the Penal System)*. London: HMSO.

Zander, M. (1968) *Lawyers and the Public Interest*. London: Weidenfeld and Nicolson.

_____ (1971) A Study of Bail/Custody Decisions in London Magistrates' Courts. *Criminal Law Review* 191.

_____ (1972) Access to a Solicitor in the Police Station, *Criminal Law Review* 342.

_____ (1974) Are Too Many Professional Criminals Avoiding Conviction? *Modern Law Review* 37: 28.

_____ (1976) Why the Royal Commission is likely to recommend reform of the divided profession. *Law Society's Gazette* 882: 27 October.

_____ (1978) *Legal Services for the Community*. London: Maurice Temple Smith.

_____ (1979) Operation of the Bail Act in London Magistrates' Courts. *New Law Journal* 129: 108.

Name Index

Abel, R., 16, 223
Abel-Smith, B., 7, 148, 154, 167, 186
Adamsdown Community Trust, 195
Aldisert, R., 70
Allen, Sir D., 39
Allott, P., 63
Americans Friends Service Committee, 136, 138-9, 143
Anderton, James, 81
Applebey, G., 165
Armstrong, G., 92
Atiyah, P., 148, 151-2
Atkinson, J., 15

Bagehot, W., 49
Baldwin, J., 15; on access to solicitor, 103, 108; city crime, 93; juries, 125, 127, 128; *Negotiated Justice*, 116-17; sentencing discount, 107, 114, 119
Bankowski, Z., 12, 129
Banton, M., 80, 82, 85
Bartlett, D., 134
Beale, H., 153, 154
Bean, P., 136
Becker, H., 9, 25, 29, 74
Bell, K., 166
Bendix, R., 13
Berman, H., 96
Birmingham Institute of Judicial Administration, 6
Bittner, E., 85
Black, D., 83, 84, 86, 87

Blom-Cooper, L., 134
Boateng, P., 92
Bordua, D., 85
Bottomley, K., 106, 111, 113
Bottoms, A., 15, 93, 102, 107, 116, 118, 123, 182
Bowles, R., 185
Box, S., 82
Bracken, D., 136, 143
Briar, S., 11, 83, 84, 86, 87
Bristow, J., 61
British Journal of Law and Society, 6
British Sociological Association, 6
Brooke, R., 148, 186
Bull, R., 121
Bullock, C., 209
Burger, Chief Justice, 114
Burgess, A., 141
Burman, S., 23, 24
Burnham, J., 36
Byles, A., 195
Byrne, P., 174, 209

Cain, M., 6, 14, 82, 85, 94
Calligan, S., 88
Campbell, C., 3, 6, 70
Carlen, P., 122
Carson, Rachel, 35
Carson, W., 11, 13, 21, 27, 29, 34, 72, 73; on Factory Acts, 30-2, 36, 37, 73
Chambliss, W., 8, 11, 12, 14, 120,

Chambliss, W., *cont.*
  204; on vagrancy, 29, 30
Christie, N., 136
Christoph, J., 45
Claiborne, L., 209
Clarke, M., 14
Clifford, B., 106, 120, 121
Clive, E., 158
Cohen, S., 9
Cooper, Lady Diana, 101
Cooper, L. Blom-, *see* Blom-Cooper
Cornish, W., 126
Cotterrell, R., 14
Coussins, J., 208, 209
Cox, B., 216, 217
Cressey, D., 205
Cross, R., 57, 59

Damaska, M., 130
Damer, S., 92, 93
Davies, C., 111, 113, 116
Davis, K.C., 80, 95
Dell, S., 116
Denning, Lord: on discretion, 57, 58;
  decisions, 60, 69; interpretation, 61,
  63, 64-5; tribunals, 168, 174
Dent, H., 121
de Smith, S., 39, 166
Devlin, Lord, 62, 64, 65, 66, 105,
  124, 185
Devons, E., 126
Diamond, A., 53
Dickson, J., 26, 29, 35, 36, 72
Dilhorne, Lord, 62
Diplock, Lord, 60, 62, 63
Drewry, G., 134
Dugdale, T., 153, 154
Duncanson, I., 224
Durkheim, E., 1, 13-14, 204
Duschinsky, M. Pinto-, *see* Pinto-
  Duschinsky
Dworkin, R., 57

Edward IV, King of England, 29
Eekelaar, J., 155, 158
Ehrlich, Paul, 35
Elston, E., 157
Engels, F., 14
Engleman, S., 218, 220
Erikson, K., 211

Fabian Society, 7

Farrar, J., 53
Feldstein, M., 187
Fitzgerald, M., 142
Forde, M., 61
Forester, T., 168
Forgan, L., 175
Foster, K., 182
Frank, J., 120, 122, 124, 129
Freeman, M., 172
Freund, Otto Kahn-, *see* Kahn-Freund
Friedman, L., 75, 222
Friedmann, W., 20, 205
Frost, A., 167
Fuller, J., 157

Galanter, M., 199, 225
Gallacher, J., 140
Gardiner, G., 7
Gault, Gerald, 139
Gibbs, J., 212
Gifford, T., 101
Gill, Owen, 86-7, 93
Glueck, E., 137
Glueck, S., 137
Goldstein, A., 163
Goodman, Lord, 186
Gouldner, A., 11
Grace, C., 14, 15, 16, 198
Grant, M., 68
Grant, W., 44
Gray, J., 41, 45
Greer, D., 120, 121
Griffith, J., 42, 65-8, 69, 70, 125
Griffiths, J., 96
Gunningham, N., 11, 34-7, 72, 73
Gusfield, J., 22-3, 24, 29, 31

Hailsham, Lord, 5
Hain, Peter, 105
Hall, J., 29, 30
Hammond, W., 212
Harman, H., 125
Harris, D., 148
Hart, H., 57
Hart, J., 49
Hay, D., 23, 24
Hazell, R., 186
Heberling, J., 117
Hewitt, C., 73
Hindell, K., 45
Hine, J., 135
Hirst, P., 14

Home Office, 208
Hood, R., 49, 52, 133, 136, 142
Hood, R., 49, 52, 133, 136, 142
Hoover, President, 207
Howard, C., 167
Hunt, A., 14, 15
Hyman, H., 209

Ison, T., 151

Jackson, George, 140
Jaffe, L., 56, 62
Jenkins, Roy, 111
Jolowicz, J., 175, 176
Joseph, M., 185
Judicial Statistics, 154, 156, 158
Justice, 110, 127, 184, 186, 193, 196
Justice for All, 7

Kadish, M., 130
Kadish, S., 130
Kahn-Freund, O., 4, 218-20
Kalven, H., 126
Kettle, M., 81
King, M., 108, 112, 123
Klare, Hugh, 46

La Fave, W.R., 83, 84, 93
Lacey, R., 136, 143
Lambert, J., 82, 85
Lancet, The, 33
Laurie, P., 107
Law in Context, 6
Law Reform Now, 7
Law and Society, 6
Law in Society, 6
Leggatt, A., 181
Legum, M., 172
Leigh, L., 99, 107
Lemert, E., 9, 10, 211
Lemon, N., 134
Lennon, P., 46
Lerman, P., 138
Levenson, H., 192
Lewis, P., 186
Lidstone, K., 102
Lipton, D., 141
Lloyd, Lord, 224
Lovenduski, J., 174, 209

Macaulay, S., 152-4, 222
McBarnet, D., 16-17, 98

McCabe, S., 78, 81, 87-9, 116, 126, 128
McClean, J., 102, 107, 116, 118, 123, 182
McConville, S., 15; on access to solicitor, 103, 108; juries, 125, 127, 128; *Negotiated Justice*,116-17; sentencing discount, 107, 114, 119
McCorquodale, S., 166
McIsaac, M., 140
Mackintosh, J., 41
McNee, Sir David, 97, 101
McWilliams, W., 135
Mack, A., 128
Manchester, A., 159
Mann, F., 185
Marcus, M., 163
Mark, Sir Robert, 89, 97, 127
Martin, A., 7
Martinson, R., 141
Marx, K., 14, 27
Matza, D., 9
Mawby, R., 93
Mead, G.H., 9
Megarry, R., 183
Miller, J., 14
Morris, A., 140
Morris, P., 186, 195
Mungham, G., 12, 129
Munro, C., 103
Murch, M., 157, 159

Nagel, S., 114
National Smoke Abatement Society, 35
National Swedish Council for Crime Prevention, 212
Newman, D., 114, 119
Nixon, President, 137
Nuffield Foundation, 6

O'Connor, P., 101
O'Higgins, P., 69
Outer Circle Policy Unit, 40, 42
Oxford Centre for Socio-Legal Studies, 6

Packer, H., 96, 215, 216
Page, B., 40
Parker, Lord, 127
Partington, M., 69, 190
Paterson, A., 65, 70
Paulus, I., 32-4, 37, 72, 73

Pearson, G., 8, 11
Pearson, Lord, 147, 151
Pease, K., 135
Phillips, A., 197, 198
Phillips, J., 185
Piliavin, I., 11, 83, 84, 85, 86, 87
Pinto-Duschinsky, M., 50
Pizzey, Erin, 48-9
Pollock, S., 188
Powis, David, 89-90
Prices and Incomes Board, 185
Purves, R., 116, 118, 119, 126, 128

Quinney, R., 8, 12

Racial Discrimination, 208
Rapoport, A., 162
Rees, T., 92
Reid, Lord, 60, 70
Reiss, A., 83, 84, 86, 87
Renner, K., 22, 27-9, 30, 72
Rock, P., 32, 34
Rodgers, H., 209
Roshier, B., 9
Ross, H., 212-13
Rough Justice, 7
Ryan, M., 46

Sachs, A., 172
Sanders, A., 127
Sawer, G., 66
Scarman, Lord Justice, 38, 53
Schur, E., 4, 214, 215, 216
Schwartz, R., 14
Scofield, M., 51
Scrutton, Lord, 68
Sealy, L., 126
Seidman, R., 14, 120, 204
Sheatsley, P., 209
Sherrington, Mr., 59
Shirley, J., 216, 217
Shklar, J., 70
Short, M., 216, 217
Simms, M., 45
Simonds, Lord, 64-5
Simpson, N.F., 119
Sinclair, A., 207
Skolnick, J., 81
Smith, B. Abel-, *see* Abel-Smith
Smith, P., 108
Society of Conservative Lawyers, 7, 194

Society of Labour Lawyers, 194
Society of Public Teachers of Law, 6
Stephenson, G., 121
Stevens, P., 92
Stevens, R., 7, 154, 167
Stinchcombe, A., 84
Stonehouse, John, 112
Street, H., 42, 101, 108
Sudnow, D., 118
Sunday Times, 216
Sutcliffe, F., 78, 81, 87-9
Sutherland, E., 205, 206, 210
Szasz, T., 140

Tangley, Lord, 52
Tarling, R., 133
Taylor, I., 9
Taylor, L., 9, 136, 143
Taylor, P., 115
Telling, D., 102
Thomas, D., 134
Thomas, P., 108
Thomson, A., 218, 220
Times, The, 58
Townsend, Cyril, 47

Wade, H., 62, 63
Walker, J., 134
Walkland, S., 41
Walmsley, R., 82
Warren, Chief Justice, 70
Weber, M., 1-2, 13, 20
Wedderburn, K., 7
Whetton, J., 159
White, R., 12, 186
White, S., 114
Whitehouse, Mary, 47
Whitelaw, William, 47
Wilberforce, Lord, 69, 175
Wilcox, A., 110
Wiles, P., 3, 6
Wilkinson, P., 14, 15, 16, 198
Wilks, J., 141
Williams, C., 80, 82
Williams, D., 63
Williams, G., 108-9
Willis, C., 92
Willok, I., 4
Wilson, G., 5
Wilson, J., 94, 95, 172
Wilson, M., 92
Wootton, B., 134

Wright, M., 45

Young, J., 11, 85-6, 211, 216
Young, M., 86

Zander, M.: on acquittal, 127, 128; bail, 111, 113, 114; compensation, 148; education, legal, 180; legal profession, 181, 182; legal reform, 7, 12, 15, 178; studies, 104; unmet need, 186
Zeisel, H., 126

Subject Index

Abortion law: and morality, 202-3,
214, 218; reform, 43, 45, 74
Abortion Law Reform Society, 44
Absconsions, and bail, 113
ACAS, *see* Advisory Conciliation and
Arbitration Services
Accessibility of law, 178, 182, 186,
187, 223; and law centres, 195,
196-7
Accident compensation, 147-52,
203
Acquittals, jury, 127-8
Acts of Parliament, 38; drafting,
58-9
Adjudication, process, 55
Administration of Justice Act 1973
164
Administrative convenience, and plea
bargaining, 118, 119
Administrative law, 63, 67, 166-8
Adulteration, *see* Food
Adversary process, 162-3; and civil
actions, 151, 161, 162-3, 175; and
discrimination, 170; and divorce,
155-6, 158, 159, 169; and industrial relations, 149; and Small Claims
Court, 164-5; trial as, 120, 122, 124;
and tribunals, 168, 172; and unrepresented parties, 164, 165; and use of
law, 204
Advertising: and discrimination, 208;
of legal services, 199
Advice to government, 49-53, 74;

Advice of government, *cont*
Law Commission, 52-3, 74; Official
Reports, 49-52, 74
Advice, legal: on plea bargaining,
115-16; right to, 103-4, 108, 225
Advisory Conciliation and Arbitration
Services (ACAS), 161, 165, 170
Advisory Council on the Penal System
(1974), 136
Advisory Liaison Service, 194
Alcohol, and driving, 212-13
Alkali Inspectorate, 27, 36, 72
Appeal Court, *see* Court of Appeal
Appearance, suspicious, 84, 89-90,
99
Arbitration, 161; Small Claims Courts,
164-5
Arbitrator, function, 161, 164
Area, and crime, 92-3
Arrest: police powers, 101-2; reasons,
83, 85, 87; *see also* Police dis-
cretion
Arrestable offences, 101-2
Assessor, insurance, 149-50
Association for Vaccine Damaged
Children, 44
Attorney-General, and public interest,
175

Bail: abuse of, 112; bargaining,
106-7, 150; and courts, 111-12;
current law, 112-14; points system,
113; from police station, 106-7,

Bail: *cont*
  150; and recognizance, 113; refusal, reasons, 112
Bail Act, 1976, 52, 111, 112-12
Bank of England, 41
Bar Council, 5, 179
Bargaining, 223: bail, 106-7; civil law, 147, 149-50, 161; criminal law, 106-7, 146, 147; and insurance companies, 149-50
Barristers: expense, 180, 183; functions, 181, 182; restrictive practices, 185
Battered women, 48-9
Battle, trial by, *see* Adversary process
Behaviour, control, 203, 205, 213
Bench effect, in Magistrates Courts, 113-4
Bias: judicial, 65; police, 79, 82, 83, 92; sentencing, 139-41
Bill of Rights, 224
Bills, Parliamentary, procedure, 40-1
Birmingham, jury trials, 125, 127
Borstal, sentencing to, 135-6, 142
Bribery, *see* Corruption
Bureaucracy: and civil law, 146, 147; and criminal law, 94; and law, 1-2, 26-7, 33, 35, 72-3; and legal aid, 192; and police, 81, 94
Bureaucratic imperatives in law-making, 25-7, 34, 72, 223
Business: crime, 210; relationships and contract law, 152-4

Cabinet committees, 40
'Cab rank' rule, 183
CABX, *see* Citizens' Advice Bureaux
Camden law centre, 195
Camden, London Borough of, and positive discrimination, 210
Canada, drugs in, 50-1
Capitalism and the law, 14, 27, 29-30, 72, 220
Capital punishment, 43, 45, 64, 74
Cardiff, duty solicitor scheme, 108
Care orders, 135
CBI, 42, 43, 44
Certainty effect, and deterrence, 212-13
Change, legal, 27-9, 30, 201, 207, 208, 211, 225
Chicago, police in, 80
Chief Constables, influence, 81

Child Poverty Action Group, 196
Children, and pornography, 47-8
Children in Trouble, 137
Children and Young Persons Act 1969, 135, 137
Chiswick Women's Aid, 48
Choice, and retribution, 137
CID: Drug Squad, 216, 217; Obscene Publications Squad, 217
Citizens Advice Bureaux, 192, 196, 197, 225
Citizens Law Centres, 200
Civil Law, 145-76; aims, conflicting, 160-1; bureaucratization, 146, 147; conciliation, 161, 169-75; courts, structure, 55; and discrimination, 170-5; and justice, 160-1, 162; legal aid, 189, 190; methods of settlement, 161-75; non-utilization, 146, 152-4, 178, 187, 195, 203-5; processes, 182-3; and secrecy, 150; tribunals, 165-8, 169; voluntary nature, 145-6
Civil Rights Movement, 7, 8
Claims consciousness, lack, 148
Class actions, 175-6
Class, social: and the law, 14, 19, 20-1, 23, 28, 37, 72; lawyers', 180; and police selectivity, 82, 92; sentencing bias, 140-1
Clean Air Act 1956, 35-7
Clerk, chambers' 183-4
Collective action, and judges, 68-9
'Colonel B' trial, 125
Colour prejudice: and police, 82, 83, 84, 92; *see also* Discrimination, racial
Commission for Racial Equality (CRE), 170, 171, 172, 174, 175
Committee: advice to government, 49-52, 74; Cabinet, 40; Official, 49-52, 74; Select, 42
Common law, 38; judicial development, 62, 65; racial discrimination, 170-1,
Community: law services, 7, 11-13, 195, 196, *see also* Law centres; and police, 94
Community Service Orders, 132
Compensation cases, 146-52; costs, 150-1; pre-war, 166; procedure, 150; and settlement, 148-52
Complaint, influence of, 84, 88
Compromise and conciliation, 169

Conciliation, 161, 169-75; industrial relations, 169-70; racial discrimination, 170-2; sexual discrimination, 172-5
Conciliation Act 1896, 170
Conciliation and Arbitration Council 44
Conciliator, function, 161
Confederation of British Industry, *see* CBI
Confessions, 102, 104, 108-9
Consensualism in law-making, 19-20, 34, 37, 41, 206, 207
Consensus, community, 64, 205, 206
Constraints on legislation, 42
Consumer law, 175, 196
Consumers' Association, 45
Continental systems of civil law, 163-4, 184-5
Contingent fees, 192-3
Contract law, 27, 28, 39; non-use of, 152-4, 203
Control: and bureaucracies, 72-3; and crime, 96, 98, 203, 205-18; and law, 16-17, 203, 205-18, 220; and police, 91, 96; of property, 27; of workers, 27, 28, 31, 32, 218-20
Conveyancing, 185, 199
Conviction, and arrest, 83
Corporations and law, 225
Corporatism, 44
Corrective role of law, 9
Corruption, police, 97, 215, 216-17
Costs, payment by loser, 150-1, 162, 193; in Small Claims Court, 165
County courts: informality, increasing, 168; legal aid, 188; and racial discrimination, 171; and sex discrimination, 173
Court of Appeal decisions: damages, time limit, 57; and House of Lords, 67; identification, rules, 105; labour relations, 61, 69; plea bargaining, 116; racial discrimination, 59-60
Court processes, 119-43
CRE, *see* Commission for Racial Equality
Creativity, judicial, 63-4, 65, 75
· Crime: control, 16-17, 96, 98, 203, 205-18; definition and police, 79; parochial nature, 92-3; rates, and area, 93-4; recording, 87-8; seriousness and

police activity, 81, 83, 91; and society, 211; tariff, 48, 133, 215; victimless, 80, 213-18
Criminal Justice Act 1967, 104
Criminal law: and control, 96, 98, 203, 205-18; courts, structure, 55; division of functions in, 129; effectiveness, 211-13; jury trial, 124; legal aid, 189; non-utilization, 204-5; operation, 78-9; plea bargaining, 116; police discretion, 82, 204-5; prosecuting agency, 109-10; sentencing, 130-43
Criminal Law Act 1967, 101-2; 1977, 104, 125-6
Criminal Law Revision Committee, Eleventh Report 1972, 97, 127
Criminal process, 96-9
Criminals, stereotypes, 82, 83, 85, 86, 89-90
Criminology: corrective stance, 9; determinism, 9, 10; interactionism, 8, 9-11; and sociology of law, 7-13; traditional assumptions, 8-9
Crown Courts: guilty pleas, 98; and solicitors, 181
'Cuffing', 87
Custody, remand in, 106, 111, 112; sentencing, 135

Damages, *see* Compensation
Dangerous offenders, treatment, 142
Death penalty, *see* Capital punishment
Debt recovery, 154, 165
Decision making: advice, 49-53; secrecy, 39-40
Declaratory theory of legislation, 54-7, 62, 64
Delay, legal, 182-3
Demeanour, suspicious, *see* Appearance
Deportation, 101
Detention, powers, 101-2, 102-4
Determinism, 9, 10, 137
Deterrence: effective, 97, 131, 211, 212; and sentencing, 131-2
Deviance, sociology of, and law, 8, 9-13
Devlin Committee (1976), 105
Director of Public Prosecutions, 109
Disability, compensation, *see* Compensation

Discount, sentencing, 107; *see also* Plea
   bargaining
Discretion: judicial, 57-8; and the law,
   223; police, *see* Police, discretion;
   role of, 1-2
Discrimination: and conciliation, 170-
   5; and police, 92; racial, 59-61, 92,
   170-2; reverse, 210; sex, 172-4, 207-
   10
Disjunctures approach, 16-17
Disputes, settlement methods, 161-75
Disqualification, driving, 133
Divorce process, 155-60; collusion, 156,
   157; and conciliation, 158-60, 169;
   current law, 157-9; 'do-it-yourself',
   156, 168; future law, 159-60; offence
   grounds, 157, 158; legal aid, 157-8,
   188, 190; previous law, 156; special
   procedure, 155, 156
Divorce Reform Act 1969, 156-7, 158,
   159
Dock briefs, 189
Domestic Proceedings and Magistrates'
   Court Act 1978, 159
'Domestics', 88-9, 93
Domestic Violence and Matrimonial
   Homes Act 1976, 48
Donovan Commission (1968), 218
Drafting of law, 58, 68
Drink: adulteration, 32-4; and driving,
   212-13
Driving, *see* Motoring
Drugs: control, 215-16; legislation,
   24-6, 214-17; Official Reports, 50-1;
   police enforcement, 85-6, 215, 216-
   17; pressure groups, 8
Drug Squad, CID, 216, 217
Due process, 3, 16, 17; and crime
   control, 98-9; and police, 96, 98, 99;
   and rehabilitative sentencing, 139;
   and retributive sentencing, 137;
   trial as, 120
Duty solicitor schemes, 108, 192, 196,
   225

Economic policy: factors affecting, 41;
   tripartism, 44
Education, legal, *see* Law, training
Effectiveness, *see* Success
Elitism, 66, 179
Emergence of legal rules, 19-29; case
   studies, 29-37

Employment, women, 173, 175, 208-9
Employment Appeal Tribunal, 168
Employment protection (Consolid-
   ation) Act 1978, 61
Enforcement of law, 204-5, 211, 213;
   consequences, 213-18
English Law Commission, 7
Entrepreneurship, moral, 24-5, 31, 34,
   35, 46-9, 72, 74
EOC, *see* Equal Opportunities Comm-
   ission
Equality: and the law, 3, 8; racial, 59-
   61, 92, 170-2; women's 172-5, 207-10
Equal Opportunities Commission
   (EOC), 170, 171, 173-4, 175
Equal Pay Act 1970, 173, 208-9
Establishment: and judges, 65-6, 70,
   75, 134; and lawyers, 179
European Community, 41, 43
Evidence, difficulty in obtaining, 214;
   see also Testimony

Fact, and law, 129-30
Factories Act 1833, 30-2
Factory Inspectorate, 27, 32, 36, 72,
   170, 210
Failure of law, 202, 203-13
Fair Trading Act 1973, 175
Family law, 159
Fault: and compensation, 149; and
   divorce, 156, 157
Fees, 192-3, 199
Finer Committee Report on One Parent
   Families (1974), 51, 159
Fines, 133
Fingerprinting, 104
First Offenders Act 1958, 52
Fisher Report (1977), 97, 108
Food adulteration laws, 32-4, 210
Food and Drink Act 1860, 33; 1875,
   33, 34
Form, legal, and reality, 15-16, 19-20,
   78, 156, 222-3
Formulation of law, 15
France, civil law, 163-4
Franchise, women, 173
Francis Committee (1971), 170
Franks Committee (1957), 167
Friends of the Earth, The, 35, 44
Funding, government: law centres, 194,
   195, 200, 225; legal aid, 189-90, 199,
   225

Fusion of legal profession, 181, 183, 184-5

Gentleman's agreements, 152
Goals, extra-legal, 146
Government departments: and Citizens' Advice Bureaux, 197; legislation, control, 41-2, 43; and pressure groups, 43-4, 45, 73; and prosecutions, 109
Graduates, in law, 179
Green Form Scheme, 189, 190, 194
Grunwick dispute, 218
Guilt, finding, 127
Guilty pleas, 98, 127; and bail, 106-7; bargaining, 114-19

Habeas corpus, 101, 103
Harassment, police, 90, 92-3
Health and Safety Commission, 44
'Helping with enquiries', 103
Hillingdon Law Centre, 195
Homeless people, 48-9
Home Office Advisory Committee, and police powers, 99; Circulars, identity parades, 105
Homosexuality, laws, 64, 74, 214; police prosecution, 82
House of Lords decisions: and Court of Appeal, 67; and intention of Parliament, 58, 129; labour relations, 69; majority verdict, 61; police procedures, 100; and precedent, 61; racial discrimination, 60
Housing (Homeless Persons) Act 1977, 48
Howard League for Penal Reform 44, 46

Identification procedures, 104-6
Ideology, law as, 23
Impartiality: judicial, 56-7, 64, 66, 69; police, 79, 82, 83, 92
Indecency with Children Act 1960, 48
Industrial injury, 149
Industrial relations: and adversary process, 149; balance of power, 219, 220; conciliation, 169; and control, 218-20; interests, divergent, 218-19; tribunals, 168
Industrial Relations Act 1971, 211, 218, 220

Industrial societies, and law, 13-14, 204, 220
Industrial tribunals, 168; and racial discrimination, 171-2; and sex discrimination, 173
Information: freedom of, 40, 42-3; importance of, 46
Inquisitorial system, 163-4
Insurance companies: and compensation, 146-7, 149-50; financing litigation, 193
Interactionism, 8, 9-11, 13
Interest: class, 21, 30; groups, *see* Pressure groups; law as expression of, 15
International constraints on legislation, 41
International Monetary Fund, 41
Interpretation, judicial, 19, 20, 39, 54-7, 59, 74-5; arguments on, 62-5; cases, 59-62; difficulty, 62; rules, 59, 70
Interpretive sociology, 14-15
Interrogation, police, 97, 102-4; regulation of, 224-5
IRA, and jury checks, 125
'Irrelevance' and Marxist theory, 21-2

Judges: bias, 65-8; creativity, 64, 65, 75; elitism, 66; function, 161, 163-4; impartiality, 56-7, 64, 66, 69; as inquisitor, 163-4; interpretation of law, *see* Interpretation; law-making, 30, 54, 57-62, arguments on, 62-5; passive role, 162; politics, 65-70; selection, 65, 66; sentencing, 134-5; training, 135
Judges' Rules, 103, 105, 111, 224; right to silence, 104
Jury, the, 124-30; acquittals, 127-8; challenge, 124-5; function, 129-30; legal provisions, 124-5; offences triable by, 125-6; research into, 126-7, 129; verdicts, 129-30; vetting, 125
Justice: and civil law, 160-1, 162; and retribution, 136
Juveniles, *see* Youth

Knapp Commission (1972), 50

Labelling, 8, 10, 69, 211-12, 215
Labour law, 61; and balance of power,

Labour law *cont*
　219; conciliation, 169-70; and judges,
　67, 68, 69; and trade unions, 196
Labour Party, and Official Secrets Act,
　39
LAG, *see* Legal Action Group
Land law, 185
Lands Tribunal, 168
Language, statutory, ambiguity of, 62,
　68
Larceny, 29
Law: administrative constraints, 166;
　aims, 203, 207, 208; and change, 27-
　9, 30, 201, 207, 208, 211, 225; and
　and community, 7, 11-13, 195, 196;
　and consensus, 19-20, 34, 37, 41, 64,
　206, 207; and crime control, 16-17,
　96, 98, 203, 205-18; enforcement,
　204-5, 211, 213-18; failure, 202, 203-
　13; formulation, 15; functions, 224;
　ideal and reality, 15-16, 19-20, 78,
　156, 222-3; limits, 201-2, 203, 207,
　210, 218; necessity for, 206; and
　oppression, 12, 14, 204; reform, 6-7,
　181; and restitution, 14, 132, 204;
　selectivity of, 8, 67, 80; and social
　class, 14, 19, 20-1, 23, 28, 37, 72;
　and sociology, conflict, 2-5, 12-13,
　198; sociology of, *see* Sociology of
　law; training, 5, 6, 179-80; *see also*
　Legal rules
Law centres, 11, 179, 187, 189, 193-7;
　achievements, 195; funding, 194,
　195, 200, 225; role, 195, 196, 199;
　type of work, 194, 196
Law Commission, 7, 49, 52-3; advisory
　role, 52-3; members, 52-3
Law Commission Act 1965, 7
Law Society: and education, 5, 179;
　law centres, 194; legal aid, 188, 189
Lawyers: radical, 11; right to contact,
　103-4, 108, 225; role, 178, 179, 198;
　training, 179-80
Le Dain commission, 50-1
Legal Action Group (LAG), 7, 44
Legal Advice and Assistance Act 1972,
　189
Legal aid, 188-93; and bail applicat-
　ions, 112; and class actions, 176;
　contingency fund, 193; contribution
　levels, 190, 199-200; elegibility for,
　189, 190, 192, 199; government

expenditure on, 189-90, 199, 225;
　insurance, 193; introduction, 179,
　188, knowledge of, 148; for matri-
　monial cases, 157, 158; means test,
　189, 190, 191; personal injury claims,
　148, 151; Royal Commission, 199-
　200; in Small Claims cases, 165; and
　tribunals, 168, 190
Legal Aid and Advice Act 1949, 188
Legal Aid Act 1974, 189; 1979, 190
Legalistic style of policing, 94
Legal profession: division, 181,
　183-4, 199; education, 179-80; fus-
　ion, 181, 183, 184-5; and law centres,
　194-5; organization, 178, 180-6; pub-
　lic sector, 179; reforms,
　181, 185-6,
　199; restrictive practices, 181, 185;
　service, inadequate, 182-3, 184; spec-
　ialization, 181, 183,　184, 185
Legal rules: aims, 201; emergence, 19-
　29, case studies, 29-37
Legal services, alternative, 187-8;
　non-utilization, 146, 152-4, 178, 187,
　195, 203-5; provision, 3, 7; Royal
　Commission, 7, 115, 178, 184, 185,
　189, 190, 196-7, 199-200; and social
　workers, 198; and unmet need, 186-
　8, 192, 196
Legislation, *see* Law
Legislative process, 37-43; and advice,
　49-53; constraints on, 42; and pre-
　ssure groups, 43-9, 73; secrecy, 39-
　40, 42; study of, 37, 39, 40-3
Limits of law, 201-2, 203, 207, 210, 218
Liverpool, police activity, 86-7, 93
Lobbying, by pressure groups, 43, 47-
　8, 74
Local authorities: and law centres, 195;
　powers, 175
Local Government Act 1972, 175
Lords, *see* House of Lords
LSE jury project, 126

Magistrates: background, 134; person-
　ality, 134; and sentencing, 133-4
Magistrates' Association, 110, 113
Magistrates' Courts: guilty pleas, 98,
　117; identification in dock, 106;
　inquisitorial procedures, 164; legal
　aid, 189, 192; police role, 109; pros-
　ecuting agencies, 109; procedures,

Magistrates Courts *cont*
122-3; sentencing variation, 133-4;
and youth, 135-6
Magistrates' Courts Act 1952, 103, 104,
106
Majority consensus, 206
Managerial revolution, 36, 37
Manchester, police activity in, 81
Manhattan Bail Project, 113
Manpower Services Commission, 44
Manufacturers: business relationships,
152-4; power, 31-2, 33-4, 36
Marijuana, legislation, 24, 25-6
Marriage: and discrimination in emp-
loyment, 173; and status, 155
Marxists, and law, 2, 12, 14-15, 19,
21-2, 28
Matrimonial Causes Act 1973, 157
Matrimonial law, 155, 156-60
Meaning of Acts, 58-9, 60, 68
Means test, and legal aid, 189, 190,
191
Media, and pressure groups, 46-9, 74
Mediation, 161, 165
Mediator, function, 161
Mental health law, 139-40
Metropolitan Police Act 1839, 99
Misuse of Drugs Act 1971, 99, 215
Monopolies, legal, 185, 199
Moral entrepeneurship, 24-5, 31, 34,
35; and law-making, 72; pressure
groups as, 46-9, 74
Morality: definition of, 23; and law,
202-3, 213-18; police sense of, 80, 81,
83-4; and privacy, 213-14
Mores, and law, 205
Motoring offences: accidents, 149; and
alcohol, 212-13; sentencing variation,
133-4

National Association for the Care and
Rehabilitation of Offenders
(NACRO), 45-6
National Council for Civil Liberties
(NCCL), 90, 92
National Deviancy Conference, 8, 9
National Economic Development
Council, 44
National Viewers and Listeners Assoc-
iation (NVALA), 47, 74
NCCL, *see* National Council for Civil
Liberties

Need, unmet, 186-8, 196
Negligence actions, 146-52
'Negotiated Justice', 116-17
Negotiation: in civil law, 161; *see also*
Bargaining
Neighbourhood law firms, 7, 193, 194;
see also Law centres
Netherlands, public consultation, 43
Norms, legal; change, 27, 71-2; emerg-
ence, 19, 22, 41, 48, 49, 71-2
North Kensington Law Centre, 194,
195
Notting Hill, drug law enforcement,
85-6
NVALA, *see* National Viewers and
Listeners Association

Obscene Publications Squad, 217
Official Reports, 49-52, 74
Official Secrets Act, 1978, 39-40
Official secrecy, 39-40, 42-3, 73;
'Colonel B' trial, 125
Ombudsmen, 165
Oppression and law, 12, 14, 204
Organization: of legal profession, 178,
180-6; and power, 225
Ormrod Committee (1971), 6, 180
Oxford Penal Research Unit jury
study, 126

Paddington Law Centre, 195
Parades, identity, 104-6
Para-legal services, 187, 197
Parkinson's law, 26
Parliament: conflict with judiciary, 38,
58; impotence, 42-3; intention of, 58;
legislative procedure, 40-1
Parole, and injustice, 142
Participation in government, 44, 45
Pearson Commission Report (1978),
147-8, 149, 168
Personality, magistrates', and sentenc-
ing, 134
Personal injury claims, 146-52
Personal rights, and judiciary, 67
Phenomenological sociology, 14-15
Picketing law, 218
Planning: and contracts, 153, 154;
law, 68
Plea bargaining, 114-19; advice on,
115-16; and bail, 106-7; case for and
against, 118-19; official model, 115-

Plea bargaining, *cont*
   16; reality of, 116-17
Pluralism in law-making, 19, 20-1, 34, 37, 41, 72, 220; limits, 46
Police, 79-109; arrest, powers, 101-2; and bail, 106-7; corruption, 97, 215, 216-217; detention, powers, 101-2,, 102-4; discretion, 79-82, 91-5, 96, 204-5, 224-5, American studies of, 82-5, 95, and control, 91, 94, 96, English studies, 85-90, and risk, 91, and setting of incident, 84-5, 87, 88-9, 91; identification procedures, 104-6; malpractice, 101, 103, 108, 214, 216-17; morality, sense of, 80, 81, 83-4; non-utilization of law, 204-5; partiality, 79, 82, 83, 92; powers, 96-107, 224-5, arguments on, 97-8; as prosecution, 109-10; questioning, 97, 102-4, 225; recording of crime, 87-8; recording of statements, 108-9; resources, limits, 80-1; search, powers, 99-101, 225; station, procedure, 98, 102-4, 224-5; and stereo-typing, 82, 83, 85, 86, 89-90, 91, 92-3, 93-4,; styles, 94-5
Politics: and judiciary, 65-70; and legislation, 38, 41, 51-2
Pollution, legislation, 34-7, 210
Poor Persons Rules, 188
Poor Prisoners' Defence Act 1903, 189
Pornography, 214, 217; child, 47-8
Poulson affair, 50
Power, and the law, 210-11, 218; *see also* Pressure groups
Precedent, importance, 4, 54; lack of, 30
Prejudice, *see* Bias
Preservation of the Rights of Prisoners (PROP), 45
Press Council, 165
Pressure groups: categories, 44; con-flicts, 45-6; and the law, 8, 12, 34-5. 41, 42, 43-9, 73-4, 196, 207, 218; legal, 7; methods, 45, 46, 47-8, 74; as moral entrepreneurs, 46-9, 74, 207; power, 46, 207, 218, 220; test cases, 196
Prevention of Terrorism (Temporary Provisions) Act 1974, 102
Prisons: overcrowding, 111; reform, 45-6

Private property, entry, police, 99-100
Problem-solving approach, 2, 3-4, 15
Procedure, legislative, 40-1
Processing of crime, 98
Professional criminals, acquittal, 127, 128
Prohibition, 202, 205, 214, 215; fail-ure, 206-7; as symbolism, 22-3, 24
PROP, *see* Preservation of the Rights of Prisoners
Property: and law, 27-8, 67; women's rights, 173
Prosecution: agencies, 109-10; inde-pendent, 109, 225
Prostitution, 214
Protection of Children Act, 1978, 47-8
Publicity, and pressure groups, 47-9
Public legal sector, 179
Public opinion, 20, 33, 45, 47-8, 73, 74, 210, 211, 218; *see also* Consensus
Public reporting of crime, 78-9
Punishment: and deterrent, 97, 131-2, 141, 212, 213

Quangos, 44, 173
Questioning, police, 97, 102-4, 225

Race Relations Act 1965, 170, 208; 1968, 59-61, 171, 208; 1976, 61, 171, 172, 208
Race Relations Board (RRB), 171-2, 206, 208
Racial discrimination legislation, 170-2, 207-10; achievements, 208
Radical Alternatives to Prison (RAP), 45, 46
Realism and law, 2, 15-17, 18, 29, 78, 156, 222-3
Recognizance, bail, 113
Reconciliation, marital, 158, 159-60, 169
Referral, by adivisory agencies, 195, 197-8
Reform, pressure for, 6-7, 199
Registrar, as arbitrator, 164, 165
Rehabilitation, 211; and sentencing, 132, 134-5, 136, 137-42, opposition to, 136, 138-42
Relationships: business, 152-4, 203; continuing, and civil actions, 146, 149, 153, 154, 203-4; and divorce,

Relationships *cont*
155, 204
Remand in custody: from courts, 111;
in police station, 106; for protec-
tion, 112
Rent Officer, 170
Reports, Official, 49-52, 74
Restitution and law, 14, 132, 204; and
sentencing, 132
Restrictive practices in legal profess-
ion, 181, 185
Restrictive Practices Court, 167, 175
Restrictive trading, 175
Retribution, and sentencing, 130-1,
135, 136-7
Rights: Bill of, 224; informing of, 97,
99, 101, 103-4
Risk, and police discretion, 91
Road accident cases, 149
Road Safety Act 1967, 212, 213
Royal Commissions, 49-50, 53: on Civil
Liability and Compensation for Per-
sonal Injury (1978), 147; on Criminal
Procedure (1977), 97, 101, 110; on
Legal Services (1976), 7, 115, 178,
184, 185, 189, 190, 196-7, 199-200;
on the Police (1962), 110; on Stand-
ards of Conduct in Public Life, 50
RRB, *see* Race Relations Board
Rules of judicial interpretation, 58,
70
Ruling class, *see* Class, social

Salmon Report (1976), 50
Scandinavia, public consultation, 43;
rehabilitative approach, 136, 138
Scotland, public prosecution system,
109, 225; youth, sentencing, 138,
140-1
Search, police powers, 99-101, 225
'Secondary picketing', 69
Secrecy, Official, *see* Official Secrecy
Select Committees, 42
Selectivity: of law, 8, 67, 80; police,
see Police, discretion
Semantic difficulty, *see* Meaning
Sentencing, 130-43; aims, 130-2, 136-
7; custodial, 135; discount, 107; discretionary, 139-40; exemplary, 132;
expertise, 134-5, 137; factors affecting, 119, 133-4; inconsistency, 132-
4; length, 135-6, 138, 142; and plea
bargaining, 114-15; and recommendation, expert, 135, 139; rehabilitative, 132, 134-5, 136, 137-42; retributive, 130-1, 135, 136-7; training,
135; as treatment, 137-8
'Service' style of policing, 94, 95
Services Divorce Division, 188
Settlement, methods of, 161-75; out-
of-court, 146, 148, 149, 150, 203;
fairness, 151; as part of tort system,
152
Severity effect and deterrence, 212,
213
Sex discrimination, 172-5, 207-10
Sex Discrimination Act 1975, 58, 171,
172, 173, 208-9
Sex Disqualification (Removal) Act
1919, 173
Sexual Offences Act 1956, 48; 1967, 82
Sheffield, crime in, 93
Shelter, 196
Silence, right to, 97, 104
Simple societies and law, 13-14, 204
Small Claims Courts, 164-5
Social class *see* Class
Social role of law, 179, 180, 199, 201-2,
203; unmet need, 186-8, 196, 197
Social Science Research Council, 6, 12
Social workers, and relationship to law
and lawyers, 198
Sociology: interactionist, 8, 9-11, 13;
interpretive, 14-15; and law, conflict,
2-5, 12-13, 198
Sociology of law: conflict within,
12-15; core, 11; definition, 2-3;
growth, 6-7
Solicitors: apprenticeship, 180; choice
of, 182; expense, 180, 183; functions,
181; and legal aid, 192; right to, 103-
4, 108, 225; role in divorce, 158, 159-
60
South Africa, law, history, 23
Standard form agreements, 152
Statements to police, authenticity,
108-9
Status: assertion, 22-3, 24, 34; and
marriage, 155
Statutes, types, and judicial intepret-
ation, 63
Stereotypes, 10, 119; police activity, 82,
83, 85, 86, 89-90, 91, 92-3, 93-4;
see also Labelling

Stop and search, police powers, 99
Success of law, 205-6
Summons, 102
Supplementary Benefits Commission,
    and legal aid, 192
'Sus' law, 92
Sussex Uniuversity law course, 180
Symbolism in law making, 22-4, 30, 34

Tape recording, 108-9, 225
Tariff: crime, 48, 133, 215; guidelines,
    133
Tax laws, 62-3
Testimony, reliability of, 120-1
Theft, in English law, 29
Tokenism, 21, 32
Tort, 39, 147; claims, 146-52;
    cost, 151
Trades unions, power, 219; *see also*
    Labour law
Trades Union Congress, *see* TUC
Training, *see* Law, training
Transactions, social, 10
Treasury, 41
Treatment, sentencing as, 137-8
Trial, the, 119-24; adversary process,
    120; drama, 119; and due process,
    120; jury, 124-30; process, 184;
    sentencing, 130-43; studies of, 120-3;
    summary, 123; testimony, 120-1
Tribunals, 165-8, 169, 179-80, 196;
    adversarial nature, 168; and Citizens'
    Advice Bureaux, 197; compared with
    courts, 167, 168; legal aid, 168, 190
Tribunals and Inquiries Act 1958, 166
TUC, 42, 43, 44, 211
'Twenty-four-hour' rule, 103

United States: bail system, 113; Civil
    Rights, 7, 8; class actions, 175-6;
    community law services, 7, 193, 194,
    196; contingent fees, 192; crimin-
    ological theory, 8, 9; drug problem,
    215-16; Freedom of Information Act
    1966, 40; judicial style, 70-1; Mari-
    juana Tax Act 1937, 24, 26; Narco-
    tics Bureau, 24, 25-6, 72; plea barg-

aining, 114-15, 118-19; police discret-
    ion, 82-5; pollution control, 34-5;
    prohibition, 22-3, 24, 202, 205, 206-
    7; racial discrimination, 209-10;
    rehabilitative approach, 136, 137-9;
    review, judicial, 71; sex discriminat-
    ion, 174-5; social engineering, 70, 71;
    Supreme Court, 70-1, 209; Voting
    Rights Act 1965, 209
Unmet need, 186-8, 196
Use of law, lack of, 146, 152-4, 178,
    187, 195, 203-5

Vagrancy Act 1824, 30, 102
Vagrancy laws, history of, 30
Victim, and police discretion, 83, 84,
    214
Victimless crime, 80, 213-18; and law
    enforcement, 214
Videotaping, 108-9
Vietnam war, protests, 8, 12
Violence in Marriage (Select Committee
    Report 1975), 48
Vocational law training, 179, 180
Votes for women, 173

Waivers, and law centres, 194
'Watchman' style of policing, 94
Welfare State: administrative tribunals,
    166-7, 168; legal services, 179
West Germany, public consultation, 43
White collar crime, 36, 210
Winn Report (1968), 150
Wisconsin, business relations, 152
Witnesses, reliability, 121, 149; at road
    accidents, 149
Women: discrimination against, 172-5;
    earnings, 208-9; protection, 48-9
Wootton Report (1968), 50-1
Wording, *see* Meaning
Working class interests, assertion, 28,
    32

Younger Report (1974), 136, 142
Youth: and police, 82, 83-4, 86-7;
    rehabilitative approach, 138; sentenc-
    ing, 135-6; as witnesses, 121